SVETOZAR MARKOVIĆ

AND THE ORIGINS OF BALKAN SOCIALISM

Светозар Марковић

Svetozar Marković

AND THE ORIGINS OF BALKAN SOCIALISM

BY WOODFORD D. McCLELLAN

PRINCETON UNIVERSITY PRESS
PRINCETON, NEW JERSEY
1964

L.C. Card: 63-23410

Publication of this book has been aided by
the Ford Foundation program to support publication,
through university presses, of works in the
humanities and social sciences

The frontispiece is taken from
Svetozar Marković: Njegov život, rad i ideje,
by Jovan Skerlić
(second edition, Belgrade, 1922).

Printed in the United States of America
by Princeton University Press, Princeton, New Jersey

TO MY CHILDREN,

MARK AND WENDY

Acknowledgments

The many debts of friendship and scholarly assistance which I have incurred in the writing of this book can never be adequately repaid, but it is gratifying to be able at least to record some of them publicly.

Professor Charles Jelavich, formerly of the University of California at Berkeley and now at Indiana University, suggested this study and gave generously of his time and his expert criticism; I am heavily in his debt. Among those who read the manuscript and gave it the benefit of their scholarly, meticulous criticism, I want especially to thank Professor Nicholas V. Riasanovsky of the University of California at Berkeley; Professor Benjamin N. Ward, also of Berkeley; Professor Wayne S. Vucinich of Stanford University; and Professor Loren R. Graham of Indiana University. Professor Carl Landauer of Berkeley read an early version of the work and made many suggestions for new and significant research.

For their many kindnesses and frank exchanges of opinion I want to record my warmest thanks to Mr. V. G. Karasëv of Moscow State University, to Professor Vasa Čubrilović of Belgrade University, and to Dr. Dimitrije Prodanović of the Institut društvenih nauka in Belgrade. Further, Professor Stephen Lukashevich of the University of Delaware made a number of thoughtful suggestions concerning my analysis, and Mr. Sergius Yakobson, Chief of the Slavic and Central European Division of the Library of Congress, answered my many queries with unfailing, scholarly assistance.

To the Ford Foundation, which provided generous support over a period of a year and a half in Berkeley and Belgrade, I am indeed most grateful. Likewise, I am greatly indebted to the Inter-University Committee on Travel

Grants for having made possible a period of study and research in the Soviet Union.

To the directors and staffs of the libraries in Berkeley, Moscow, Leningrad, Belgrade, and Novi Sad I extend my sincere thanks for their invaluable assistance. I am especially indebted to the Istoriski arhiv Beograda and to its director, Mr. Veljko Kuprešanin, for having given me the opportunity to see several rare and valuable collections. I should also like to record my thanks to the directors and staffs of the Državni arhiv Narodne Republike Srbije and of the Državna arhiva F.N.R.J. for their many kindnesses.

The writing of this book was completed during my tour of active duty (1961-65) with the United States Army, a tour which was for the most part spent as an instructor in the Department of Social Sciences at the United States Military Academy. I am indebted to the head of that department, Colonel George A. Lincoln, for his scholarly understanding of the problems involved in preparing a study of this nature.

Finally, my warmest thanks to Miss Miriam Brokaw, Managing Editor of Princeton University Press; her exacting editorial standards saved me from many pitfalls.

It is understood that none of the individuals or organizations named above is in any way responsible for any opinions, judgments, or statements of fact expressed in this book. I alone am accountable for what follows.

W.D.M.

West Point, August 1963

Abbreviations

UNPUBLISHED MATERIALS

Dokumental'nye materialy: Dokumental'nye materialy o prebyvanii serbskikh urozhentsev Markovicha i Knezhevicha v Institute Inzhenerov Putei Soobshcheniia, S. Peterburg, 1866-69.

DANRS: Državni arhiv Narodne Republike Srbije, Belgrade.

IAB: Istoriski arhiv Beograda, Belgrade.

PUBLISHED MATERIALS

C.d.: Celokupna dela Svetozara Markovića, Belgrade, 1891-1912.

Skerlić: Jovan Skerlić, *Svetozar Marković: Njegov život, rad i ideje,* second edition, Belgrade, 1922.

UZIS: Uchënye zapiski Instituta Slavianovedeniia, Moscow.

Vlada Milana, I: Slobodan Jovanović, *Vlada Milana Obrenovića,* I, Belgrade, 1926.

NOTE: All dates in text and footnotes, unless otherwise specified, are according to the Julian Calendar (Old Style).

NOTE ON SERBO-CROATIAN PRONUNCIATION:

c = ts as in flats
č = ch as in chimney
ć = same as č but slightly softer
đ = hard j as in just
š = sh as in mesh
ž = zh as in Zhukov or s as in pleasure

Table of Contents

SVETOZAR MARKOVIĆ

AND THE ORIGINS OF BALKAN SOCIALISM

CHAPTER I

The Problem and the Setting

IN MARCH OF 1875 European socialist journals mourned the death of Svetozar Marković, the founder of the Serbian radical-socialist party. The first Balkan socialist of European stature, Marković had created a party which enjoyed wide and growing support among the Serbian peasantry. The minuscule Serbian working class was virtually unanimous in its adherence to the radical-socialist program, and many of the intellectuals were followers of Svetozar Marković.

The radical-socialists had among their leaders a number of talented, capable men. Nikola Pašić, later to become prime minister of Serbia and Yugoslavia, was for a time one of Marković's closest associates. Adam Bogosavljević, parliamentary leader of the radical-socialists, was an influential deputy in the National Assembly. Vasa Pelagić, a respected and intelligent Bosnian priest, joined others in propagating Marković's socialist teachings beyond the borders of tiny Serbia.

Despite its outward indications of strength, however, the radical-socialist party began to disintegrate shortly after Marković's death. Marković had dominated the party completely, and only his strong personality had held its manifestly disparate components together. Nikola Pašić abandoned the fold a few years after Marković's death and helped found a new party which retained only the "radical" label. Adam Bogosavljević lost much of his parliamentary influence after the Balkan Crisis of 1875-78 and died in 1880. Vasa Pelagić was expelled from Serbia and spent much of the 1880's in Austrian jails in Bosnia; he finally returned to Serbia, only to die in the Požarevac prison in 1899. No new leaders of Marković's caliber emerged, and for many years no socialist party figured prominently in Serbian politics.

The decline of the Serbian radical-socialist movement largely explains the obscurity which has until recently been the fate of Svetozar Marković. Within a few years after his death Marković was forgotten by all but a handful of his countrymen. In European socialist circles only Benoit Malon and Karl Kautsky paid homage to the man who had introduced socialist theories into the Balkan Peninsula. And among Western historians Marković has been not so much forgotten as never known.

Insofar as they have investigated nineteenth-century Balkan history, historians in the West have delved chiefly into diplomatic history and, increasingly of late, into the problems created by the recession of the Ottoman Empire toward Asia Minor. Intellectual currents, with the admittedly important exception of the Yugoslav movement, have been largely ignored. Karl Marx's arrogant designation of the Balkan peoples as "unhistorical" has received wide, if tacit, confirmation from Western historians. Such a view—or, more precisely, the absence of one—reflects a distorted image.

The Balkan "cultural gap" to which Western historians frequently refer did indeed exist, but it narrowed significantly in the nineteenth century. The resumption—if the word be applicable after a hiatus of several centuries—of diplomatic and economic ties with Europe was followed by the development in the Balkans of political and intellectual movements which endeavored to give substance to the reunion. Western conservative and liberal political ideologies vied with each other and with Eastern autocratic traditions for the allegiance of the Balkan peoples. By the middle of the century the influx of romanticist currents had given birth to modern, national literatures. Social reform movements, based upon both Western and Russian models, came into existence in the latter half of the century; of these, the most important was the socialist movement.

Though present in one form or another throughout the Balkans, socialist teachings found particularly fertile soil in the South Slav lands. In Bulgaria men like Vasil Levsky, Hristo Botev, and Liuben Karavelov created a revolutionary, quasi-socialist tradition which in the twentieth century was perpetuated by genuine socialists like Dimitar Blagoev, Yanko Sakuzov, and Christian Rakovsky. In Serbia the movement founded by Svetozar Marković was shaken out of the doldrums at the end of the century when a number of socialist parties were formed. Most of those parties paid scant attention to Marković's teachings in their official platforms, but many individual socialists—in Bulgaria no less than in Serbia—acknowledged his influence.

Early in this century the most important Serb historian, Slobodan Jovanović, wrote a lengthy, critical analysis of Marković's thought and work.[1] Jovanović's father had been a bitter political enemy of Svetozar Marković, and filial piety colored the historian's search for truth; his study of Marković was one of his least satisfactory works. A few years after the appearance of Jovanović's book, the socialist writer Jovan Skerlić produced the first full-scale biography of Svetozar Marković.[2] Skerlić, who had been expelled from the Serbian Social-Democratic party in 1904 because of his opposition to its new Marxist orientation, attempted to justify his own ideological position in his book on Marković. Though his was on the whole a laudatory biography,

[1] "Svetozar Marković," *Političke i pravne rasprave*, II of *Sabrana dela* (*Collected Works*), Belgrade, 1932. The work was originally published in 1903.

[2] *Svetozar Marković: Njegov život, rad i ideje* (*Svetozar Marković: His Life, Work and Ideas*), 2nd edition, Belgrade, 1922.

Skerlić joined with Slobodan Jovanović in seeking to prove that Marković could in many respects be identified as the predecessor of both Radical ("bourgeois") and socialist parties in Serbia.

These two works were followed, in the years before World War II, by a number of Yugoslav monographs on Marković. The flow was uneven, however, both quantitatively and qualitatively, and it remained to the Yugoslav communists to build Marković into a national hero. Upon their seizure of power in 1945 the communists, lacking a native Marxist of any stature, adopted Svetozar Marković as a spiritual if not an ideological ancestor. The veritable flood of literature on Marković which has issued forth from Belgrade, Novi Sad, and Zagreb has unfortunately been of limited value, due primarily to its generally tendentious ideological coloring. The same is true of the Soviet works on Marković; Soviet researchers entered the field in 1950, though their motive was at that time scarcely one of scholarly collaboration.[3]

A NOTE ON SOCIALISM

The official communist view of Marković is deceptively straightforward. Having apparently overcome some of the differences that divided them in the period 1948-55, Yugoslav and Soviet historians now agree that Svetozar Marković was, despite his utopianism, the most important native Yugoslav socialist of the pre-Marxian era. This thesis has gone unchallenged in the West. To be sure, the challenging of it merely for the sake of argument would be both gratuitous and facile. Pokrovsky's dictum that "history is politics projected backward" is obviously the motto of all communist historians and indeed of some in the West, and

[3] V. G. Karasëv, *Svetozar Markovich (Sotsial'no-politicheskie vzgliady)* (*Svetozar Marković: His Socio-Political Views*), unpublished Ph.D. dissertation, Moscow State University, 1950.

to attack it is as pointless as it is pharisaically gratifying. But we can at least attempt to clarify and refine our own position; in the case of Svetozar Marković it seems clear that we can indeed marshal sufficient evidence to present a valid alternative to the communist view.

We should begin with a definition of terms. When Yugoslav and Soviet writers refer to Marković as an agrarian, utopian socialist, we can undoubtedly agree with them upon the meaning of "agrarian." The rest of the subsumption, however, deserves our close attention, for the term "utopian socialist" has been used with such reckless abandon that it no longer—if indeed it ever did—conveys a precise image. Marx borrowed it from Blanqui and applied it to all socialists who had preceded him (Marx). As in the case of his designation of the Balkan peoples as "unhistorical," Marx's definition of "utopian socialist" has received a deplorably wide acceptance in the West. Let us examine the problem in detail.

One of communist historiography's major guidebooks defines "utopian socialism" as "socialist teachings which, contrary to the theory of Marx's scientific socialism, constructed wide and universal plans for the reorganization of society, plans divorced from the reality of society and the class struggle. The socialist-utopians grounded their socialist ideals purely idealistically, not understanding the primary role of the conditions of the material life of society in its historical development."[4] Marx and Engels noted in *The Paris Commune* that the "utopians" "belong to that period when the working class had not yet been sufficiently schooled and organized by the pace of the development of capitalist society itself in order to become an active entity in the world arena; nor had the material conditions of its [the working class's] liberation sufficiently ripened in the

[4] *Kratkii filosofskii slovar'* (*Short Philosophic Dictionary*), Moscow, 1955, p. 497.

guts of the old world. The poverty of the working class existed, but the conditions for [the creation of] its own movement did not yet exist."[5] Our problem is now resolved into two questions: (1) Is the definition advanced by Marx and the Marxists applicable to Svetozar Marković? (2) Is that definition valid?

We shall attempt in the present work to answer the first question; the classification of Marković's socialism is indeed one of our major tasks. The second question, however, requires an immediate answer: Is the Marxist definition of utopian socialism valid? It is at once obvious that it is too broad, too all-inclusive. Beyond the fact that it is simply absurd to characterize all socialists who preceded Marx as utopian, there are a multitude of objections to the Marxist definition. There is an enormous gulf between the statist utopians—Plato and Sir Thomas More, to mention only two—and the quasi-anarchist utopians like Owen, Fourier, and St.-Simon. Furthermore, it is clearly impossible to syncretize these two schools with a third, the anarchist utopians: William Godwin and Michael Bakunin have little in common with other "utopians." Finally, the methods through which the various utopians sought to achieve "utopia" have varied greatly, and of course "utopia" itself has assumed numerous forms.

If we pretermit the formidable semantic obstacles and define "utopia" as "perfect society" and the latter as a "society free from injustice," we are inescapably drawn to the conclusion that only the anarchists and *Karl Marx* can be classified as true utopians. Only Marx and the anarchists envisioned a society not only free from injustice but also devoid of machinery to ensure against injustice. It can of course be argued that "justice" does not necessarily imply the existence of machinery to establish and maintain justice, but an examination of history would seem to indicate

[5] Quoted in *ibid.*, p. 497.

a necessity for that machinery. The statist utopians recognized the essence of the problem in that they foresaw not a perfect but an ideal society; the same can be said of the quasi-anarchist utopians, though their theories lacked the philosophical refinement of the statists. Plato and Sir Thomas More recognized, as Marx and the anarchists did not, that nothing in the history of mankind suggests that man is ultimately perfectible. Whether original sin, egoism, the law of self-preservation, or some other motive force is held responsible for the human predicament is a matter of futile debate. Man remains imperfect man, and, as the statist utopians perceived, the continued existence of the state, which attempts to regulate relations among men, is an inevitable necessity. In this fundamental regard, upon which all social theories must ultimately stand or fall, the statists were much closer to reality than Marx and the anarchists: they not only recognized but also accepted man's limitations.

We cannot, therefore, accept the Marxist-communist definition of utopian socialism. But in admitting the existence of the phenomenon we presuppose that it is susceptible of reduction to readily understood terms. The Marxists have a definition for everything, and their critics in the West are all too frequently content with a mere rejection of the Marxist argument. We must proceed further.

The historian, as the recorder and interpreter of past events, has in mid-twentieth century accepted the fact that his traditional methods and tools are inadequate for at least half his purpose. The recording of events is the occupation of the chronicler and the annalist; their interpretation requires far more complex and diverse skills. In connection with our present problem—that of finding an acceptable definition not only of utopian socialism but of socialism in general—the eminent French sociologist Emile Durkheim has provided the historian with a guide to its solution. In his brilliant study of socialism Durkheim wrote that "socialism . . . is entirely oriented toward the future. It is above all a plan for the reconstruction of societies, a program for a collective life which does not exist as yet or in the way it is dreamed of, and which is proposed to men as worthy of their preference. It concerns itself much less with what is or was than what ought to be."[6] And with incisive eloquence Durkheim further noted that "socialism is not a science, a sociology in miniature—it is a cry of grief, sometimes of anger, uttered by men who feel most keenly our collective *malaise*. Socialism is to the facts which produce it what the groans of a sick man are to the illness with which he is afflicted, to the needs that torment him."[7]

In these passages Durkheim makes no distinction between "utopian" and "nonutopian" socialism: in his view there are no basic differences between them. Despite varieties of form the substance of all socialist creeds tends to be basically identical. All socialist theories are indeed "oriented toward the future," and we scarcely need be reminded that neither socialist—of whatever school—nor any other theory can predict the future with any degree of exactitude. Marx essayed such a prediction, basing it upon his often valuable analysis of the development of capitalism, and failed miserably. But despite his failure he remains unquestionably the most influential socialist of all time, and it is obvious that Marx, more than any other single individual, answers Durkheim's description. No socialist has ever felt more keenly the social malaise, and none has cried out against it more eloquently or angrily. Again confirming Durkheim's analysis, Marx created no "system": if his diagnosis of the past and of contemporary society was dogmatic, his vision of the future was not, and this is where his strength lies.

[6] Emile Durkheim, *Socialism*, New York, Collier Books, 1962, p. 39.
[7] *Ibid.*, p. 41.

It is a tribute to the truth inherent in Durkheim's thesis, and further evidence of its applicability to Marx, that Marx has had such a great appeal for many intellectuals in backward societies. One of those intellectuals, Jawaharlal Nehru, has outlined some of the reasons for the continuing power of socialism in general and Marxism in particular in such societies: "Marx may be wrong in some of his statements, or in his theory of value. . . . But he seems to me to have possessed quite an extraordinary degree of insight into social phenomena, and this insight was apparently due to the scientific method he adopted. This method, applied to past history as well as current events, helps us in understanding them far more than any other method of approach, and it is because of this that the most revealing and keen analyses of the changes that are taking place in the world today come from Marxist writers. . . . The whole value of Marxism seems to me to lie in its absence of dogmatism, in its stress on a certain outlook and mode of approach, in its attitude to action. That outlook helps us in understanding the social phenomena of our own times and points out the way of action and escape."[8]

It is symbolic that Nehru here both contradicts himself and misunderstands Marx: these are two common characteristics of intellectuals in "emerging nations." The absence of dogmatism in Marx's vision of the future is due in large measure to the amorphism of that vision; and Marx the diagnostician of the evils of the past and present is the most dogmatic of thinkers. But to Nehru it is the form rather than the content of Marxism that is the important thing, and he has provided yet another confirmation of Durkheim's thesis.

Durkheim's definition of socialism applies to Nehru's views no less than to those of Karl Marx; it also describes accurately the position of Svetozar Marković, whom we have

[8] Jawaharlal Nehru, *Toward Freedom*, New York, 1941, p. 349.

neglected during this lengthy digression. Marković, like Nehru, was a product of a subjugated, backward society which moved in his lifetime toward political independence. Both men were educated outside their native lands, and both were influenced by radical social teachings including, in both instances, Marxism. The parallelism perhaps ends there, but the similarities we are able to see between the careers of Marković and Nehru are of considerable significance.

We should bear in mind the obvious but frequently ignored fact that radical social teachings can flourish in advanced as well as in backward societies: we need look no farther than the strong Marxist parties in Western Europe to be reminded that socialism does not necessarily have to feed on poverty. Nevertheless, socialism has enjoyed its greatest successes and its most spectacular perversions in backward countries, and it is to the experience of those countries that we turn in our attempt to understand it.

While it is certainly true that not *all* intellectuals in the "underdeveloped nations" turn to radical social teachings, it is equally true that, in the modern world, the great majority of them *do* opt for programs and "solutions" which promise the most immediate and sweeping social reforms. To such men, socialism is indeed "a cry of grief, sometimes of anger," and the *promise* it seems to hold for the future is of infinitely more importance than its *program* for the future. They are impatient, skeptical men, and they are not prepared to wait for God to smile on their lands as on Columbia: the noble American experiment, most of them believe, succeeded largely due to overwhelming good fortune. For such men the world moves too swiftly to allow their potential Jeffersons and Hamiltons and Marshalls sufficient time to create a stable, democratic society: the new society must be created now, and egalitarianism must precede democracy.

Rightly or wrongly, the majority of intellectuals in backward countries hold such beliefs. It is the historian's task to determine why they do so. In the present work we shall, through an historical and theoretical analysis of the work and thought of Svetozar Marković, attempt to point the way toward an answer to the problem. And by incorporating Marković's intellectual biography the book can perhaps help bring him the recognition he richly deserves. Finally, it may—hopefully—serve as a small testament to the historicity of the Balkans.

THE NATURE OF SERBIAN SOCIETY IN THE NINETEENTH CENTURY

In order to understand Svetozar Marković we must understand the nature of the society in which he lived. The multifarious problems of nineteenth-century Serbia were such that they had by the 1860's produced a psychological milieu which led Marković and many of his fellow intellectuals to see their resolution through socialism. What was the nature of that milieu?

Problems of State-Building. Turning first to politics, we should note that, after more than four centuries of Ottoman rule, the Serbs had no real political traditions. Memories of their great medieval empire provided scant foundation upon which illiterate and inexperienced peasant masses could build a modern state. Significantly, when the Serbs did finally rise against their Turkish masters, their original purpose was to restore the benevolent rule of the last governor of the province, Hadji Mustapha.

The Serbian Revolution (1804-12), which developed into a full-scale national liberation movement, was an event of no small significance in modern European history. The revolution occurred at a time when, due to the international situation, no power was willing or able to aid the Serbs. There was none of the European enthusiasm for the

Serbs that one witnesses in the case of the Greeks during their War of Independence (1821-30); the latter, of course, came at a time when Napoleon had departed from the European scene. The Serbs were unable to secure a European united front against the Turks; rather, they were left largely to themselves. As a result Serbian independence had to come slowly over a lengthy period.

Despite their isolation, however, by 1815 the Serbs had won a considerable measure of autonomy through their own efforts. In 1815 Miloš Obrenović, one of the leaders of the revolution, was recognized by the Ottoman sultan as supreme *knez* (prince) in Serbia; fifteen years later Miloš was proclaimed *hereditary* prince and Serbian autonomy was officially decreed. All estates belonging to Turkish landowners were expropriated (with compensation to the owners) in 1830, taxation was established on an annual basis, and the Turks agreed to restrict their garrisons to eight frontier towns.[9]

Events were to prove that Serbian autonomy had been dearly bought. In 1817 Miloš inspired the murder of Black George Petrović (Karađorđe), the original leader of the revolution, and sent his head to the sultan. The stage was thus set for the Obrenović-Karađorđević feud which was to torment Serbian politics for nearly ninety years. Further, the newly autonomous principality was in a difficult diplomatic situation. Manifestly unable to stand alone against the Ottoman Empire, still its suzerain, Serbia was obliged to look either to Austria or to Russia for support. After the revolution Austria quickly established strong economic ties

[9] Cf. Mihajlo Gavrilović, *Miloš Obrenović*, I (1813-20), Belgrade, 1908. See also B. Kunibert, *Srpski ustanak i prva vladavina Miloša Obrenovića* (*The Serbian Uprising and the First Reign of Miloš Obrenović*), Belgrade, 1901. On the revolution see Ivan Avakumović, "Literature on the First Serbian Insurrection (1804-1813)," *Journal of Central European Affairs*, vol. 13, no. 3, October 1953, pp. 257-260, and Wayne S. Vucinich, "Marxian Interpretations of the First Serbian Revolution," *Journal of Central European Affairs*, vol. 21, no. 1, April 1961.

with Serbia, and Russia was now the chief enemy of the Turks.

In the opinion of many Serbs Russia had done little to help her Balkan Slav brothers in their revolution. This perhaps not altogether fair opinion was shared and reinforced by many of the Austrian Serbs who had crossed the Danube to assist in the revolt and help build an autonomous Serbia (the while making a handsome living as state servants). Some of the latter, reared in the Western culture of the Habsburg lands, encouraged the Serbian Serbs to turn their attention away from backward Russia and concentrate upon winning the friendship and imitating the culture of Austria. But many Serbs found it impossible to turn away from the Russians, their kinsmen by blood and faith, and the problem of Serbia's dual "allegiances" was to haunt that country's politics and divide its citizens for over a century. The situation was frequently exacerbated through Austrian and Russian political pressures which invariably were reflected in Serbian politics.

After 1815 Miloš Obrenović ruled Serbia as his personal despotate. He exercised direct supervision over all state affairs, including the most routine administrative problems; he appropriated some of the best lands for his own use; he regulated trade to suit his personal financial interests; and he installed his relatives and friends (together with scores of the Austrian Serbs) in the upper echelons of the bureaucracy. Miloš dispensed justice personally, acting as both judge and jury, and took little notice of the National Assembly which had been established in 1815. The Assembly met only when he summoned it and was in any event dominated (at least in the early years of his reign) by his friends.

Having overthrown an alien autocracy, the Serbs were in no mood to tolerate a native one. Opposition to Miloš' rule mounted steadily, and the dissident elements in Serbia found support in both Constantinople and St. Petersburg. The sultan and the tsar, both hoping to extend a greater degree of control over Serbia, jointly demanded that Miloš grant a constitution embodying wide powers for an advisory council.[10] The two powers were certainly not motivated by any newfangled enthusiasm for democracy; both wished on the contrary to establish a Serbian oligarchy which would, they hoped, be more tractable than Miloš.

Understandably reluctant to relinquish power, Miloš stalled and made a rather feeble attempt to enlist British support on his side. Late in 1838 he was suddenly confronted with a *fait accompli* when the sultan issued a *hatt-i sherif* (organic decree) which established an advisory body to maintain a check on the prince. Unable to endure the curb on his powers, Miloš abdicated within half a year and went into voluntary exile.[11]

Milan Obrenović succeeded his father but died less than a month after his election by the new advisory council. A second son, Michael, then became prince under the tutelage of a regency. Despite his youth (he was seventeen) Michael did not prove the malleable figurehead wanted by the regents and the advisors. After three years of confusion and conflict the Belgrade politicians deposed Michael and elected in his stead Alexander Karađorđević, the son of the leader of the first uprising.

During Alexander's reign (1842-58) the council of advisors and the bureaucracy were the real rulers of Serbia.[12] Interpreting the 1838 *hatt-i sherif* to their own advantage, these "defenders of the constitution" effectively under-

[10] Grgur Jakšić and Dragoslav Stranjaković, *Srbija od 1813 do 1858* (*Serbia from 1813 to 1858*), Belgrade, n.d., pp. 67ff.

[11] Gavrilović, *Miloš Obrenović*, III.

[12] The standard work on the period is Slobodan Jovanović's excellent *Ustavobranitelji i njihova vlada (1838-1858) (The Defenders of the Constitution and their Rule* [*1838-1858*]), Belgrade, 1912.

mined the power of the prince. A Civil Code modeled closely on that of Austria (and thus indirectly on the *Code Napoleon*) was adopted in 1844, and the rule of the advisors and bureaucrats was patterned, in the 1840's and 1850's, after the Metternich and Bach regimes in Austria.

In the realm of foreign affairs the weak Alexander was torn between the "Russian party," which favored close ties with St. Petersburg, and the budding national-liberal movement which was oriented toward the West. Alexander's cautious, uncertain foreign policy during the revolutionary year of 1848-49 and later in the Crimean War cost him what little support he enjoyed in the country, and in 1858 he was forced to call for the convocation of a National Assembly.

The St. Andrew National Assembly (so called because it met on that day) convened late in 1858 and as its first order of business deposed Alexander.[13] Many of the delegates, disgusted with the corrupt and inefficient rule of the bureaucrats, demanded the return of the old autocrat, Miloš Obrenović. Despite some opposition there was indeed no reasonable alternative, and Miloš was recalled from exile to rule his countrymen a second time. He was summoned, paradoxically, by a National Assembly dominated by the growing liberal party. Though not averse to a strong ruler, the liberals insisted that the government be responsive to the wishes and needs of the nation. These liberals, schooled in the West, had become a potent force in the life of the nation. Were they to gain the upper hand in the government, the problem of Serbia's dual allegiances would be resolved in favor of the West.[14]

[13] Slobodan Jovanović, "Sastanak Svetoandrejske skupštine" ("The Convocation of the St. Andrew National Assembly"), *Sabrana dela*, v, Belgrade, 1933, pp. 376-420; Živan Živanović, *Politička istorija Srbije u drugoj polovini devetnaestog veka* (*The Political History of Serbia in the Second Half of the 19th Century*), I, Belgrade, 1923, pp. 32-59.

[14] *Vlada Milana*, I, pp. 230ff.

But in Serbia, as in all "developing nations," much depended upon the strength and character of the ruler. Miloš lived only until 1860, but in the two years of his second reign he clearly demonstrated his intention to return, as far as possible, to his old autocratic ways. Upon his death he was again succeeded by his son Michael, who likewise was not inclined to permit any significant curb on the princely powers.[15]

Michael Obrenović proved to be the most capable ruler Serbia was to find in the nineteenth century. A cultivated, intelligent, and ambitious man, he quickly left no doubt that he intended to rule without interference from the liberals or any other political faction. One of his first acts was to promulgate a new constitution which strengthened the powers of the prince and weakened those of the National Assembly. Ministerial rule, which had earned a deservedly unsavory reputation under Alexander, was replaced by the quasi-autocratic rule of the prince.

Michael enjoyed his greatest successes in the field of foreign affairs. When the Turks bombarded Belgrade in 1862 over a minor, local quarrel, Michael turned the incident to his own advantage and secured the withdrawal of Turkish troops from four of the eight garrison towns. Early in 1867, when the Turks were occupied with the Cretan insurrection, Michael pressured the sultan into withdrawing the remainder of his troops. Serbia was now a vassal in name only: no more than token Ottoman suzerainty remained in the land.[16]

In an attempt to form a Balkan alliance against the Turks, Michael concluded secret offensive agreements with Rumania, Montenegro, Greece, and a Bulgarian revolutionary society. Arms and supplies were collected and

15 Slobodan Jovanović, *Druga vlada Miloša i Mihaila* (*The Second Reign of Miloš and Michael*), Belgrade, 1923.

16 Živanović, *Politička istorija Srbije*, I, pp. 126ff.

stored, and a concerted uprising was planned for 1868. Before it could be launched, however, Michael was assassinated. Upon his death the entire project collapsed. The same fate befell Michael's dreams of eventual Balkan unity.[17]

Michael's death led to a grave political crisis in Serbia, out of which there developed a system of party politics. The problem of Serbia's political and cultural orientation came to a head in the decade 1868-78, and Svetozar Marković and his followers were to play an important role in the attempt to resolve it.

The Land and the People. The political and cultural problems which confronted Serbia in the crucial decade after the assassination of Prince Michael were inextricably linked with and to a large extent conditioned by socio-economic developments during the first half century of autonomy. In 1815 Serbia embraced an area of roughly 38,000 square kilometers and had a population of a little over one million.[18] The overwhelming majority (about 90.5 per cent in 1850) of the population lived in rural areas and earned its living exclusively from the land.[19] During the Turkish period the towns were inhabited almost exclusively by the Turks and other foreign elements (Greeks, Jews,[20] Magyars, Germans, and others), but in autonomous

[17] For an interesting recent analysis of Michael's schemes see Vasa Čubrilović, *Istorija političke misli u Srbiji XIX veka* (*The History of Political Thought in Serbia in the 19th Century*), Belgrade, 1958, pp. 229-236.

[18] See the irregularly published *Državopis Srbije* (*Statistique de la Serbie*) of the Ministry of Finance, Belgrade. For other early statistics see M. Ć. Milićević, "Serbskaia obshchina" ("The Serbian Commune"), *Russkaia Beseda* (Moscow), vol. 6, 1859, pp. 49-64.

[19] Vladislav Milenković, *Ekonomska istorija Beograda* (*The Economic History of Belgrade*), Belgrade, 1932, chaps. I and II. See also Nikola Vučo, *Privredna istorija Srbije do prvog svetskog rata* (*The Economic History of Serbia to the First World War*), Belgrade, 1955.

[20] Until the latter part of the nineteenth century Jews were not permitted to live outside Belgrade; exceptions were, however, occasionally allowed. See Zh. (Živojin Žujović), "Serbskoe selo" ("The Serbian Village"), *Sovremennik* (St. Petersburg), no. 5, May 1865, p. 126.

Serbia the urban population rapidly shifted in favor of the Serbs.

The Middle Class. Before turning to the peasantry let us examine for a moment this growing urban population. It was composed of bureaucrats, tradesmen, craftsmen, some of the clergy, foreigners, and others. There was a tiny urban professional class of doctors, lawyers, teachers, and a handful of engineers, but its growth, like that of the educated class in general, was a painfully slow process.

The old system of guilds (*esnafs*) which had prevailed under the Turks had of course embodied the interests of the foreign craftsmen in the towns. With the influx of Serb artisans after 1815, however, the system was disrupted. Certain crafts (e.g., fez-making) disappeared entirely, and others suffered serious decline due to the importation of manufactured wares, chiefly from Austria. Nevertheless, the number of individuals employed in the crafts rose steadily throughout the nineteenth century. The government attempted to regularize the guild system by law in 1847; by the 1870's, however, the guilds had lost much of their influence. They were finally abolished in 1910.[21]

The bureaucrats, tradesmen, and the few entrepreneurs formed the nucleus of a tiny but growing middle class. By 1865 there were over 21,000 urban dwellers who paid direct taxes; by way of comparison, there were in the same year nearly 200,000 such taxpayers in rural areas.[22] After the abdication of Prince Miloš in 1839 the embryonic middle class, despite its numerical insignificance, controlled the economic and political life of Serbia. The rapidly swelling bureaucracy—a characteristic phenomenon in "emerging nations"—created an administrative despotism which

21 On the guilds see Nikola Vučo, *Raspadanje esnafa u Srbiji* (*The Disintegration of the Guilds in Serbia*), Belgrade, 1954. On the opposition to the guilds see Karasëv, *Svetozar Markovich*, p. 76.

22 Žujović, "Serbskoe selo," p. 126.

placed an ever-growing tax burden upon the peasantry.[23]

A small but nevertheless important influx of foreign capital, coupled with the development of native enterprises, accelerated the transition from a natural to a money economy. The net effect of the growing capitalist system in Serbia was to increase the exploitation of the peasantry. By the 1870's the situation had become intolerable, and the peasants and their sympathizers in the urban areas began to call for radical reforms of the social and economic structure of the country.

Despite the distress of the peasantry, however, we should see the growth of Serbian capitalism in its true perspective. Capitalism in Serbia remained of the commercial rather than the industrial variety until very late in the nineteenth century. As late as 1875 there was only one factory worthy of the name in the country; the bulk of the "enterprises" were small undertakings of no great consequence economically or socially.[24] The claims of some Marxist writers that the artisan class was being proletarianized throughout the century[25] are simply not in accordance with the facts. It was not the urban "workers"—even the term is misleading—who were being exploited but rather the peasants; and the exploitation of the peasantry can be traced directly to the inevitable upheavals and dislocations which accompany the shift from a natural to a money economy.[26]

The Peasantry. The Serbian peasant was indeed in serious economic difficulties during the first half century of autonomy, and his plight grew steadily worse. The un-

23 Slobodan Jovanović, "Svetozar Marković," pp. 105-132.

24 V. G. Karasëv, "Osnovnye cherty sotsial'no-ekonomicheskogo razvitiia Serbii v kontse 60-kh-nachale 70-kh godov XIX v." ("The Fundamental Characteristics of the Socio-Economic Development of Serbia at the End of the Sixties and Beginning of the Seventies of the 19th Century"), *UZIS*, v, p. 212.

25 Žarko Plamenac (Árpád Lebl), "'Realizam' i—realnost. Nova nauka" ("'Realism' and Reality. The New Science"), *Pregled* (Sarajevo), vol. 13, no. 158, 1937, pp. 91-93.

26 See below, chap. v, pp. 198, 206-209.

shackling of the Turkish yoke was followed by a series of economic disarrangements which had not spent themselves even in the middle of the twentieth century. The old natural, primitive economy of the Serbian *zadruga* (extended family commune) began to fall apart as early as 1815.[27] During the Turkish period the overwhelming majority of the Serbs had lived in self-sufficient *zadrugas* and had had little contact with the outside world—little indeed even with neighboring villages.

In the first years of Prince Miloš' rule land was cheap, and many peasants left the restrictive confines of the patriarchal *zadrugas* to build their own farms. Immigrants from Bosnia-Hercegovina and other areas inhabited by Serbs flocked into the newly autonomous principality and received free land and tax preference—a situation which thus added a further stimulus to the tendency toward private farming. All too often, however, the peasant who rushed to establish his own farm quickly found himself reduced to subsistence farming. Usurers rapidly established themselves in the villages and exploited the peasants unmercifully. Local merchants likewise played upon the ignorance of the peasants to drive them still deeper into debt.

Peasant indebtedness, and the decline of the communalist *zadrugas*, was further accelerated by the introduction of a money economy. It was now no longer possible for the *zadruga* to be merely self-sufficient: taxes had to be paid in money rather than in kind, and the peasants were obliged to produce for the market. Resentment at being forced to share in the new responsibilities of the *zadruga* drove many peasants to leave it; the old laws and regulations prohibiting the alienation of the communal land were thrown to the winds as the peasants increasingly came to demand the liquidation of the venerable family commune and the division of its property.[28]

27 See below, chap. VI.

28 Jozo Tomasevich, *Peasants, Politics, and Economic Change in Yugoslavia*, Stanford and London, 1955, pp. 160-202.

The proud Serbian peasant, now the owner of his land, was faced with the problem of producing cash crops and selling those crops and his livestock in the market place in competition with other small farmers. Primitive and inefficient agricultural practices, coupled with a lack of familiarity with the intricacies of the business world, quickly led the peasant into grave financial difficulty. Peasant indebtedness increased astronomically; having no state credit institutions to which he could turn,[29] the peasant was driven into the clutches of the village usurer.

The steady growth of the urban population, the bureaucracy, and the army worsened the economic plight of the peasantry. By the middle of the nineteenth century nearly ten per cent of the population had left the ranks of the producers; the percentage was neither unusual nor of momentous import per se, but the ever-increasing tax burdens upon the peasants—a seemingly inevitable concomitant of a reduction in their numbers—did have the effect of compounding their distress.

The Serbian government early recognized the fundamental importance of the peasant problem and endeavored to solve it through legislation. In 1815 Prince Miloš secured the abolition of the Turkish *chifliks* (fully heritable land) in Serbia, and fifteen years later *all* land owned by Turkish landlords was confiscated and turned over to the peasants. Further in his attempt to base his rule upon a landed peasantry rather than on a landlord class, in 1836 Miloš passed a unique "Homestead Act" designed to guarantee the peasant a "protected minimum" of land and movable property which could not be taken from him under any circumstances.[30] There were, however, a number of loopholes in the law (e.g., it did not apply if the peasant wished

29 The first state credit bank was established in Belgrade in 1862, but it had no branches in the interior of the country.

30 Jelenko Petrović, *Okućje ili zaštita zemljoradničkog minimuma* (*The Protected Minimum Homestead*), Belgrade, 1930.

to give up farming altogether), and in any event it was not incorporated into the Civil Code of 1844.

With the development of a centralized bureaucratic state, local self-government, which had flourished in Serbia during the Turkish era, began to break down. In the 1870's Serbia was divided into 17 provinces (*okrugs*), 57 districts (*srezes*), 48 urban areas, and 1,041 rural communes (*opštinas*).[31] The *opština* had long been the basic unit of local autonomy and had functioned smoothly without serious interference from Belgrade officialdom. In the reign of Alexander Karađorđević, however, the *opštinas* began to fall into the hands of bureaucrats appointed by the central government. The old town-meeting kind of rough democracy which had prevailed in the communes gave way before the growth of a modern state apparatus. Such a development was perhaps inevitable, but the fact remains that the curbs on local self-government imposed by the Belgrade authorities contributed to the spread of dissatisfaction among the peasantry.[32]

Thus the peasants, a class of small proprietors with strong if increasingly repressed traditions of communal autonomy, had by the early 1870's been driven to a point of economic and political exasperation. Proud of the fact that he had driven the hated Turk from his land, the Serbian peasant was perplexed by the lack of freedom he had under a government of his own countrymen. His land was less securely his own than in Turkish times, his taxes were higher, his government more obtrusive into his affairs. To the peasant it seemed that he had indeed exchanged one set of masters for another; and in many respects the new masters were worse than the old, for they were of his own kind.

To whom was the peasant to turn for relief? His gov-

31 Karasëv, "Osnovnye cherty," p. 209. The term "opština" was also used for districts within the larger cities.

32 Cf. Vladimir Jovanović, "Obština" ("The Commune"), *Glasnik srpskog učenog društva*, vol. 34, 1872, pp. 86-150.

ernment promised much in the way of redress of grievances but produced little or nothing. The Serbian peasant increasingly came to feel that his enemies included not only the usurer and the merchant but also the government. When the economic crisis of the early 1870's struck, the peasant turned to the only group in Serbia which promised to help him fight this oppressive triumvirate: the radical-socialist party of Svetozar Marković.

The Intelligentsia. The radical-socialist party which came into being in 1869 was a natural product of the social and economic development of autonomous Serbia. During the first few decades after 1815 an educated class slowly came into existence, but it had not, by the middle of the century, found the leadership and coherence necessary to free the minds of the Serbs from the stagnation of the Turkish era. Two early intellectuals, Dositej Obradović (1739-1811) and Vuk Karadžić (1787-1864), endeavored to bring their countrymen into contact with the ideas of the Enlightenment and the romantic movement, respectively. Their efforts were, however, limited to the educated class, which even at the time of Karadžić's death numbered only a few thousand individuals.

In 1857 there were in Serbia 11,461 males and 959 females attending schools ranging from local grammar schools to the *lycée* in Belgrade.[33] As late as 1874 the literacy rate in the country was between five and ten per cent.[34] Since there were no educational institutions above the level of the one *lycée,* Serbian students who wished to continue their education were obliged to go abroad. Obviously, most of these students returned home steeped in the ideas of the lands in which they had studied. The Serbs who were educated in Germany, Austria, and France returned to Serbia familiar with the ideas and ideologies of those

[33] Milićević, "Serbskaia obshchina," p. 50.
[34] Karasëv, "Osnovnye cherty," p. 209.

countries; those who studied in Russia (a very small minority prior to the 1870's) were exposed to the intellectual currents prevalent there.

The ideas of the Russian Slavophils and Pan-Slavs penetrated Serbia through some of the students who studied in Russia (as well as through Pan-Slav propaganda), but it would seem that the students who brought back such ideas were few in number and lacking in influence. The majority of the Serbs who studied in Russia in the 1860's and 1870's were attracted to the Russian revolutionaries; it was the influence of the latter which colored the social and political *Weltanschauung* of the Serbian intelligentsia —the alienated segment of the educated class which became determined to reform Serbian society. This intelligentsia brought back to Serbia revolutionary democratic theories learned in Russia; the theories were of Western origin, but it was through their refraction in the Russian prism that they influenced the Serbian—and the Bulgarian—intelligentsia.

The challenging task of analyzing a revolutionary movement becomes still more complex in those cases where theories coined for advanced, industrialized countries are applied in *backward* societies in which conditions are ostensibly not at all favorable for their implementation. The fact that Western revolutionary theories (or Russianized versions of them) traveled from Russia, a backward country, to still more backward Serbia is of major significance. Neither Russia nor still less Serbia had any "right" to those theories, which were fashioned to fit the alleged needs, and to conform with the political and socio-economic background of Western Europe. There is no zealot like a converted zealot, but more significant than his zeal are the causes of his conversion; it is important to point out at this juncture that the greatest "conversion-ground" to Western radical thought was, for the Balkan intelligentsia, Russia.

The revolutionary ferment for which the Balkan Peninsula became notorious was spurred by Serbs and Bulgars who received their education in Russia. Of these revolutionaries, the first and in a number of respects the most important was Svetozar Marković, a typical representative of the Serbian intelligentsia.

Most of the young men of the Serbian educated class were employed by the state. Lucrative careers were open to them in the bureaucracy, and comparatively few were those who renounced what was known to be an easy and comfortable life. But those who did decline a bureaucratic career were a significant group. Their reasons for pursuing their minority path were many, and, by and large, it was personal choice rather than lack of opportunity which led educated Serbs to refuse to work for the state. For such individuals, however, there remained the problem of making a living. Those whose fathers were merchants were frequently able to enter the family business, but the educated sons of artisans and peasants were extremely reluctant to work with their hands, and those from families of bureaucrats who did not choose to follow in their fathers' footsteps found it difficult to secure suitable employment.

The intellectuals among this group of unemployed members of the educated class were often, precisely because of their education at the hands of the Russian revolutionaries, unable to work within society. They could not be used in society, for they were psychologically outside it and alienated from it.

Being on the outside, this alienated intelligentsia, in order to have the authority to reform society, had to speak on behalf of a well-defined class *within* society, a class of unquestionable historical and social significance. All serious revolutionaries have to adopt, at least until they come to power, the interests of an established class in society and, moreover, of a class which is in real or potential economic difficulty.[35] In Serbia and in the rest of the Balkans that class could only be the peasantry, and it was to the peasants that Svetozar Marković and his fellow alienated intellectuals turned as the class upon which to build a socialist society in Serbia.

[35] In his essay "The Intelligentsia," Arthur Koestler, speaking of the intelligentsia of the 1930's, made the point in sledge-hammer fashion: "An intelligentsia deprived of this prop of an alliance with an ascending class must turn against itself and develop that hot-house atmosphere, that climate of intellectual masturbation and incest, which characterized it during the last decade." *The Yogi and the Commissar*, New York, Collier Books, 1961, p. 72.

CHAPTER II

The Serb in the Smorgon Academy

ACCORDING to the family legend, Svetozar Marković's grandfather and two great-uncles, prominent, prosperous men in the Kosovo region of Old Serbia, were forced to flee to the Belgrade *pashalik* (Serbia) in the second decade of the nineteenth century. One of the girls in the family had been abducted by a Turk; the offender was hunted down and killed by the Marković brothers. The authorities immediately ordered the arrest and execution of the brothers, but before Turkish justice could be done the entire family escaped.

The Serbia into which the Markovićes came was in revolt against the Ottoman Empire, and the family was safe from prosecution. The brothers and their families established themselves in the village of Donja Sabanta and soon recovered some of their former prosperity. Svetozar Marković's father, Radoje, benefited from the family's recovery to the extent of receiving an elementary education, no mean accomplishment in early nineteenth-century Serbia.

In the late 1830's, when the documentation of the affairs of the Marković family permits the researcher to leave the realm of legend, Radoje Marković entered the service of Prince Miloš as a minor provincial functionary.[1] The loyalties of the Markovićes, however, lay not with the Obrenovićes but with the son of Black George Petrović (Karađorđe), the leader of the first Serbian uprising. Radoje Marković supported Alexander Karađorđević in the dynastic upheavals of 1838-39, and was rewarded with a promotion when Alexander became prince. Radoje's ca-

[1] *Skerlić*, p. 11; *Pravda*, Belgrade, May 6, 1933, p. 8.

reer was not hampered when he married the daughter of the district prefect; from the marriage were born four daughters and two sons, Jevrem and Svetozar. Svetozar, the second son, was born in the town of Zaječar in September of 1846.[2] Immediately after his birth his father applied to Belgrade for a promotion, calling attention to his loyalty to Prince Alexander and citing his "poor situation" as the basis for his application. Radoje Marković's request was granted, and he was posted to the village of Rekovac.[3]

MARKOVIĆ'S EARLY YEARS

Young Svetozar attended the first two grades of grammar school in Rekovac, and his formal education was supplemented with regular lessons from his father. By the time Svetozar had completed the second grade he was reading newspaper accounts of the Crimean War to his family; his exploits in the world of learning amazed the peasants in his district and made him a favorite of his teachers.[4] The Marković family moved to the town of Jagodina in the autumn of 1854, and Svetozar continued his education in the local grammar school. Though he himself, apparently because of his academic prowess, generally escaped the wrath of his teachers, Svetozar later wrote of the torments endured by some of his young schoolmates. A favorite form of discipline consisted of forcing an errant schoolboy to stand on one leg, holding a pitcher of water in one hand and hanging onto the bell rope with the other; if the water spilled or the bell rang, the unfortunate was severely

[2] S. M. Prvanović, "Gde je rođen Svetozar Marković?" (Where was Svetozar Marković born?"), *Arhivski pregled,* Belgrade, no. 1-2, 1956, pp. 44-46. A lengthy controversy over Marković's birthplace has been waged in Yugoslav journals for half a century; Prvanović presents ample evidence to establish Zaječar as the scene.

[3] *DANRS,* Ministarstvo Unutrašnjih Dela, I, 173/1845.

[4] Marković, "Kako su nas vaspitavali" ("How We Were Raised"), *Sabrani spisi,* I, pp. 31-32.

beaten. The teacher who introduced this variant of pedagogical sadism frequently cursed his pupils in German and Magyar, with the result that they went about the village, as Svetozar noted, shouting words not found in any dictionary.[5]

For reasons of an obscure personal nature, in 1856 Radoje Marković and his children moved to Kragujevac, the chief town in the Šumadija region of Serbia. There Svetozar entered the *polugimnazija* (junior high school). The curriculum was devoted to the study of the medieval trivium —grammar, rhetoric, and logic—but some natural science was also taught. Competent and human teachers, according to Svetozar, were rare exceptions, and he and his classmates revolted against both teachers and curriculum by discarding books and knowledge at the first opportunity.[6]

Svetozar managed to finish at or near the top of each grade, and in 1860 he was admitted to the *gimnazija* (high school) in Belgrade. His father had died in 1858,[7] and he was now supported by his older brother, Jevrem, who had become an officer in the army. When Svetozar first came to Belgrade he lived in the home of one of his brother's fellow officers, Lieutenant Jovan Dragašević, then a professor at the Artillery School.[8]

5 *Ibid.*, pp. 32-33.

6 *Ibid.*, pp. 33-40. For a corroborative account see Momir Veljković, "Marginalije Pavla Mihajlovića na 'Svetozaru Markoviću' od Dr. J. Skerlića" ("Pavle Mihajlović's Marginalia on Dr. J. Skerlić's *Svetozar Marković*"), *Književni sever*, Subotica, vol. 8, 1932, no. 6, pp. 178-179.

7 There has been some confusion concerning the date of Radoje Marković's death. One of his daughters recalled a half a century later that he had died in 1858 of shock occasioned by the overthrow of the Karađorđe dynasty (*Skerlić*, p. 13). Some investigators, noting that Svetozar Marković collected his share of his father's estate in 1868, have claimed that Radoje died in that year (*Knijiževnost*, 1946, no. 9, p. 108). Svetozar could not, however, obtain his inheritance until he came of age, and there is no evidence whatsoever to suggest that his father lived beyond 1858.

8 Jovan Dragašević, *Istinske priče: Avtobiografija u odlomcima* (*True Tales: A Fragmentary Autobiography*), Belgrade, 1891, pp. 281-283. In

The Belgrade *gimnazija,* like all the schools in Serbia, was modeled on the German "classical" schools. In his article on his education Svetozar Marković sharply criticized the classical tradition and its application in Serbia. The Serbian schools attempted to provide culture rather than education, he insisted, for rhetoric, poetry, and Greek and Latin paradigms were emphasized at the expense of mathematics and science; Serbia should renounce the "classical" schools in favor of the *Realschule.* Although the Belgrade teachers were, according to Marković, almost as incompetent as those in the provinces, he nevertheless blamed the system rather than its agents for what he had come to regard as the abysmal state of Serbian education.

In 1863, having completed the course at the *gimnazija,* Svetozar Marković enrolled in the Technical Faculty of the Belgrade *Velika Škola* (*lycée*), the highest educational institution in Serbia. Looking back at the institution from the point of view of a sophisticated young college student, Marković wrote a few years later that the *Velika Škola* was incapable of providing Serbian students with a satisfactory education. Courses in the Technical Faculty, he recalled, were often conducted without practical experiments, and the Faculty had yet (1868) to graduate a single scientist competent in his field. The Law Faculty was equally derelict in its responsibilities, he insisted, for its professors were themselves poorly trained and the courses they gave dealt with legalisms rather than the concept and administration of justice; significantly enough, he noted, the graduates of the Law Faculty were better qualified to be bureaucrats than lawyers.[9]

addition to being a respected army officer Dragašević was also a scholar of some note and a minor poet. At one time he was a member of the Serbian general staff, and upon retirement was given the honorary rank of general.

9 "Kako su nas vaspitavali," pp. 55-56.

This rather bombastic indictment of the *Velika Škola* was on the whole justified. While Marković's own diploma indicates that students in the Technical Faculty devoted considerable time to the study of mathematics and the physical sciences,[10] the fact that in the latter disciplines they did not regularly perform experiments (due to the lack of both equipment and competent instructors) revealed a serious shortcoming in the curriculum. The *Velika Škola* was, to be sure, only a *lycée*, but its graduates often found themselves inadequately prepared when they went abroad to continue their studies.[11] In the case of the Law Faculty there were indeed few capable professors, and it was certainly true that most students entered that Faculty with the sole purpose of securing a well-paid government position. P. A. Rovinsky had in mind the professors and students of the Law Faculty when he wrote in 1870 that "idealism, in the sense of devotion to some sort of idea, is absolutely foreign to the Serb."[12]

The private life of the Belgrade students was wholly undisciplined. Belgrade citizens admonished one another to refrain from permitting students or soldiers to enter their homes, and "he staggers like a drunken student" was a common expression. Though little is known of Marković's own activities, it would appear that he was as fond of gambling, drinking, and related pursuits as were the majority of his contemporaries. He later referred to his student days as "the rotten years," and his earliest extant

10 *Dokumental'nye materialy*, Marković *Velika Škola* diploma.

11 On the *Velika Škola* (the forerunner of Belgrade University) see the articles by two of its rectors: Kosta Branković, "Razvitak Velike Škole" ("The Development of the Velika Škola"), *Glasnik srbskog učenog društva*, XVIII, pp. 1-24; Svetomir Nikolajević, "Kraljevsko-srpska Velika Škola za pedeset njenih godina" ("The Royal Serbian Velika Škola over Fifty Years"), *Godišnjica Nikole Čupića*, XII, 1891, pp. 202-232.

12 P. A. Rovinsky, "Belgrad, ego ustroistvo i obshchestvennaia zhizn' " ("The Structure and Social Life of Belgrade"), *Vestnik Evropy*, May 1870, part II, p. 137.

letter is one to his stepmother[13] in which he begged her forgiveness for his behavior. She had come to Belgrade on a visit and had found him, apparently intoxicated, in a gambling den.[14]

Despite the flamboyance which characterized all his writings and most of his actions, Svetozar Marković was haunted throughout his life by a sense of personal inadequacy. The roots of the problem, it seems clear, lay deep in Marković's emotional constitution, but the lack of any but peripheral sources renders speculation hazardous. He later admitted that he lacked confidence in himself during his student years in Belgrade; he had been well liked by everyone, he noted, and had had many friends, but he had come to believe that that friendship had been extended only because of his "weak character." "I could always 'agree' with everyone," he wrote in 1868, and "that 'agreement' corrupted me terribly."[15] It was a theme to which he often returned in later years. He detested any sign of weakness in himself and those around him, but he frequently confused weakness with honest doubt. Part of the "weakness" he saw in himself was possibly a reflection of his relations with the opposite sex. Though the evidence is scanty, it is clear that Marković maintained a normal and healthy interest in women, but it is likewise clear that his relations with them were never completely satisfactory.[16]

The "agreement" to which Marković referred in self-reproach concerned the rather vague liberalism to which he had subscribed during his student years in Belgrade.

[13] Radoje Marković remarried (about 1856) after the death of his first wife; Svetozar was devoted to his stepmother, and turned over to her his share of his father's small estate.

[14] *IAB*, Svetozar to Marija Marković, Belgrade, December 6, 1862, letter no. 1.

[15] *Sabrani spisi*, I, p. 83.

[16] See his frequent references to such matters in his letters to Milica and Anka Ninković in *Izbrannye sochineniia*.

By 1868 he had come under the influence of the Russian revolutionary democrats, and in the zeal of his conversion he regarded his earlier association with the Serbian liberals as proof of the weakness of his character.

Some writers, eager to prove the "progressive" character of Marković's work, have claimed that he left the liberals and embraced the philosophy of Russian revolutionary democracy even before he left Belgrade. One such writer has claimed that Marković and his friends in the *gimnazija* and the *Velika Škola* were known as the "seven apostles" of the teachings of Herzen, Chernyshevsky, and Pisarev;[17] another has declared that Marković shared a room in Belgrade with Liuben Karavelov, the Bulgarian revolutionary who was educated in Russia and who was active in *avant-garde* Serbian literary circles.[18] There exists no known evidence to support either contention, and it is beyond question that Svetozar Marković, during his student years in Belgrade, formed his still vague and indecisive political views wholly under the influence of the Serbian liberals. His political mentor was then Vladimir Jovanović, sometime professor at the *Velika Škola* and the foremost exponent of liberalism in nineteenth-century Serbia.

VLADIMIR JOVANOVIĆ AND THE LIBERALS

The career of Vladimir Jovanović (1833-1922),[19] especially in the critical decades between the Crimean War and the Russo-Turkish War of 1877-78, reflected the position and the aspirations of the Serbian liberals. The liberals held the allegiance of most of the young members of the

17 Todor Marković, "Ljuben Karavelov u srpskoj književnosti" ("Liuben Karavelov in Serbian Literature"), *Srpski književni glasnik*, series 1, vol. 24, 1910, p. 357.

18 Božidar Kovačević, "Život Svetozara Markovića" ("The Life of Svetozar Marković"), *Književnost*, 1, 1946, no. 9, p. 112.

19 I am indebted to Mr. Veljko Kuprešanin, Director of the Belgrade Historical Archives, for making available to me Vladimir Jovanović's unpublished *Avtobiografija* (*Autobiography*).

educated class in the 1860's, and a brief examination of Vladimir Jovanović's activities will perhaps serve to give some indication of the nature of the liberal movement which influenced Svetozar Marković and his contemporaries. Jovanović entered politics as a young man and was one of the chief ideologists of the Serbian liberals in the 1858 St. Andrew National Assembly.[20] He was briefly exiled in 1860 because of his political views but returned to Serbia after the death of Miloš. When the Turks bombarded Belgrade in 1862 the Serbian government sent Jovanović to London to plead its case against the sultan. In the British capital Jovanović published a brochure outlining the Serbian position which brought him to the attention of William Gladstone.

The Grecophile chancellor of the exchequer met Jovanović and suggested to him that a "Greco-Slavic union" —apparently Gladstone's personal idea—in the Balkans could count on the moral support of Great Britain. Jovanović also met Richard Cobden, many of whose views he adopted. Giuseppe Mazzini was also in London at the time, and he and Jovanović had several meetings. Jovanović's account of Turkish persecution inflamed the Italian liberal, who discussed with Garibaldi the possibility of forming a group of European volunteers to assist the Serbs; it was probably fortunate that the project was never realized. Jovanović met yet another well-known figure in London, the Russian anarchist-revolutionary Michael Bakunin. The sensible, proper Jovanović was more at home in the company of men like Gladstone and Cobden and Mazzini, but he was still a Slav and he noted after one of his meetings with Bakunin that "the Russo-Serbian ideal was: A UNION OF FREE AND INDEPENDENT SLAVIC PEOPLES."[21]

[20] Cf. Traian Stoianovich, "The Pattern of Serbian Intellectual Evolution 1830-1880," *Comparative Studies in Society and History*, I, no. 3, March 1959, p. 255.

[21] Jovanović, *Avtobiografija*, pp. 8-13.

After spending nearly a year in London propagandizing the cause of Serbian independence, Jovanović moved on to Italy, where he met the Hungarian revolutionary Louis Kossuth. He returned to Belgrade in the summer of 1863 and resumed his position at the *Velika Škola,* but in the following year he was summarily discharged for having proposed the names of Garibaldi and N. G. Chernyshevsky for honorary membership in the Serbian Literary Society. The Serbian government was apparently suspicious of his contacts with foreign revolutionaries (a category in which the Englishmen scarcely belonged!) and was furthermore reluctant to bestow honor on Chernyshevsky, who had just (May 1864) been tried and convicted for revolutionary activities in Russia.[22]

Upon his dismissal from the *Velika Škola* Jovanović left Serbia and went into voluntary exile in Switzerland. Settling in Geneva, he quickly made contact with the Russian revolutionary *émigrés* Herzen and Ogarëv.[23] Also among his circle of acquaintances were Lev Mechnikov, a member of Garibaldi's Thousand and a former associate of Chernyshevsky; Nikolai Utin, one of the founders of the Russian Section of the First International; and various Polish and Czech *émigrés.*[24]

One of Jovanović's major tasks in Switzerland was to edit a newspaper setting forth the views of the Serbian liberals. The liberals had not gained a voice in the government of Prince Michael, who saw in them the chief threat to his autocratic rule. Determined to make themselves heard, the liberals commissioned Jovanović to act as

22 Stanoje Simić, "Prilozi za građu o počecima socijalističkog pokreta u Srbiji" ("Contributions to the Materials on the Origins of the Socialist Movement in Serbia"), *Delo,* Belgrade, I, no. 5, July 1955, p. 580.

23 Herzen enjoyed great popularity among the Serbian liberals, who regularly received from London the *Kolokol* (*The Bell*); Todor Marković, "Ljuben Karavelov u srpskoj književnosti," pp. 534-540.

24 Jovanović, *Avtobiografija,* p. 17.

their propagandist.[25] From 1864 until 1866 Jovanović edited and published in Geneva the bilingual weekly *Sloboda-La Liberté*.[26] The newspaper proclaimed the goals of the Serbian liberals to be the achievement of complete independence from Turkey and the establishment of a constitutional monarchy on the British model. *Sloboda-La Liberté* resembled in many respects the *Kolokol* that Herzen had edited in London; Jovanović's liberalism reflected above all else the views of Herzen and Cobden.[27] The Serbian liberal spokesman bitterly attacked Prince Michael in his journal, accusing the prince of putting the welfare of the Obrenović dynasty above that of the nation; Michael was less interested in Serbian liberation, Jovanović charged, than in securing his own position.[28]

Despite the attempts of the Serbian government to prevent Jovanović's journal from entering Serbia,[29] *Sloboda-La Liberté* was regularly received and eagerly read throughout the principality. The journal faithfully reflected the views of the Serbian liberals who, having been inspired and encouraged by the events of the St. Andrew National Assembly in 1858, were now, in the reign of Prince Michael, disappointed and embittered over their exile to the political wilderness. Particularly frustrated were the impetuous young students who had come under the influence of

25 Vladimir Jovanović, *Les Serbes et la Mission de la Serbie dans l'Europe d'Orient*, Paris-Brussels, 1870, p. 209.

26 In 1865 the name was changed to *Srpska Sloboda-La Liberté Serbe*. Slobodan Jovanović has denied a charge that his father's newspaper was financed by Princess Persida, the wife of Alexander Karađorđević; *Jugoslovenski istoriski časopis*, II, books 1-4, pp. 243-246.

27 Kovačević, "Život Svetozara Markovića," p. 121.

28 Cf. the collection of articles from *Sloboda-La Liberté Serbe* which Vladimir Jovanović published as *Za slobodu i narod* (*For Freedom and the Nation*), Novi Sad, 1868. Jovanović and his associates in Geneva also published translations of foreign political works, among them Engel'son's "What is the State?"; cf. Božidar Kovačević, "Studenti u Cirihu oko godine 1870—prvi srpski socijalisti" ("The Students in Zürich Around 1870—the First Serbian Socialists"), *Književnost*, XI, no. 1, January 1956, p. 82.

29 Marković, *Sabrani spisi*, I, p. 363.

Jovanović and the older liberals; in October of 1865 several of those students wrote to Jovanović, praising his work in the cause of Serbian freedom and progress. In answer to his call for the formation of a liberal youth movement, the young Serbs wrote to Jovanović: "You appeal to the youth and in this you are not mistaken. The seeds which you sowed as a professor did not fall upon stones, but upon fertile soil. . . . The voice of freedom, with which you speak in the name of all true Serbs (despite the opposition of the 'parasites') is not a voice in the wilderness. Receive these few words with your heart, for we send them from the heart of Serbdom."[30] One of the signatories of the letter, and from the style quite possibly the author, was Svetozar Marković, then nineteen years old and in his last year at the *Velika Škola*.[31]

Svetozar Marković was an adherent of the liberal movement during his student years in Belgrade, and it was only after spending a year in Russia that he came to feel that he had joined the liberals for the sake of conformity rather than conviction. Although the lack of sources has made difficult the task of determining the precise nature of the views Marković held in Belgrade, it seems clear that, while he did go along with his colleagues in espousing liberalism, he was less enthusiastic about the criticism of Prince Michael. Michael was an energetic and capable ruler, and for many Serbs it was difficult to ignore the real accomplishments of his reign. The opposition of the liberals to Michael was opportunist rather than substantial; the rather pretentious aspirations of the liberals to create a constitutional monarchy on the British model reflected at once a commendable espousal of democratic principles and a distressing lack of political realism. The Serbia of the 1860's, caught between three rival empires, Austro-Hungarian, Ot-

[30] *Ibid.*, pp. 3-4, 363.
[31] *Jugoslovenski istoriski časopis*, II, pp. 243-246.

toman, and Russian, was in no position externally or internally to indulge in political experimentation. A strong and gifted ruler (the conclusion is inescapable) was needed, and Serbia had found such a man in Michael; she was to learn to her sorrow what the lack of such a ruler would mean for the state.

Though Svetozar Marković, as his later writings proved, was unable to agree fully with the liberals' view of Michael, he nevertheless remained in the liberal camp. By his own admission the most *avant-garde* writer he knew in Belgrade was Eugene Sue, whose *Story of a Proletarian Family* he returned to the library unread after having been unfavorably impressed by a brief glance.[32] Certainly there is no truth in the suggestions of some modern writers that Marković was an adherent of Russian revolutionary democracy during his years in Belgrade. He may have had a vague acquaintance with that movement, however, for the Serbian press had devoted a certain amount of attention to it. As early as 1861 a Serbian newspaper had printed a lengthy account of the Russian intelligentsia, singling out Herzen, Ogarëv, and Bakunin.[33] In 1863 a young Serb of vaguely socialist leanings, Živojin Žujović, wrote an article for Chernyshevsky's *Sovremennik;* since Žujović was well known in Belgrade, it is unlikely that his article (or a second one he published in the same journal in 1865) went unnoticed.[34] It has been established that *Sovremennik* was

[32] *Sabrani spisi,* I, p. 51.

[33] K. A. Koperzhinskii, "Serbskie deiateli 60-70kh godov i peredovaia russkaia literatura" ("Serbs of the 60's and 70's and Progressive Russian Literature"), *Nauchnyi Biulleten' Leningradskogo Universiteta,* no. 11-12, 1946, pp. 65-69.

[34] Zh. Sklav (Živojin Žujović), "Slavianskii iug" ("The Slavic South"), *Sovremennik,* no. 6, June 1863, pp. 259-274, and Zh. (Živojin Žujović), "Serbskoe selo" ("The Serbian Village"), *Sovremennik,* no. 5, May 1865, pp. 125-162. Žujović's authorship of the two articles is established by V. Bograd in *Zhurnal "Sovremennik" 1847-1866 (The Journal Sovremennik 1847-1866),* Moscow-Leningrad, 1959, p. 425. Chernyshevsky was of course no longer associated with *Sovremennik* when Žujović published his articles;

received in Prague in the early 1860's, and the probability of its penetration into Serbia can be assumed.[35] And despite the dismissal of Vladimir Jovanović from the *Velika Škola* for having proposed their names, Chernyshevsky and Garibaldi, along with Cobden and Herzen, in 1864 were elected to honorary membership in the Serbian Literary Society.[36]

But the fact remains that Western liberalism rather than Russian revolutionary democracy dominated the thinking of the educated Serbs in the 1860's. Certainly the Soviet historian B. P. Koz'min was correct in noting that Herzen and Chernyshevsky enjoyed considerable popularity in Serbia during the decade, but his assertion that the Russians helped shape the Serbian *Weltanschauung* in the sixties requires qualification.[37] Herzen, a liberal who leaned toward socialism, was known in Serbia almost exclusively for his liberalism; Chernyshevsky was regarded primarily as a victim of autocratic oppression. In the 1860's few Serbian students had gone to Russia to continue their education; the majority went to Austria, Germany, or France. The education they received in those lands led them to return home full of enthusiasm for the intellectual currents prevalent there. With the collapse of the revolutions of 1848-49 the Serbs turned to the liberal and national-revolutionary (but not the republican) doctrines of, primarily, Giuseppe Mazzini. The unification of Italy, which the Serbian liberals attributed to Mazzini rather than to Cavour, had an enor-

---

also on those articles see S. A. Nikitin, "Iuzhnoslavianskie sviazi russkoi periodicheskoi pechati 60-kh godov XIX veka" ("The South Slav Ties of the Russian Periodical Press in the 60's of the 19th Century"), *UZIS*, VI, 1952, p. 109.

35 Nikitin, "Iuzhnoslavianskie sviazi," pp. 110-111.

36 Jovan Skerlić, *Omladina i njena književnost ("Youth" and its Literature)*, Belgrade, 1906, p. 138.

37 B. P. Koz'min, *Revoliutsionnoe podpol'e v epokhu "Belogo Terrora" (The Revolutionary Underground in the Epoch of the "White Terror")*, Moscow, 1929, p. 42.

mous influence upon the Serbian educated class; Serbian liberalism and nationalism became inextricably linked, and together they dominated the thinking of the educated Serbs.[38] A final proof of the fact that the theories of the Russian revolutionary democrats were not well known in Serbia is indicated by the lack of translations of their works. A few of Pisarev's short articles were translated in 1869, and Chernyshevsky's *What is to be Done?* followed in the same year.[39] Russian was not a fashionable language in Serbia, and most of the Belgrade students, their attention riveted on developments in the West, studied German and French.[40] It was only when Svetozar Marković returned to his homeland in 1870 to popularize the theories of the Russian revolutionary democrats that Chernyshevsky and the other Russian "men of the sixties" came to exercise considerable influence in Serbia.

STUDY IN RUSSIA

Graduates of the *Velika Škola* being obliged to go abroad to continue their education, Svetozar Marković applied in 1865 for one of the scholarships offered by the Russian Ministry of Foreign Affairs.[41] The majority of his predecessors had gone to universities and technical schools in Central and Western Europe, but the number of Russian

38 Cf. Čubrilović, *Istorija političke misli u Srbiji*, pp. 240-245, 249-255.

39 For an incomplete chronological list of the translations of Russian works into Serbo-Croatian see G. Chuich, "Russkaia literatura na serbskom iazyke. Opyt bibliografii perevodnoi russkoi literatury za period s 1860-go po 1910-i god" ("Russian Literature in the Serbian Language. A Tentative Bibliography of Translated Russian Literature in the Period 1860-1910"), *Trudy Voronezhskogo Gosudarstvennogo Universiteta*, III, 1926, pp. 116-140. The Chuich article is indeed "tentative," and contains many gaps including much of the Russian literature published in Svetozar Marković's newspapers in the 1870's.

40 Such was the case with Svetozar Marković; cf. Momir Veljković, "Marginalije," pp. 178-179, and Marković, *Sabrani spisi*, I, p. 5.

41 *DANRS*, Ministarstvo Prosvete, F III, no. 444, k 1/865, Svetozar Marković's letter dated June 2, 1865.

scholarships available increased substantially after 1865 and more young Serbs were induced to continue their studies in Moscow, St. Petersburg, and Kiev. Both the Russian government and various Pan-Slav organizations offered financial assistance to students from the Slavic West and South.[42]

In the spring of 1866 Marković was awarded a four-year scholarship to attend the Institute of Ways and Communications in St. Petersburg. Though the scholarship ostensibly was sponsored by the Asiatic Department (responsible for Balkan affairs) of the Foreign Office, it is probable that it was financed by the St. Petersburg Slavic Committee. There were no conditions attached to the scholarship, but certainly both the Russian government and the Pan-Slav organizations were interested in acquiring as many friends as possible among the future leaders of the Balkan Slavs.

Soon after graduation from the *Velika Škola*[43] Marković left for Russia. With him traveled Aleksa Knežević, who had graduated the previous year and had also won a scholarship to the Institute of Ways and Communications. Journeying through Vienna, Prague, and Warsaw, the two young Serbs reached St. Petersburg early in August of 1866. Renting a small apartment at No. 30 Voznesensky Prospekt (now Prospekt Maiorova) not far from the institute, Marković and Knežević settled down and prepared to enter the student life of the capital.[44]

The St. Petersburg to which they came was, as Peter Kropotkin later said, "not the St. Petersburg of Chernyshevsky but already that of Trepov."[45] When he became

42 S. A. Nikitin, *Slavianskie komitety v Rossii v 1858-1876 godakh* (*The Slavic Committees in Russia, 1858-1876*), Moscow, 1960, pp. 96ff.

43 At his graduation Marković was one of the two remaining students from the class of four which had entered the Technical Faculty in the autumn of 1863; cf. Kovačević, "Život Svetozara Markovića," p. 113.

44 Marković, *Sabrani spisi*, I, p. 4; K. A. Pushkarevich, "Svetozar Markovich v Peterburge" ("Svetozar Marković in St. Petersburg"), *Trudy Instituta Slavianovedeniia Akademii Nauk SSSR*, I, 1932, pp. 347-348.

45 Quoted in Vladimir Viktorov-Toporov, "Svetozar Markovich," *Golos Minuvshago*, I, no. 3, March 1913, p. 36.

governor of St. Petersburg in 1866 General F. F. Trepov already had behind him, as Franco Venturi noted, "a remarkable career of brutality." Trepov, who had been chief of police in St. Petersburg since 1860, had earned his reputation both in the Russian capital and in Warsaw, where he had helped crush the uprising of 1863. After Dimitry Karakozov, a young revolutionary, tried to assassinate Tsar Alexander II in April of 1866, Trepov was promoted to the post of governor of St. Petersburg and given carte blanche to suppress the revolutionaries. He immediately instituted a régime of severe repression. Hundreds of arrests were made, and the unfortunates who fell into the hands of the police were occasionally tortured and often held incommunicado for weeks during intensive questioning. A rigid censorship was imposed; Chernyshevsky's *Sovremennik* (now edited by Nikolai Nekrasov) and *Russkoe Slovo,* the journal with which Pisarev had been associated, were suppressed in June of 1866. The educational system was revised; an uncompromising classicism was introduced in the secondary schools, and the universities were divested of their corporate organizations.

The dissident students were driven to form secret underground societies in which they occupied themselves with endless, fruitless internal debates. They had been caught largely by surprise when Karakozov at a stroke brought forth a new era in the fatal duel between revolutionaries and government, the era of the "White Terror."[46] Karakozov was executed in October after what has generally been considered a fair trial; his fate was no worse than that which befell several Irish contemporaries who attempted to assassinate Queen Victoria. Most of those of his circle who had been arrested were sentenced to prison or Si-

[46] The standard work on the period is B. P. Koz'min's *Revoliutsionnoe podpol'e v epokhu "Belogo Terrora."* General Trepov later added to his notoriety by managing to get himself shot by Vera Zasulich in 1878; on that famous case see A. F. Koni, *Vospominaniia o dele Very Zasulich* (*Recollections of the Vera Zasulich Affair*), Moscow-Leningrad, 1933.

berian exile. Trepov's "White Terror" quickly and effectively reestablished order and serenity, and to all outward appearances Russia had sunk once more into the deep and lifeless calm of the reign of Tsar Nicholas I (1825-55).

In the struggle against the revolutionaries the Russian government seemed to enjoy the support of the majority of the population. The revolutionaries had neglected to establish any genuine rapport with the class whose interests they professed to champion, the peasantry. The peasants were ignorant of the aims of the revolutionaries, and in most cases the reverse was also true. Neither the peasants nor the gentry nor the inchoate working class harbored any sympathy for the revolutionaries, whose program was as nebulous and ill-defined as their methods were, in the eyes of many, contemptible and inhuman. Isolated, vilified, and despised by the loyal elements of the population, the revolutionaries were considered the enemies of all men, the would-be ravishers of Mother Russia.

Such was the St. Petersburg and the Russia which Svetozar Marković and Aleksa Knežević found in the summer of 1866.

At the request of the Asiatic Department of the Ministry of Foreign Affairs, the Ministry of Communications directed the Institute of Ways and Communications to admit Marković and Knežević as first-year students. The request was approved by the director of the institute, General Sobolevsky, on September 2, 1866.[47]

The Emperor Alexander I Institute of Engineers of the Ways of Communications[48] was founded in 1809. Originally

[47] *Dokumental'nye materialy*, Ministerstvo Putei Soobshcheniia, August 11, 1866, no. 341; M.I.D., Department Aziiatskii, August 19, 1866, no. 2841; Institut Inzhenerov Putei Soobshcheniia, September 2, 1866, no. 1015; letter from Marković to General Sobolevsky, St. Petersburg, August 16, 1866.

[48] The French *Ponts et Chaussées* conveys more precisely the meaning of the Russian term, which I have elsewhere rendered as the Institute of Ways and Communications—less precise but also less clumsy than a literal translation.

staffed by foreign engineers, its first inspector was Lt. General Augustine de Betancourt, a noted engineer who had served both the Spanish Bourbons and Napoleon. The institute graduated many of the engineers who developed the Russian railway system, and later in the century, under the guidance of General Sobolevsky, it became one of the outstanding technical schools in the country.[49]

Marković and Knežević each received scholarships of three hundred rubles, payable at twenty-five rubles a month.[50] Despite the fact that the Serbian Ministry of Education granted both students a perquisite of fifteen rubles a month,[51] Marković, due partly to his own poor management, soon found himself in serious financial difficulties. Winter came early in 1866; the first snow fell in St. Petersburg on October 2, and Marković impulsively bought a fur coat which cost him more than a month's income. He likewise bought a pair of fashionable boots for eleven rubles; apparently he was not altogether satisfied with his purchases, for he complained in a letter to his brother that he was regularly "fleeced" by Russian tradesmen. He was furthermore troubled by the fact that he had to accept his scholarship payments in paper rubles, which were worth twenty per cent less than silver ones.[52]

Throughout his life Marković was plagued by financial problems. His attitude, particularly during his years abroad, frequently seemed to be that of a rather selfish individual who feared above all for his own comfort. He

49 See S. M. Zhitkov, *Institut Inzhenerov Putei Soobshcheniia Imperatora Aleksandra I*, St. Petersburg, 1899; A. M. Larionov, *Istoriia Instituta Inzhenerov Putei Soobshcheniia za pervoe stoletie ego sushchestvovaniia, 1810-1910* (*The History of the Institute of Engineers of the Ways of Communications During its First Century, 1810-1910*), St. Petersburg, 1910.

50 *Dokumental'nye materialy*, institute records. By way of comparison, the director of the institute received a salary of 4,200 rubles a year; Zhitkov, *op. cit.*, p. 469.

51 *DANRS*, Ministarstvo Prosvete, no. 961, k 1/868.

52 Marković, *Sabrani spisi*, I, pp. 4-6.

regularly borrowed money from his brother, money which he apparently never bothered to repay. In 1867 a Serbian creditor succeeded in attaching his scholarship after he had failed to pay a debt;[53] his troubles probably stemmed more from carelessness than from more serious personal shortcomings, but Marković was nevertheless somewhat self-centered and often displayed a disturbing lack of consideration even for his friends.

Though Marković was not as careful with his limited funds as he might have been it was in fact difficult for most students to maintain themselves adequately in Russia. High prices, inadequate scholarships, and a generally nonchalant attitude toward practical matters kept most students—Russians as well as foreigners—on the verge of disaster. One of the Bulgarians (Naiden Gerov) who studied in Russia sent a note of bitter warning to his countrymen: "He who does not wish to starve . . . had better not come here without money or a definite job awaiting him."[54]

The Slav students were brought to Russia by the various Slav committees. The Moscow Slavic Philanthropic Committee was founded in 1858 for the purpose of assisting non-Russian Slavs to study in Russia. From the outset the committee had a quasi-official character, for it was in direct contact with the Asiatic Department of the Russian Foreign Ministry.[55] Similar committees were subsequently established in St. Petersburg, Kiev, Odessa, and Kazan, but the Moscow committee remained the most active of the organizations and a considerable number of Slavic students came to Russia under its auspices. Serbs formed only about

53 *DANRS*, Ministarstvo Prosvete, F II/171, 1868.

54 Quoted in Nikitin, *Slavianskie komitety*, p. 97.

55 *Ibid.*, pp. 9-40. Further on the Slavic committees see the valuable article by K. A. Pushkarevich, "Balkanskie slaviane i russkie 'osvoboditeli' (Slavianskie komitety i sobytiia na balkanakh pered russko-turetskoi voinoi 1877-1878gg)" ("The Balkan Slavs and the Russian 'Liberators' [The Slavic Committees and Balkan Developments before the Russo-Turkish War of 1877-1878]"), *Trudy Instituta Slavianovedeniia AN SSSR*, II, 1934, pp. 189-229.

ten per cent of the total number of students sponsored by the Moscow committee, the majority of whom were Bulgarians.[56] In the period 1868-88 the St. Petersburg committee, which probably financed the scholarships awarded to Marković and Knežević, brought one hundred and four men and sixteen women students to Russia. Fifty-eight of the men and six of the women were from Serbia.[57] Various factors contributed to the increase in the number of students from Serbia: the 1862 bombardment of Belgrade by the Turks and the resultant wave of Russian indignation and sympathy, the revolutionary situation in Bosnia-Hercegovina in the 1870's and the Russian interest in the fate of the Ottoman Empire, the Russo-Turkish War of 1877-78, the Russian desire to counter Serbia's dependence upon Austria after the Congress of Berlin, and, finally, the penetration of Russian radical social theory into Serbia in the 1870's led not a few young Serbs to seek further education in Russia.[58]

There were several other Serbian students in St. Petersburg with Marković and Knežević in 1866, some of whom later played important roles in the military and civil affairs of their country. Sava Grujić, a young artillery officer who had fought (along with Svetozar Marković's brother Jevrem) with the Poles in the revolt of 1863, came to Russia in 1864 and stayed seven years. A colleague of Svetozar Marković until 1875, he became minister of war in 1876

56 Nikitin, *Slavianskie komitety*, p. 94.

57 Akademiia Nauk SSSR, *Obshchestvenno-politicheskie i kul'turnye sviazi narodov SSSR i Iugoslavii. Sbornik statei* (*The Socio-Political and Cultural Ties between the Peoples of the USSR and Yugoslavia*), Moscow, 1957, p. 112.

58 The noted Soviet scholar Professor S. A. Nikitin has written (*Slavianskie komitety*, pp. 77-81) that commercial interests in Russia played no role in the efforts of the Slavic committees to bring foreign students to Russia. Despite the absence of conclusive evidence one way or another it would seem a far-fetched assumption; according to Professor Nikitin's own Marxist dogma commerce would certainly have taken precedence over Slavic brotherhood in the minds of the Pan-Slavs.

and in the following thirty-five years held various high positions including a brief term as prime minister in 1906. Dimitrije Đurić, also an artillery officer, spent the period 1865-67 at the Tsar Nicholas I General Staff Academy. Returning to Serbia in 1867, he was attached to the general staff. He attained the rank of general in 1893, and served in several capacities including director of the military academy and minister of war.

Svetozar Marković and Aleksa Knežević were the only non-Russian Slavs among the one hundred and forty-eight students who began the academic year at the Institute of Ways and Communications. They were enrolled in the first-year course along with thirty-six other students, nearly all of whom were of middle-class origin: their fathers' occupations are listed in the institute's records as provincial secretary, military officer, teacher. Only three of the thirty-eight were of lower-class origin: one was the son of a Cossack noncommissioned officer, one of an artisan, and one of a druggist.[59] Marković and Knežević, both sons of minor governmental officials, were apparently the only students in the first-year class who were supported by scholarships.[60]

General Sobolevsky excused Marković and Knežević from the first-year mathematics and physics courses at the institute. He informed his superior, the minister of communications, that their satisfactory completion of those courses at the *Velika Škola* eliminated the need to repeat them. According to Marković's own evaluation of the curriculum at the Serbian *lycée,* however, and in the light of his subsequent academic performance, it would seem that it was not the good record of the two students but rather their status as potential Serbian leaders that led the institute to lighten the academic load they were required to

59 A peasant's son, one of the outstanding students at the institute, was in an upper class.

60 *Dokumental'nye materialy, Institut Inzhenerov Putei Soobshcheniia,* 1866 register of students.

bear during their first year. The subjects the two Serbs were obliged to take were chemistry, geology, geodesy, mechanical drawing, statistics, and theology.[61]

Marković wrote to his brother early in October of 1866 that he now understood Russian quite well but still had considerable difficulty in speaking the language. He noted that the instruction at the institute was excellent, and that "one can read for hours on any subject" in the "enormous" library of the university.[62] In this same letter he wrote that "if only the Lord grants me good health" he would be able to do his work satisfactorily. Unfortunately, his hopes were in vain. The records of the institute show that he entered the infirmary in November of 1866 for treatment of swollen lymphatic glands; his illness was diagnosed as scrofula.[63] It was the first indication of the disease which was to end his life a few short years later. The ill-health which dogged Marković all his life was in no small measure responsible for the impatience and arrogance he often displayed. The frenetic character of much of his activity was due largely to his repeated insistence that time was somehow against him.

Despite scanty evidence it would seem probable that Marković came into contact with several of the Russian revolutionaries during his first year in St. Petersburg. One of his fellow students at the institute was Dimitry Rikhter, a follower of Peter Lavrov; Rikhter, like Marković, later went to Zürich to continue his education, although the two men were not in the city at the same time. Marković may also have known the revolutionary V. M. Aleksandrov, whose brother studied at the institute.[64] Marković's associations during the early part of his stay in St. Petersburg

61 *Ibid.* Church attendance was compulsory for all students.

62 *Sabrani spisi,* I, pp. 4-6.

63 *Dokumental'nye materialy,* institute infirmary records for November 1866.

64 *Ibid.*, register of students, and V. G. Karasëv, *Svetozar Markovich,* p. 129.

were, however, primarily with his own countrymen. In January of 1867 he participated in the founding of an organization called the Serbian Commune (*opština*). Dimitrije Đurić was president, Sava Grujić vice-president, and Svetozar Marković secretary. The goal of the Commune was stated to be the establishment of fraternal relations among all Serbs in Russia with a view to cooperation for the "general progress" of the Serbian people and nation. The Commune emphasized in an open letter to the Serbs in Russia that it "agreed completely" with the principles of the youth organization of the Serbian liberals, *Omladina* (Youth), an organization of which the Commune considered itself the "Russian wing."[65]

OMLADINA

Omladina had been founded the previous year on the initiative of the Serbian student society *Zora* (Dawn) in Vienna. The members of *Zora*, inspired by Vladimir Jovanović's call for the formation of a liberal, Pan-Serb youth movement, summoned all Serbs to send delegates to a meeting in Novi Sad (in the Hungarian-ruled Vojvodina). Five hundred Serbs from all over the Balkans responded, and out of their congress in August of 1866 *Omladina* was created.[66] The organization quickly won the allegiance of the overwhelming majority of the Serbian students and educated young men. Bearing a strong resemblance to Mazzini's Young Italy movement, *Omladina* was during its first four years completely dominated by Vladimir Jovanović and the liberals. Jovanović used the organization as a forum in his fight to establish a constitutional monarchy in Serbia; inevitably *Omladina* came into conflict with the Serbian authorities. Nationalism was a key plank of its platform, and its militancy embarrassed Prince Michael in his nego-

[65] *Skerlić*, pp. 26-27.

[66] In general on *Omladina* see Skerlić, *Omladina i njena književnost.*

tiations with the other Balkan states.[67] In addition to the liberals there were also in *Omladina* "panslavist dreamers . . . ideological democrats dreaming of a Balkan Republic which would form part of a democratic Republic of European United States, and a few socialists."[68] In actual fact, the only socialist in the organization prior to 1870 was Vasa Pelagić, a young priest who later became an adherent of Svetozar Marković; the socialists entered *Omladina* in strength only after Marković's return to Serbia in 1870 to found the radical-socialist movement.

In the St. Petersburg Serbian Commune's first annual report, Secretary Marković noted that the organization had thirty-five members and a cash reserve of 443 rubles. A great many contacts had been made with other non-Russian Slavs and with Serbian student societies in other countries, and the organization was renamed the South Slav Commune to indicate the broadened scope of its activities.[69] Three Bulgarians were elected to office in the organization, and a "brother Russian" had brought back to the Commune a glowing report of the second *Omladina* congress.[70]

The "brother Russian" to whom Marković referred was Ivan Bochkarëv, an outstanding though little-known figure in the Russian revolutionary movement. Bochkarëv, who attended the university as an auditor, operated a small printing establishment in St. Petersburg. In October of 1866 he sold his business and traveled about Russia, returning to the capital in January of 1867, the month in which the Serbian Commune was founded. Franco Venturi has written that Bochkarëv himself founded the Commune.[71] While no evidence has been discovered to

[67] Slobodan Jovanović, "Omladina protiv Mihaila" ("'Youth' versus Michael"), *Sabrana dela*, VI, Belgrade, 1933, pp. 336-403.

[68] Viktorov-Toporov, "Svetozar Markovich," p. 34.

[69] *Skerlić*, p. 26.

[70] Marković, *Sabrani spisi*, I, pp. 18-22.

[71] *Roots of Revolution*, London, 1960, p. 352. Venturi did not have access to the Russian archives.

support such a contention, it seems certain that Bochkarëv was in touch with the Serbian students in St. Petersburg early in 1867. They surely must have encouraged him to accept the invitation he had received to attend the second *Omladina* congress later in the year. Bochkarëv, along with four Russian students from Moscow University, did indeed attend the August congress after traveling in France and Italy.[72]

The *Omladina* leaders had asked Bochkarëv to prepare a speech on the subject of Slav unity. He complied with the request, but before he could deliver his address the Serbian government, alarmed at the militant liberalism displayed at the congress, forced its dissolution. The text of his speech has, however, been preserved; echoing the views of Chernyshevsky, Bochkarëv proposed the creation of a Slav confederation, with each separate group retaining complete internal autonomy but united with one another by the bond of "one common literary-political Slavic language." Such a confederation, Bochkarëv wrote in his notes, would "confound Old Europe by its startlingly simple [!] solution of the 'Slavic problem.' " Although he was unable to deliver his speech, Bochkarëv participated in the organizational work of *Omladina*. When the question of female participation in the organization was raised, he presented the views of the Russian intelligentsia, which insisted upon the complete emancipation of women; his influence helped pass a compromise resolution which provided for the establishment of a women's auxiliary to *Omladina*.[73]

Bochkarëv's presence at the second congress of the Serbian youth organization was a significant milestone in the history of the relations between the intelligentsia in the various Slav lands. Not since Michael Bakunin had participated in the 1848 Slav Congress in Prague had the Russian

[72] Koz'min, *Revoliutsionnoe podpol'e*, pp. 38-48.
[73] *Ibid.*, pp. 48-51.

revolutionaries actively concerned themselves with their brothers in the Slavic West and South. Svetozar Marković and Ivan Bochkarëv worked together during the period 1867-69 in an attempt to establish a close collaboration between the Russian and Serbian radicals; as we shall see shortly, their efforts failed principally because of the intervention of the Russian political police.

In May of 1867 Marković wrote to General Sobolevsky requesting permission to travel to Serbia during the coming summer vacation in order to attend to personal matters. He also asked that the institute provide him with free round-trip rail passage; with extraordinary (for Russian bureaucracy) dispatch his requests were granted. The Russian authorities were willing to go to considerable lengths to accommodate the young Slavs upon whom they wished to make a favorable impression.[74]

Several authors, notably the Soviet scholar V. G. Karasëv, have speculated that Marković went to Odessa in the summer of 1867, where he participated in the founding of the "Slavic-Serbian Society."[75] The lack of documentary evidence has made it impossible to trace his activities during that time, though it is established that he was in fact in Serbia.[76] One of the members of the Smorgon Academy was in Odessa during the summer of 1867,[77] and it is certainly possible that Marković was also there either before or after his trip to Serbia. But virtually nothing is known of the

[74] *Dokumental'nye materialy*, Marković's letters to the institute dated St. Petersburg, May 20 and 23, 1867. Marković could travel by train only to the border of the Vojvodina, for there were no railroads in Serbia in 1867.

[75] V. G. Karasëv, "Serbskii revoliutsionnyi demokrat Svetozar Markovich (Ocherk obshchestvennoi i publitsisticheskoi deiatel'nosti)" ("The Serbian Revolutionary Democrat Svetozar Marković [A Sketch of his Social and Publicist Work]"), *UZIS*, VII, 1953, p. 354.

[76] Marković, *Sabrani spisi*, I, pp. 6-10.

[77] B. P. Koz'min (ed.), *Nechaev i Nechaevshchina* (*Nechaev and the Nechaev Era*), Moscow and Leningrad, 1931, p. 198; see also *Revoliutsionnoe podpol'e*, p. 129.

Odessa "Slavic-Serbian Society,"[78] and for the student of Marković's work the summer after his first year at the institute remains a mystery.

Although Ivan Bochkarëv participated in the 1867 *Omladina* congress Svetozar Marković did not, and the young Serb student returned to St. Petersburg in time for the beginning of the fall session at the institute. Presumably he still resided at No. 30 Voznesensky Prospekt with Knežević, who had also successfully completed the first-year course. It was during his second year in the Russian capital that Svetozar Marković was fully accepted into the secret, underground circles of the Russian revolutionaries. He was closely associated with the mysterious Smorgon Academy almost from its inception.

THE SMORGON ACADEMY

The Smorgon Academy was an outgrowth of one of the "communes" often formed by students in Russia (cf. the Serbian Commune). The members of the academy lived communally and made their living by writing or tutoring. Their organization came into being in 1867 and took its name from the Smorgon Woods in the Urals where the gypsies trained bears for the circus—a wry indication of the bearlike, slovenly appearance of the male members of the academy.[79] For the first time in such societies women had full membership—a fact which indicates the ever-growing sentiment for the emancipation of women. There are

78 The Slavic-Serbian Society in Odessa was a highly secret revolutionary organization which seems to have had as its goal the fomenting of revolution in Bosnia-Hercegovina; the organization apparently disintegrated about 1871. See E. N. Kusheva, "Iz russko-serbskikh revoliutsionnykh sviazei 1870-kh godov" ("On Russo-Serbian Revolutionary Contacts in the 1870's"), *UZIS*, I, 1949. See also Skerlić, *Omladina i njena književnost*, p. 118.

79 In nineteenth-century Russia the term "Smorgon Academy" also indicated a nonprestigious school.

few archival materials concerning the Smorgon Academy; none of its members published any reminiscences of the organization, and there are no reliable police reports on the academy due to the fact that the Third Section (political police) learned of its existence only in 1870, a full year after its demise. The report which the police finally assembled is untrustworthy; the Third Section agents, anxious to conceal their ignorance of the academy's activities, minimized its significance and embellished their own haphazard investigation. Catering to the tastes of their superiors rather than to fact, the agents reported that the members of the academy had enticed into their ranks a "beautiful nihilist" (Ekaterina Kozlovskaia), an "unquenchably depraved" woman who sold herself for the benefit of the communal fund.[80]

The leaders of the academy, according to the 1870 police report, were D. A. Voskresensky and A. E. Sergievsky. Both individuals had been members of Nikolai Ishutin's "Organization" (from which Karakozov had sprung), and both had been imprisoned for several months following Karakozov's attempt on the life of the tsar. It is possible that the terrorists Sergei Nechaev and Vladimir Orlov were associated with the academy, and Peter Tkachëv, leader of the Jacobin wing of the revolutionary movement, was, if not a member, at least a trusted friend of the organization. Finally, the gradualist revolutionary Peter Lavrov was in contact with the Smorgon Academy, although he did not become one of its members.[81]

The program of the Smorgon Academy, all of whose members were disciples of N. G. Chernyshevsky, involved the organization of a revolution in Russia, the liberation

80 Koz'min, *Revoliutsionnoe podpol'e*, p. 138.

81 *Ibid.*, pp. 136-137; see also B. P. Koz'min, *Iz istorii revoliutsionnoi mysli v Rossii* (*From the History of Revolutionary Thought in Russia*), Moscow, 1961, p. 355.

of Chernyshevsky from his exile in Siberia, and the establishment of relations with the First International.[82]

Svetozar Marković, along with Sava Grujić, was apparently introduced into the academy by Bochkarëv. The latter, the report of the police notwithstanding, was probably the outstanding member of the organization and certainly his was the broadest revolutionary experience. Through Bochkarëv the two Serbs met another academy member, Varlaam Cherkezov, late in 1867 or early in 1868. One writer, Max Nettlau, has claimed that Cherkezov weaned Marković and Grujić away from the theories of the Slavophils and the Pan-Slavs and introduced them to the socialist thought of Chernyshevsky.[83] While Cherkezov may have influenced the two Serbs, he was certainly not responsible for awakening them to Chernyshevsky, for they could scarcely have lived in St. Petersburg a week without coming into contact with the followers of the exiled martyr.

MARKOVIĆ AND N. G. CHERNYSHEVSKY

What is to be Done?, the novel which Chernyshevsky wrote during his imprisonment (1862-64), was the bible of the young revolutionaries. Though it had no literary merit the novel effectively described the life of the "new people," the emancipated intellectuals. The Smorgon Academy and other revolutionary societies were modeled after the communes described by Chernyshevsky. With its thinly disguised call for the overthrow of the political and social order and the establishment of a socialist society, *What is to be Done?* exerted a powerful influence not only on the radical youth of the sixties and seventies but on later generations as well.[84]

82 V. G. Karasëv, *Svetozar Markovich*, p. 120.

83 Quoted in Koz'min, *Revoliutsionnoe podpol'e*, pp. 117-118.

84 Cf. Avrahm Yarmolinsky, *Road to Revolution*, London, 1957, p. 118.

The teachings of Chernyshevsky, based as they were upon the thinking of Feuerbach, Fourier, and others in the West, were not limited in their influence to Russia. Through the Serbs and Bulgars who studied in Russia in the 1860's Russian versions of Western theories gradually began to penetrate the Balkans. In Svetozar Marković's case those theories were first expressed in a rather vague and unsophisticated manner; Marković began his career as a journalist during his second year (1867-68) at the Institute of Ways and Communications, and his first published writings, as well as his letters of the period, reflected a gradual shift to the revolutionary democratic principles of Chernyshevsky and his disciples in the Smorgon Academy.

As early as 1866 Marković had written to his brother expressing his support for the "revolutionary movement" in Bosnia-Hercegovina,[85] but by 1868 he had become downright militant concerning the necessity for revolution in the twin provinces and for the liberation of all the lands inhabited by Serbs. Paradoxically, Marković and the Serbian liberals moved toward a position in which each adopted the views formerly held by the other. Whereas Marković had previously disagreed with the liberals in supporting Prince Michael's aggressively nationalist foreign policy, he now, in 1867-68, became convinced that that policy had (as the liberals had maintained for a decade) as its primary aim the strengthening of the Obrenović dynasty rather than the liberation of the Serbs. While the liberals were coming to a reconciliation with the dynasty, Marković, under the influence of the Russian revolutionaries, developed an implacable opposition to the monarchy. Warning of his impending break with the liberals, Marković wrote to Vladimir Jovanović that "*the greatest misfortune for the Serbian people would be to be liberated*

[85] Marković, *Sabrani spisi*, I, p. 5.

under the Obrenović dynasty. I want liberation through popular revolt—through revolution."[86]

His break with the liberals was not yet complete, however, for he urged all "true Serbs" to support the liberal-dominated *Omladina,* and with the liberals he enjoined the Serbian youth to follow the national-revolutionary example of the Greek Philike Hetairia and Mazzini's Young Italy.[87] Further adding to the confusion, Marković expressed views which served the interests of the reactionary Pan-Slavs when he wrote in January of 1868 that the Russian people were "very anxious" to go to war with Turkey in order to liberate the Serbs and Bulgars. Displaying a naïveté from which he never completely freed himself, Marković wrote enthusiastically of the selfless brotherly love of the Russians for the South Slavs, a love for which the Russians were prepared to die in battle.[88]

Probing more deeply into the intricacies of Russianized versions of Western theories, Marković wrote in February of 1868 of the absence of class distinctions in Serbia, a fact which set that country apart from (and, by implication, above) Western Europe.[89] A few months later he developed the theme in a lengthy article the very title of which ("What must we do?") was taken from Chernyshevsky.[90] Western society, argued Marković in a liberal Belgrade newspaper, had become divided into rulers and ruled. Serbia, having thus far escaped such a division, could avoid the capitalist stage of economic development which had brought misery to the West. An enlightened intelligentsia (an idea he borrowed from Pisarev and Tkachëv, who had taken it from Blanqui) would lead the nation to the establishment of a new society based, he hinted, on the collectivism of the *zadruga.*

86 *Pančevac* (Pančevo), December 4, 1870, no. 87.
87 *Sabrani spisi,* I, p. 25.
88 *Ibid.,* p. 13.
89 *Ibid.,* p. 7.
90 *Ibid.,* pp. 58-72.

Marković went on to redefine "rulers and ruled" as "government and people" and then further as "rich capitalists and proletariat." His use of the latter two terms probably stemmed from Chernyshevsky, who had referred to such a division in the West. But the problem of identifying the sources of his views becomes more intriguing when we note that in the same article Marković went on to write that capitalists only exploit the wealth accumulated by previous generations and do not themselves create new wealth. Further, he noted, capital itself is merely stored-up human labor.[91] Marković did not elaborate upon either point, and it is therefore difficult to determine the exact source of his ideas. Both concepts originated with the labor theory of value and the variants upon it which followed in the 1820's and 1830's. Since these theories were known and discussed in Russia, it is possible that Marković was merely displaying a rather superficial acquaintance with Ricardian socialism. But there remains the interesting and, on the basis of the available evidence, more likely possibility that he had come into contact with Marxism; Karl Marx had of course adopted and fashioned for his own use both the concepts mentioned by Marković.

It has generally been thought that Marxism did not begin to penetrate Russia until the 1870's. Bakunin had translated the *Communist Manifesto* into Russian in 1862; a few copies were smuggled into Russia from Geneva, but the work seems not to have aroused any great interest in *avant-garde* circles. *Das Kapital* was published in Russian translation in 1872, and Marx's *Critique of Political Economy* sold moderately well in Russia in the late 1870's. But it was not until the formation of Plekhanov's "Liberation of Labor" in 1883 (in Switzerland) that a Russian Marxist organization came into being.[92]

91 *Ibid.*

92 The latest study of the origins of Russian Marxism is Iu. Z. Polevoi's

Despite the fact that Marxism was not widely known in Russian intellectual circles in the period 1865-70 it is clear that there were individuals who were well acquainted with the movement. Peter Tkachëv was the first Russian to make a serious study of Marx's works, and as early as 1865 he was discussing with his friends the concepts of historical and dialectical materialism.[93] Even earlier, N. V. Shelgunov's review in *Sovremennik* in 1861 of one of Engels' works stimulated wide discussion of Marxist theories.[94] These two examples alone would seem to indicate a certainly earlier and probably wider acquaintance with Marxism on the part of Russian intellectuals than historians have indicated; clearly there is room for a great deal of research on the problem. Svetozar Marković certainly learned something—however little—of Marxism during his stay in Russia; not long after his final departure from St. Petersburg he referred to Marx in a letter and indicated that he had studied his critique of the capitalist system.[95] He was surely introduced to Marxism by Peter Tkachëv; both men were associated with (though neither was a member of) the Smorgon Academy, and Tkachëv exercised considerable influence upon Marković's intellectual development during the years 1867-69.

A further indication of Marković's growing addiction to Russian revolutionary democracy was contained in his article describing a meeting of nihilists at a seamstresses' artel. The first thing that struck him about the nihilists, Marković wrote, was the manner in which the young women conducted themselves: "I have never seen such a

---

undistinguished *Zarozhdenie marksizma v Rossii* (*The Origins of Marxism in Russia*), Moscow, 1959.

93 B. P. Koz'min, *P. N. Tkachev i revoliutsionnoe dvizhenie 1860-kh godov* (*P. N. Tkachëv and the Revolutionary Movement of the 1860's*), Moscow, 1922; see also Venturi, *Roots of Revolution*, pp. 389-428.

94 "Rabochii proletariat v Anglii i vo Frantsii," *Sovremennik*, 1861, No. 9, pp. 131-172, No. 10, pp. 485-518, No. 11, pp. 205-270.

95 Marković, *Sabrani spisi*, I, pp. 130-132.

number of women so *modestly dressed.* The great majority come in black, brown and grey dresses buttoned to *the throat.* There are some whose dresses are noticeable because of their special simplicity: black wool, without crinoline. All of them have their hair cut short, and some wear blue or green eyeglasses. These are the Russian nihilists. They are women who have renounced male tutelage and who have decided to earn their bread with their own hands. . . . They form associations in order to free themselves from dependence upon someone else's capital; they are showing the world that humanity *is not using half its intellectual resources . . . they are the heralds of the new era.*"[96] Contrary to the Serbian custom, Marković noted, there was no dancing at the meetings of the Russian youth. The evening he spent with the nihilists began with the presentation of two short plays, following which several writers read from their literary and critical works. Among those present was the most famous nihilist of all, Dimitry Pisarev, who utilized a discussion of Heine's work to deliver a savage attack upon the Russian liberals. Marković observed in his account of the evening that Pisarev and Chernyshevsky were jointly responsible for the fact that the term "liberal" had become one of mockery in Russia.[97]

After completing his second year at the institute Marković spent the summer vacation of 1868 in Serbia. One of his reasons for returning home had to do with his father's estate; having come of age, he was now legally entitled to receive his share of the estate. He immediately turned the small sum over to his stepmother, Marija Marković;[98] it was a warm and generous gesture which indicated that

[96] *Ibid.*, pp. 27-29. It is interesting to compare Marković's account with a police agent report quoted in Yarmolinsky, *Road to Revolution*, p. 123.

[97] One writer has claimed that Marković met Pisarev at a meeting of the Smorgon Academy; V. K. Zaitsev, "Svetozar Markovich," *Vestnik Leningradskogo Universiteta*, 1957, no. 14, Seriia Istorii, iazyka i literatury, vypusk 3, p. 125.

[98] *DANRS*, Ministarstvo Inostranih Dela, F VI, R 140/869.

he was not entirely the selfish individual he sometimes seemed to be in his relations with his brother and his creditors. Marković wrote his "What must we do?" at this time, and spent most of his days in the offices of the liberal newspaper which published the article.

THE SERBIAN CRISIS OF 1868

The summer of 1868 in Serbia was a difficult period for all but the staunchest supporters of the Obrenović dynasty. Prince Michael had been murdered in June, and the regency which was established to rule during the minority of the new prince, Michael's cousin Milan, undertook a brutal campaign to purge the principality of dissident elements. The Karađorđe family and its adherents were blamed for the murder of Michael and were severely persecuted. Torture was freely employed by the police; for a time Serbia seemed to lapse into Oriental barbarism reminiscent of the days when Miloš Obrenović had sent Black George Petrović's head to the sultan.[99]

The Habsburg press attacked the Serbian liberals, accusing them and the "Karađorđevists" of having plotted Michael's assassination through the "revolutionary" *Omladina* organization. The conservative Serbian newspapers echoed the charges made in Vienna and Budapest, but so palpably false were their accusations that the regency was obliged to order them toned down.[100] The liberals, perhaps understandably anxious to shed the role of scapegoat, insisted that "republicans, socialists and communists" were behind the assassination. Svetozar Marković, on the verge of a complete break with the liberals, replied that Serbia did indeed have such elements, a grand total of three: the "republican" Dragiša Stanojević, a professor at the *Velika*

[99] Vladimir Jovanović, *Les Serbes et la Mission de la Serbie dans l'Europe d'Orient*, pp. 78-79. See also Rovinsky, "Belgrad," part II, pp. 137-138.

[100] Jovanović, *Les Serbes*, pp. 77-117.

Škola, was absent on leave at the time of the assassination; the "socialist" Živojin Žujović was on his deathbed in Dalmatia; the "communist" Svetozar Marković was in Russia.[101]

The Habsburg authorities, to whom Pan-Serbism was no more palatable than liberalism, pressed their attack on the Serbian liberals. At the time of Michael's assassination Vladimir Jovanović was working as the chief editorial assistant to Svetozar Miletić, editor of the liberal newspaper *Zastava* (*The Banner*) and mayor of Novi Sad. Apparently at the request of the Serbian regency Jovanović and Miletić were jailed on suspicion of complicity in the murder "plot."[102] Arrested with them was Liuben Karavelov, the Bulgarian revolutionary who was prominent in Serbian *avant-garde* literary circles.[103] Miletić was too prominent a citizen to be held long on the palpably false charge of conspiring to assassinate Michael, and the Hungarian authorities soon released him. No such considerations obtained in the case of Jovanović and Karavelov, both of whom languished in jail for months.

Despite the fact that many of its leaders were in prison, *Omladina* held its third congress in August of 1868 in the

101 *C.d.*, VII, pp. 100-101. The identifications were Marković's, and there was a rather impulsive, belligerent air about them. Stanojević was indeed a republican, but Žujović's connection with socialism was exceedingly vague, and in 1868 no one had yet called Marković himself a communist.

102 Jovanović, *Avtobiografija,* pp. 21-23; see also Georgi Konstantinov, *Vođi bugarskog narodnog pokreta: Rakovski-Karavelov-Botjov* (*The Leaders of the Bulgarian National Movement: Rakovski-Karavelov-Botëv*). Belgrade, 1939, pp. 131-134. Konstantinov mistakenly places Jovanović and Karavelov in Belgrade at the time of the assassination.

103 In 1867 a Serbian journal began to serialize Karavelov's *E li kriva sudbina?* (*Is Fate Guilty?*), a didactic revolutionary democratic treatise which immediately came to be regarded as a Balkan *What is to be Done?* See Marković, *Sabrani spisi,* I, pp. 91, 94-95. See also Jovan Skerlić, *Istorija nove srpske književnosti* (*The History of Modern Serbian Literature*), 3rd edition, Belgrade, 1953, pp. 336-340. An excellent bibliography on Karavelov is contained in Mikhail Dimitrov, "K voprosu ob ideologii Liubena Karavelova" ("On the Problem of Liuben Karavelov's Ideology"), *UZIS,* XVI, 1958, pp. 78-108.

Banat town of Veliki Bečkerek. Svetozar Marković again failed to attend the congress; having gone to visit relatives in Jagodina, he merely sent a telegram wishing the delegates success in their work.[104] Returning to St. Petersburg in September of 1868, he settled at a new address on Ekateringofsky Prospekt in the Spassky Quarter. He apparently lived alone; Aleksa Knežević had become seriously ill with scrofula (seemingly an occupational hazard for Balkan students in Russia) the previous spring and did not return to St. Petersburg for the new academic year, going instead to Zürich.[105]

Before his departure from Serbia Marković had detected signs of the imminent *rapprochement* between the liberals and the regency, and in the autumn of 1868 he made a decisive break with his former friends. In an article which Svetozar Miletić published in *Zastava*,[106] Marković accused the liberals of attempting to create, in the confused situation which prevailed after Michael's death, a highly centralized state under the domination of the Belgrade bureaucrats (many of whom had gone over to the liberals). Furthermore, he charged, the "Great Serbia" foreign policy being put forth by liberal spokesmen was clearly designed to replace one set of oppressive masters, the Turks, with another, the Belgrade bureaucrats and the liberal leaders. Such a policy, he insisted, could only end in the loss of civil freedom in Serbia and the certain alienation of all Serbs outside the principality. As an alternative to "Great Serbia" Marković proposed a "free union" of Bulgars, Croats, and Serbs; such a union, he maintained, would provide the political foundation for the liberation of the Balkan peoples.

104 *Sabrani spisi*, I, p. 77.

105 *Dokumental'nye materialy*, infirmary records of the Institut Inzhenerov Putei Soobshcheniia for June 1867; Aziatskii Department, letters of May 1 and 7, 1868.

106 *Sabrani spisi*, I, pp. 97-115.

Marković's call for a South Slav union was, like Bochkarëv's proposal at the 1867 *Omladina* congress, based upon the views of Chernyshevsky.[107] But in his attempt to propagate those views Marković dissipated the force of his argument by outlining an incredibly vague domestic "program." He wrote that internal policy should be "in the interests of the people," and in explanation of that term he quoted Vladimir Jovanović's statement "that things be good for each and all." He dismissed with heavy sarcasm the "literary charlatans" who were so "extraordinarily foolish" as to question his meaning.[108] Marković's criticism of the liberals was, like his call for a South Slav union, interpreted by many as a defense of Prince Michael; he was forced into a tedious amplification of his views which largely obscured his original purpose.

THE REVOLUTIONARY UNDERGROUND

In the winter of 1868-69 Marković's association with the Russian revolutionaries deepened into conspiracy. Late in October he wrote to a Serbian friend in Berlin that Ivan Bochkarëv had been arrested by the Third Section and charged with plotting with the revolutionary *émigrés* in Switzerland; there was, however, Marković noted, hope that he would soon be released.[109] He did not mention the fact that two of his own manuscripts had been found in Bochkarëv's possession and that he was now certain to be placed under surveillance.[110]

[107] N. G. Chernyshevsky, *Polnoe sobranie sochinenii* (*Complete Collected Works*), v, Moscow, 1950, p. 642. The Ukrainian Society of SS. Cyril and Methodius, the chief goal of which was the promotion of Ukrainian nationalism, had in the 1840's proposed a union similar to that outlined by Chernyshevsky.

[108] *Sabrani spisi*, I, p. 100.

[109] *Ibid.*, p. 82.

[110] V. G. Karasëv, "Dva novykh avtografa Svetozara Markovicha" ("Two New Pieces by Svetozar Marković"), *Slaviane*, no. 9, September 1956, p. 38.

After attending the 1867 *Omladina* congress Bochkarëv had spent several days with Vladimir Jovanović in Novi Sad before returning to St. Petersburg in September. Because of his extensive contacts with the Russian *émigrés* in Switzerland and Germany, the Smorgon Academy sent him abroad again in January of 1868 to discuss with the *émigrés* the problems of revolutionary organization and the liberation of Chernyshevsky. Forced by lack of funds to return to Russia after two months, Bochkarëv stayed a month in the capital before setting off once more for Central Europe.[111] He went first to Prague, where he visited the noted Czech nationalist and historian František Palacký, whom he had perhaps met at the Moscow Pan-Slav congress in 1867.[112] From Prague he moved on to Vienna, Zürich, Geneva, and Berne. In the latter city he attended the 1868 congress of the League of Peace and Freedom, a pacifist, liberal organization.

After the League congress Bochkarëv returned to Russia by way of Prague, Leipzig, Dresden, and Berlin; it was probably in the latter city that he acquired Marković's manuscripts, for one of Marković's closest friends, Ljubomir Belimarković, was at the time a student in Berlin. Arrested as he crossed the Russian frontier in October of 1868, Bochkarëv was taken to the Peter-Paul Fortress in St. Petersburg and questioned intensively. He denied having had contact with the revolutionary *émigrés,* but was sorely compromised by the abject confession made by I. G. Rozanov, an erstwhile revolutionary also arrested in October upon his return from Switzerland. Rozanov's

111 Koz'min, *Revoliutsionnoe podpol'e,* p. 117. On his first trip in 1868 Bochkarëv carried with him fifty rubles donated by Varlaam Cherkezov to help defray the cost of publishing Chernyshevsky's *What is to be Done?* in Switzerland.

112 On the Slav congresses see S. A. Nikitin, "Slavianskie s'ezdy 60-kh godov XIX veka," *Slavianskii sbornik. Slavianskii vopros i russkoe obshchestvo v 1867-1878 godakh,* edited by N. M. Druzhinin, Moscow, 1948, pp. 16-92.

confession conclusively linked Bochkarëv with Nikolai Utin and M. K. Elpidin, two of the leaders of the Russian *émigrés*. Bochkarëv had indeed seen both men, but ironically they had considered him a tsarist agent and refused to believe him an emissary from the Smorgon Academy, of which they knew nothing.

Max Nettlau, the biographer of Michael Bakunin, has written that Bochkarëv did not meet the famous anarchist-revolutionary in 1868, and Bochkarëv himself denied to the Third Section that such a meeting had taken place. Among the effects taken from him upon his arrest, however, was the first issue of *Narodnoe Delo* (*The People's Cause*), a revolutionary journal edited by Bakunin and Utin.[113] Furthermore, it is known that Bakunin attended all the congresses of the League of Peace and Freedom (his ubiquity approached saturation), and it would therefore seem unlikely that he did not meet Bochkarëv.[114]

Convicted of conspiring with enemies of the state, Bochkarëv was sentenced to confinement in his native town, Ostashkov, in the Tver department. Arrested again and imprisoned during the Nechaev affair,[115] he managed to have the charges against him dismissed. Once more he returned to Ostashkov and devoted himself to his small estate and to improving the caliber of instruction in the local schools. According to a police report his activities in the latter field brought him the hatred of the parents in the area, who complained of his dissemination of "criminal propaganda." Twice he escaped from Ostashkov; after his second attempt he was exiled to Krasnyi Yar in the Astrakhan province. He was regularly arrested in the fol-

[113] One writer has identified S. Chubarov as the individual who brought the first issue of *Narodnoe Delo* into Russia; J. M. Meijer, *Knowledge and Revolution: The Russian Colony in Zürich (1870-1873)*, Assen, 1955, p. 39.

[114] Koz'min, *Revoliutsionnoe podpol'e*, pp. 86-122.

[115] In November of 1869 the terrorist Sergei Nechaev and three colleagues killed I. I. Ivanov, a fellow revolutionary whom Nechaev mistakenly suspected of challenging his leadership.

lowing years, and only in the 1880's was he able to return to his home for any length of time. From 1895 until 1901 he lived near Leo Tolstoy at Yasnaya Polyana; the two men, sharing an aversion to formal religion and a predilection for vegetarianism, became firm friends. Bochkarëv eventually returned to Ostashkov, where he died in 1915.[116]

One of the most capable and intelligent of Chernyshevsky's disciples, Bochkarëv had an enormous influence upon Svetozar Marković and the members of the Smorgon Academy. His great physical and intellectual courage marked him, and not, as the Third Section had claimed, A. E. Sergievsky, as the outstanding member of the Smorgon Academy. No one played as significant a role as Bochkarëv in converting Svetozar Marković to the revolutionary democratic socialism of Chernyshevsky; Marković's views on Slav union, the social and political emancipation of women, and revolutionary organization stemmed from Bochkarëv's interpretation of Chernyshevsky.

Marković began to see himself as the leader of a "radical party" which would lead the struggle against antiquated and anachronistic institutions and mores in Serbia, against the forces which were attempting to introduce Western capitalism into the country. But Marković accepted only those elements of Russian revolutionary democracy which in his view were applicable to Serbia; the eclecticism which was to be the distinguishing feature of his socialist ideology was developed during his years in Russia. As his Russian teachers had borrowed liberally and at will from a wide variety of Western theories, so Marković attempted a fusion of several currents of the Russian versions of those theories. He early departed from Chernyshevsky and many of the Russian revolutionaries in refusing to advocate the violent overthrow of the existing form of government in Serbia; he rationalized his departure by maintaining that

116 Koz'min, *Revoliutsionnoe podpol'e,* pp. 155-160.

conditions in Serbia were much more favorable than those in Russia for the peaceful, legal establishment of a new society. A *social* revolution was unnecessary in Serbia, he insisted, for the country had neither landless peasantry nor exploited urban proletariat. The situation of the peasants was deplorable, he admitted, and they were indeed being victimized by the usurers and the bureaucrats; nevertheless, the existing evils could be cured by peaceful means. Marković was a national rather than a social revolutionary, and he could not agree with those in the Smorgon Academy (the followers of Tkachëv) who sought violent social upheaval. He remained much closer to the gradualist Lavrov, and later he wrote that "I do not understand and can never understand these socialists who expect to consolidate socialism with bayonets."[117]

Despite the certainty that he was under surveillance following Bochkarëv's arrest, Marković did not abandon his contacts with the Russian revolutionaries. On the contrary he participated even more frequently in the secret meetings of the Smorgon Academy and in those of the slightly more circumspect organizations (i.e., the artels). It is from Marković, who apparently got his information from the Academy, that we have the first mention (November 1868) of the plans of Maxim Antonovich and Yuly Zhukovsky to publish a new "scientific" journal to replace the proscribed *Sovremennik,* on which they had collaborated after Chernyshevsky's arrest.[118] The new journal, *Kosmos,* appeared as a weekly during the first half of 1869 and as a monthly thereafter.[119] *Kosmos* frequently published the works of leading Western natural scientists, and continued the work begun by Pisarev in popularizing Darwinism and

[117] Marković, *Izbrannye sochineniia,* p. 817.

[118] *Sabrani spisi,* I, p. 84.

[119] When Marković went to Zürich in 1869 he regularly received *Kosmos;* see his frequent references to the journal in *ibid.,* pp. 225-361.

materialism.[120] Marković wrote to a friend in Serbia that he would send him a subscription to *Kosmos* rather than *Nedelia* (*The Week*), which he had previously considered the finest post-*Sovremennik* journal in Russia.[121] Marković himself wrote at least one article for *Nedelia*,[122] and tried unsuccessfully to publish his work in other St. Petersburg journals.[123]

Serbian editors were more willing to accept Marković's work, and he regularly published in liberal journals in Belgrade. It was during his last year in St. Petersburg that he wrote and published in Novi Sad his article "Poetry and Thought."[124] His major piece of literary criticism, the article at once reflected the realism of Chernyshevsky and Dobroliubov and the iconoclasm and preoccupation with science of Pisarev.

Science, Marković wrote, had destroyed the old dualist concept of human nature, and the task of literature was therefore to depict humanity as science had revealed it. But a mere scientific understanding of man is not enough; literature must have a practical, socially useful purpose—*littérature oblige*. Art for art's sake is an intellectually dishonest creed, and is furthermore a product of the "childhood stage" of intellectual development (a stage which had produced, Marković noted, the *Iliad* and the *Odyssey*). Modern literature, the work of an intellectual elite edu-

120 The nominal editor of *Kosmos* was L. N. Simonov, but Antonovich and Zhukovsky were in full editorial control. The journal frequently attacked the liberal Russian press, and insisted that Chernyshevsky and Dobroliubov, not the liberals, were the true heirs of Belinsky. Cf. A. G. Dement'ev, *Russkaia periodicheskaia pechat' 1702-1894* (*The Russian Periodical Press*, 1702-1894), Moscow, 1959, p. 520.

121 *Sabrani spisi*, I, p. 84.

122 "Korrespondentsiia iz Belgrada" ("Correspondence from Belgrade"), *Nedelia*, 1868, no. 52, pp. 1832-1834. I am indebted to Mr. V. G. Karasëv for bringing this article to my attention. The article is unsigned, but the style and content identify it as almost certainly the work of Marković.

123 M. Milićević, *Dodatak pomenika od 1888*, Belgrade, 1901, p. 87.

124 *Sabrani spisi*, I, pp. 85-96.

cated in science, must be preceptive: the enlightened few must disperse the fables and romanticism which hinder the intellectual development of the masses. Concluding his article, Marković praised the works of Liuben Karavelov ("our brother Bulgarian") and called upon Serbian writers and dramatists to emulate his example. Marković's article was well received in Serbian intellectual circles, and he quickly became (with Karavelov) one of the heralds of the new realism. As we shall see in chapter IV, Marković's influence upon Serbian literature in the latter part of the nineteenth century was not inconsiderable.[125]

Although the arrest of Bochkarëv had not had any apparent effect upon Marković's work at the institute, and had certainly not curtailed his contacts with the revolutionaries, he began in the autumn of 1868 to think of leaving St. Petersburg. He wrote to a friend that he felt the five years he had spent in studying to be an engineer were wasted, for he wanted only to be a "political worker." He could no longer divert his energies to useless study, he observed, for to do so would blunt his political acumen and leave him but a Don Quixote on the fringes of society. Earlier Marković had planned to remain at the institute until June of 1869, at which time he would go to Switzerland to become better acquainted with his "brother revolu-

[125] Among the many works dealing with Marković's influence on Serbian literature the following should be noted: Živojin Bošković, "Uticaj Svetozara Markovića na srpsku književnost" ("The Influence of Svetozar Marković on Serbian Literature"), *Letopis Matice Srpske* (Novi Sad), vol. 358, 1946, pp. 126-134; Žarko Plamenac (pseud., Arpad Lebl), "'Realizam' i—realnost. Nova nauka" ("'Realism' and Reality. The New Science"), *Pregled*, Sarajevo, XIII, 1937, no. 158, pp. 153-159; Momčilo Miletić, "Svetozar Marković i Đura Jakšić," *Književnost*, III, 1946, pp. 303-305; Jovan Popović, "Svetozareva buktinja nad našom književnošću" ("Svetozar's Guiding Light for our Literature"), *ibid.*, I, 1946, no. 9, pp. 9-25; Vicko Zaninović, "Literarna fizionomija Svetozara Markovića" ("Svetozar Marković's Literary Physiognomy"), *Život i Rad*, Belgrade, III, 1929, no. 13, pp. 60-64; no. 14, pp. 137-144; no. 15, pp. 220-224.

tionaries"; now, in November of 1868, he made his decision to leave St. Petersburg as soon as possible.[126]

On Christmas Eve (Old Style) Marković wrote to his friend Ljubomir Belimarković, who was studying in Berlin, that he wanted to come to see him as soon as possible. He noted that one of his "progressive young friends," a doctor, would give him a certificate testifying to the harmful effect of the St. Petersburg climate upon his health, thus giving him an excuse to leave the institute in the middle of the academic year. In the same letter, which reflected his increasingly great concern for his own safety, Marković noted that Bochkarëv (to whom he always referred as "B") was still in the Peter-Paul fortress, the police not having completed their interrogation.[127]

There was good cause for Marković's obvious uneasiness. Agitation among student groups in St. Petersburg and Moscow became more and more vociferous in the winter of 1868-69; protest meetings and petitions for redress of student grievances led the authorities to predict an outburst of violence.[128] In January of 1869 the St. Petersburg chief of police requested a complete dossier on Svetozar Marković from the director of the institute, General Sobolevsky. Although Bochkarëv had steadfastly denied his acquaintance with revolutionaries inside or outside Russia, the fact that Marković's manuscripts had been found upon him was more than enough evidence to direct the attention of the police to the young Serb. For many months Marković had moved freely in revolutionary circles; the Third Section, it will be remembered, had even at this late date no knowledge whatsoever of the existence of the Smorgon Academy. But now, in the winter of his last year in the

126 *Sabrani spisi,* I, pp. 83-84.

127 *Ibid.,* pp. 118-121.

128 "Revoliutsionnoe i studencheskoe dvizhenie v otsenke III otdeleniia" ("The Third Section's Appraisal of the Revolutionary and Student Movement"), *Katorga i ssylka,* 1924, no. 3, pp. 106-121.

Russian capital, Marković became suspect and was obliged to share some of the grim side of the revolutionaries' life.[129]

Marković was unable to leave St. Petersburg in the winter, but in March of 1869 he suddenly acquired four hundred Swiss francs and wrote to Belimarković that he hoped to leave for Berlin by the middle of the month.[130] It is not clear how Marković came into possession of such a large sum of money. His biographer, Jovan Skerlić, wrote that his brother had "assisted" him to leave Russia,[131] but it would seem at least as likely that he obtained the money from the Smorgon Academy. One writer, V. G. Karasëv, has speculated that the long-standing desire of the Academy to establish relations with the revolutionary *émigrés* was not the least reason why Marković chose to leave Russia in 1869.[132] Certainly Marković would have been an ideal emissary: he was on friendly terms with the revolutionaries, had been compromised by Bochkarëv's arrest, and as a foreigner it was relatively easy for him to leave the country; he also had the excuse of his poor health.

There were numerous precedents for the undertaking which the Smorgon Academy may well have assigned Marković. Chernyshevsky had made an unsuccessful trip to London to attempt a reconciliation with Herzen. The revolutionary Khudiakov went to Switzerland in 1865 and brought back to Russia the first detailed account of the recently founded First International. Varfolomei Zaitsev, whom Marković may have known, left for Switzerland in March of 1869 and established contact with Bakunin's friends in Geneva; he later founded a cell of the International in Turin. The Jacobin terrorist Sergei Nechaev also

129 Cf. Pushkarevich, "Svetozar Marković v Peterburge," p. 349.

130 *Sabrani spisi,* I, p. 130.

131 *Skerlić,* pp. 29-30. Jevrem Marković could have afforded to send his brother such a sum, for he had married a widow who brought as her dowry title to fifty-three acres of the best land in the Vojvodina.

132 "Serbskii revoliutsionnyi demokrat Svetozar Markovich," p. 356.

left for Switzerland about the time of Marković's departure. Finally, there were the several unsuccessful attempts of Bochkarëv to establish contact with *émigré* groups in Central Europe.[133] The probability is that the Smorgon Academy commissioned Marković to create a link between the revolutionary groups in Russia and those in Switzerland; as we shall see in the following chapter, Marković did indeed enter into Russian revolutionary circles in Zürich and Geneva. But the full story remains unknown, primarily because of the refusal of the Soviet authorities to release the pertinent documents, even to their own scholars.[134]

Immediately after obtaining the four hundred francs Marković requested permission to withdraw from the institute and leave Russia, citing poor health as the basis for his application. His request was forwarded to the Ministry of Foreign Affairs, which quickly gave its consent; he was free to make his departure.[135] Curiously enough, General Sobolevsky replied to the request for a dossier on Marković only on March 28, two months after he had received it and two weeks after Marković's departure from Russia. Even then he merely noted that Marković had been a student at the institute since 1866 and that he had recently been unconditionally released at his own request. No reason has been discovered for the lengthy (in matters of this nature) delay.[136]

133 Venturi, *Roots of Revolution*, pp. 328, 342.

134 The *Fond Bochkarëva* (*Bochkarëv Collection*) in the Central State Historical Archives in Moscow contains many key documents concerning Svetozar Marković's association with Russian revolutionaries. During a period of research in the Soviet Union in 1960 and 1961 I was not permitted to utilize those documents. The Soviet scholar V. G. Karasëv likewise did not use them in his 1950 Ph.D. dissertation on Marković, nor do his many articles on Marković cite them.

135 *Dokumental'nye materialy*, Institut I.P.S. to Aziatskii Department M.I.D., no. 278, March 6, 1869; Aziatskii Department to Institut I.P.S., no. 876, March 8, 1869; Institut I.P.S. certificate, no. 286, March 11, 1869.

136 B. P. Koz'min, "Po stranitsam knig i zhurnalov. Liuben Karavelov

Marković left St. Petersburg about March 14, barely in time to avoid almost certain arrest. On March 13 disorders erupted among the students at the Medical-Surgical Academy as a result of the severe disciplinary measures which the new inspector, Colonel Smirnov, had attempted to enforce. The academy was quickly closed and the student leaders arrested. A few days later new outbursts of student protest struck the Technological Institute, and on March 20 the disorders spread to the university.[137] The police moved swiftly to quell the disturbances, and within a week the capital was again quiet. Many students were expelled, some permanently, and others received severe reprimands. A stricter police surveillance was placed upon all institutions of higher education.[138]

One consequence of the intensified campaign of repression was the dissolution, later in the spring, of the Smorgon Academy. That remarkable organization, having survived undetected for over two years, quietly disbanded in April and May of 1869.[139] The demise of the Academy, coming as it did immediately after Marković left Russia, was a fitting close to his education at the hands of the Russian revolutionaries. He had come to St. Petersburg an immature, untutored young man whose first thoughts were of money and fashionable clothes. His political views amounted to little more than a deep love of his country and a desire to see it liberated from the last vestiges of Turkish oppression; his adherence to Vladimir Jovanović's liberal-

---

i Svetozar Markovich v ikh sviazi s russkimi revoliutsionerami" ("Through the Pages of Books and Journals. The Relations of Liuben Karavelov and Svetozar Marković with Russian Revolutionaries"), *Katorga i ssylka,* 1933, no. 4-5, pp. 145-155.

137 S. G. Svatikov, "Studencheskoe dvizhenie 1869 goda (Bakunin i Nechaev)" ("The 1869 Student Movement. Bakunin and Nechaev"), *"Nasha Strana" Istoricheskii Sbornik,* no. 1, 1907, pp. 196-201.

138 *Katorga i ssylka,* 1931, IV, 77, p. 109.

139 Koz'min, *Revoliutsionnoe podpol'e,* p. 139.

ism was shallow and uncritical, and did not long survive his exposure to Russian revolutionary democracy.

The concept of revolutionary democracy which Marković developed during his stay in Russia was derived from a wide variety of sources. It is important to note that all of the Russians who influenced him were themselves under the influence of *Western* social theories; there was little that was peculiarly "Russian" in the ideas of the Russian revolutionary democrats, none of whom can be called a truly original thinker. Chernyshevsky, Dobroliubov, Lavrov, Pisarev, and Tkachëv had studied the socialist, the visionary, the materialist, and sometimes the crackpot ideas of the West and had attempted to mold those ideas to suit Russian conditions. Marković, in his turn, took Western theories that had been reworked for Russia and attempted to apply them to his own Serbia. From the teachings of Pisarev and Tkachëv he adopted the concept of an enlightened intelligentsia leading the masses to socialism; the apparent contradictions between this egotistical elitism and revolutionary "democracy" disturbed neither Marković nor the Russians, as indeed they had failed to disturb the man from whom the Slavs borrowed the idea, Auguste Blanqui. From Peter Lavrov Marković derived a gradualist approach to socialism which was to determine the nature of his work in Serbia: the intellectual elite which Marković envisioned was in essence reformist rather than revolutionary.

The spirit of Marković's socialism was derived almost exclusively from N. G. Chernyshevsky. Chernyshevsky had taught that Russia, a latecomer into the modern era, could escape or hold to a manageable minimum the capitalist stage of economic development. Although he did not idealize the venerable *obshchina* (commune) he insisted that there was in it the nucleus of a communal society; using the modernized *obshchina* as a guide, Russia could proceed directly from the existing semifeudalism to socialism, thus escaping capitalism and its concomitants of pauperization and proletarianization. By socialism Chernyshevsky understood a democratic, decentralized society based upon agricultural-industrial associations; he owed a great debt to the Western visionaries, especially Charles Fourier.

Svetozar Marković became a true *narodnik,* a disciple of Chernyshevsky's Populist socialism, and applied his master's analysis of Russia to Serbia. He went to Switzerland to complete his socialist education, but the influence of his Russian master was to remain decisive throughout his life.[140]

140 An interesting comment upon the influence of Russian revolutionary democracy on Marković is contained in B. Boshkovich, *Krest'ianskoe dvizhenie i natsional'nyi vopros v Iugoslavii* (*The Peasant Movement and the National Problem in Yugoslavia*), Moscow, 1929, p. 19. After Marković left Russia the Russian consul in Belgrade, Shishkin, asked the Serbian government to name a replacement without delay; a Bulgarian wanted Marković's scholarship, and Shishkin urged the government to act quickly to preserve it for a Serb. A minor governmental official, Ljubomir Mutavdžić, was named to succeed Marković, but I have been unable to determine whether he actually went to Russia. *DANRS,* Ministarstvo Inostranih Dela, F VIII, R 70/869; Ministarstvo Inostranih Dela, F VIII, R 71/869.

CHAPTER III

Materialism, Marxism, and the First International: Marković in Switzerland

IN THE SPRING of 1869 the *Materialismusstreit* was at its zenith in continental intellectual circles. Originating early in the decade, the movement was essentially an artificial fusion of Feuerbachian materialism and Darwinism; it preached an uncompromising materialism which Feuerbach, an idealist almost in spite of himself, specifically condemned, and a distorted Darwinism which Darwin, humanitarian as well as scientist, could not accept. Led by the Germans Ludwig Büchner and Karl Vogt and the Dutchman Jacob Moleschott, the *Materialismusstreit* was one of the more extreme products of the reaction against romanticism.[1]

The materialist movement had spread from Central Europe to Russia, where Svetozar Marković first came into contact with its teachings. Chernyshevsky was a disciple of Feuerbach, and he and his followers made materialism a cornerstone of Russian revolutionary democracy; one of the revolutionaries, Kravchinsky, once observed that a non-materialist among the radical youth in Russia was "as rare as a white crow."[2] Pisarev had popularized the works of Moleschott, Vogt, and Büchner; *Kraft und Stoff*, in which Büchner set forth his views, was second only to the writings of Chernyshevsky in its influence upon the revolutionaries of the sixties and seventies.[3] After the exile of Cherny-

[1] Marx and Engels called the philosophy of the *Materialismusstreit* "vulgar materialism," and the appellation has stuck.

[2] Quoted in *Skerlić*, p. 201.

[3] Cf. J. A. Rogers, "Darwinism, Scientism and Nihilism," *The Russian*

shevsky, who was basically hostile to Darwinism, that doctrine gained virtually universal acceptance among his followers. Svetozar Marković had come of age in this Russian milieu, and further study in Switzerland served to intensify the materialist convictions he had begun to develop in Russia.

Marković's first stop after leaving Russia was Berlin, where he spent a few days with his friend Ljubomir Belimarković. He failed to convert Belimarković to the principles of Russian revolutionary democracy, but we learn from his letters that he discussed with his friend the analyses of capitalism made by Chernyshevsky, Marx, and John Stuart Mill; only they, he told Belimarković, had correctly understood the system which ruled the West.[4]

Moving on to Zürich, Marković took a small room at Prediger Hof 22 and at once began to prepare for the Polytechnikum entrance examinations. He devoted himself to statics, German, and French, the subjects in which he was deficient, and qualified in June to enter the third-year course the following September. On the basis of his success in the examinations he obtained a Serbian government scholarship; he was thus relieved of his financial worries, although he and the other Serb students in Zürich had regularly to urge Belgrade to send their monthly stipends on time.[5]

There were at least five Serbian student engineers in Zürich when Marković arrived, including his former roommate in St. Petersburg, Aleksa Knežević. Nikola Pašić, later to become prime minister of Serbia and Yugoslavia, was also among the small group of Marković's countrymen who were studying in the Swiss city.

Review, vol. 19, no. 1, pp. 10-23; Masaryk, *The Spirit of Russia*, II, pp. 71-72; Venturi, *Roots of Revolution*, pp. 288-289.

[4] Marković, *Sabrani spisi*, I, pp. 130-132; see also pp. 82-84.

[5] *DANRS*, Ministarstvo Prosvete, F V, 1122/870; Ministarstvo Prosvete, VII, k 9, 1756/1868; F VIII, 1756, k 9/1869.

SERBIAN POLITICS

Late in the spring of 1869 the *rapprochement* which Marković had foreseen between the Serbian liberals and the regency became an accomplished fact. Under the terms of the agreement, the admittedly repressive régime which had been in power since the assassination of Prince Michael was to be replaced by a constitutional form of government based upon popular representation. The accord also stipulated that the armed might of Serbia was to be "organized and prepared" for the creation of a "Great Serbia" which would embrace all the Serbs.[6] A new constitution, written by the liberals, was promulgated in July of 1869.[7] It provided for a democratically elected National Assembly which did not, however, have the right to initiate legislation; that was a privilege which resided solely with the Council of Ministers, which was appointed by the regency. The National Assembly was obliged to accept or reject en masse all ministerial legislation, and could not amend bills. In the event that the Assembly refused to approve legislation it could be enacted into law by ministerial fiat, and a simple decree was sufficient to pass a money bill. Thus popular representation existed but had no meaning; the Assembly was virtually powerless, for the ministers were responsible only to the regency.

The agreement between the liberals and the regency was the work chiefly of one of the regents, Jovan Ristić. Historian, diplomatist, and ardent monarchist, Ristić later entered the liberal party and served three terms as prime minister. Vladimir Jovanović, then the titular leader of the liberals, took no part in the agreement; he was still in confinement in Novi Sad.[8] Many of the rank-and-file lib-

[6] Jovanović, *Avtobiografija*, p. 24; Alex N. Dragnich, *The Development of Parliamentary Government in Serbia*, unpublished Ph.D. dissertation, University of California, Berkeley, 1945, pp. 64-66.

[7] Dragnich, *op. cit.*, pp. 67-84.

[8] Jovanović, *Avtobiografija*, p. 25.

erals were dissatisfied with the *rapprochement* in general and the constitution in particular and expressed bitter criticism of the Belgrade group which had made them.[9] The strongest criticism, however, came from the tiny "radical party" which Svetozar Marković created after the news of the accord had reached Switzerland. Nikola Pašić, Pera Velimirović, and Dimitrije Rakić had joined with Marković to form a party which would, in Marković's words, "strike at everything that is old in Serbia, destroy the old and lay the foundation for a new edifice."[10] Đura Ljočić, a Serbian engineer who was studying in Paris, passed through Switzerland and immediately joined the four Zürich "radicals," as Marković had insisted his group be called.[11]

BIRTH OF THE RADICALS

Svetozar Marković's incisive critique of the 1869 constitution became the credo of the infant radical party. Writing in Svetozar Miletić's Novi Sad newspaper *Zastava*, Marković pointed out that the army, the *appointive* judiciary, the ministers (i.e., the government), and the prince himself were all outside the constitution and in no way controlled or limited by it. The National Assembly was wholly lacking in effective power, and the State Council, an appointive, advisory body, was merely a "second edition of the government." Freedom of the press did not exist: the constitution provided only for the passage of a "special law" governing the press. Further, Marković charged, the wide powers allocated to the police clearly indicated a powerful threat to the most basic civil freedoms. The constitution was, in short, Marković wrote, that worst of political frauds, a tyranny imperfectly disguised in a cloak of paper

9 Dragnich, *op. cit.*, p. 78.
10 Quoted in *Skerlić*, p. 36.
11 *Ibid.*

freedoms; it created a "popular" government in which the people played no part.[12]

Not content with a critique of the constitution, Marković went on to tear apart the fabric of Serbian politics. Parties (he used the term in the sense of power elites), he maintained, rule the world: popular sovereignty and the popular will are merely illusions. Parties have the resources of wealth and power necessary to maintain themselves in office; occasionally they do so under a cloak of legality, as in the France of Napoleon III, but nothing can conceal the essential truth that the "popular will" can be manipulated in any direction by the ruling circles. Having written in Russia that Serbia had thus far escaped the division of the population into "rulers and ruled," Marković now reversed himself. The so-called intellectuals, he claimed, had created in Serbia the "bureaucratic party," a self-perpetuating group including the regents, the ministers appointed by the regents, and all state officials down to the lowliest village policeman; the only goal of the bureaucrats was "back stairs intrigue" and the exploitation of the nation for their own gain. At the other end of the spectrum, Marković wrote, was the great mass of the Serbian people (i.e., the peasants), the "ruled" whose obligations involved the payment of taxes and the performance of the "most undesirable tasks," and who were encouraged to consider their greatest happiness the "right" to die for their masters.[13] To correct this situation, Marković demanded the "*destruction of the bureaucratic system.*"[14]

Marković displayed a not inconsiderable polemical skill in his denunciation of the bureaucracy, which in later writings he seemed to regard as a true socio-economic *class.* It is manifestly obvious that Marković's struggle against the bureaucracy was to a certain extent a sciamachy. Among

[12] "Srpske obmane" ("Serbia Defrauded"), *Sabrani spisi,* I, pp. 153-187.
[13] *Ibid.,* p. 159. [14] *Ibid.,* p. 167.

the writers who attacked Marković's views on the bureaucracy was Slobodan Jovanović (the son of Marković's contemporary, Vladimir Jovanović), who held that the bureaucracy was numerically insignificant and its abuses a symptom of political growth rather than a fundamental cause of peasant misery.[15] Marxist writers have also challenged Marković; they agree with him that the bureaucracy did indeed play a role in the "original accumulation of capital," but they insist that its significance had largely expired by the end of the 1860's, when "commercial capitalism" began to be replaced by "industrial capitalism." It was the latter, with its "inevitable concomitants" of *zadruga* disintegration, peasant pauperization, and urban proletarianization which was, according to the Marxists, the real cause of the economic distress which gripped Serbia in the third quarter of the nineteenth century.[16]

Although Marković may have committed serious errors in his analysis, there was nevertheless an element of truth in his view of the bureaucracy. He recognized the role of the bureaucracy in the developing capitalism in Serbia, and it was to inhibit that development that he attacked

15 Slobodan Jovanović, "Svetozar Marković," *Političke i pravne rasprave*, Belgrade, 1932, pp. 105-132, 244. Jovanović has used as a statistical source his father's "Statističan pregled našeg privrednog i društvenog stanja, sa obzirom na privredno i društveno stanje drugih država" ("A Statistical Survey of our Economic and Social Situation in Relation to that of Other States"), *Glasnik srpskog učenog društva*, vol. 50, 1881, pp. 165-588; see esp. pp. 343ff. Vladimir Jovanović claimed that there was only one bureaucrat for every 314 inhabitants; P. A. Rovinsky ("Belgrad," part 1, p. 531) put the figure much higher, noting that Belgrade alone had over 450 policemen. Since Svetozar Marković included the army in the ranks of the bureaucracy, it is clear that, in his view, its numerical strength was considerable.

16 The best examples of the Marxist view are Veselin Masleša, "Svetozar Marković," in *Dela*, vol. 3, Sarajevo, 1956, pp. 12-100, and V. G. Karasëv, "Osnovnye cherty sotsial'no-ekonomicheskogo razvitiia Serbii v kontse 60-kh—nachale 70-kh godov XIX v." Masleša was intoxicated with the "original accumulation of capital" theme (cf. *Das Kapital*, chap. XXXII), while Karasëv is exceedingly fond of discussing the Serbian "unfinished bourgeois revolution."

its agents. Industrial capitalism, despite the Marxist claims, was not really in sight in Marković's time; as late as 1875 Serbia still had but one factory (an arms plant in Kragujevac) worthy of the name, there were no railroads whatsoever, and except for land and livestock there was no real capital in the country. Like Chernyshevsky in Russia, Marković refused to recognize capitalism as inevitable, and he insisted that timely action could "save" Serbia from what he later referred to as the capitalist "purgatory." A socialist society, he maintained, could be built without prior pauperization and proletarianization. To give him credit, Marković recognized as few in the nineteenth century did (Engels later developed a view not unlike that of Marković) the growing quasi-independent nature of bureaucracies. He attacked the narrow-minded, grasping, smug *činovnici* (bureaucrats) as an arrogant band of legal bandits whose goal was not service but preservation of their sinecures. His indictment was perhaps too sweeping, but he diagnosed a problem which has never found a satisfactory solution.[17] And his analysis of the situation in Serbia was supported by some of his contemporaries; after a trip to Serbia in the late 1860's, a Russian reporter noted that the Serbian bureaucrat "regards the people as something absolutely foreign to him, something to which he owes nothing, something with which he has nothing in common; the people for their part regard the bureaucrat in a still worse light: they see in him their enemy, detest him, and do not allow him in their society. . . ."[18]

Marković's critique of the 1869 constitution and his first attack on the bureaucracy were printed in the Novi Sad *Zastava* under the by-line "A Serb from the Principality."

[17] For Marković's amplification of his views on the bureaucracy see *Sabrani spisi*, I, pp. 187-201; *Narodnoe Delo* (Geneva), nos. 2 and 3, May 1870; *Pančevac*, nos. 64 and 65, August 1870.

[18] "Belgrad," part II, p. 164; see also "Partii v Serbii" ("Parties in Serbia"), *Otechestvennye zapiski*, vol. 175, book 1, November 1867, pp. 307-327.

The Serbian government demanded that Svetozar Miletić, editor of the journal, reveal the name of the author; Miletić refused, but the government was apparently advised anonymously to direct its attention to Marković.[19] The Minister of Education and Religion, Dimitrije Matić, was ordered to conduct an investigation. But even before Matić began his inquiry Marković had in effect been condemned by the Serbian government. Đura Ljočić had returned to Serbia after the founding of the radical party in Zürich in the summer of 1869, and had immediately begun to win converts among the Belgrade students. Two of the young men who joined the movement were sons of a minor bureaucrat, Kosta Mihailović. The regents summoned the elder Mihailović and informed him of their displeasure with the conduct of his sons. Ristić observed that the government had planned to give one of the Mihailović brothers a desirable post in the bureaucracy and the other a scholarship to study abroad; those plans might have to be reexamined, he noted, if the young men persisted in associating with "extreme elements" among the "enemies of the dynasty."[20]

Shortly after Marković's article on the constitution was published, Dimitrije Matić (who was personally not unfavorably disposed toward Marković)[21] wrote Marković a private letter suggesting that he could clear himself of all suspicion by openly disavowing the article.[22] Marković did not reply. After risking the wrath of his superiors for his delay, Matić wrote to Marković again in January of 1870 and noted that he was now obliged to "recommend" that

19 *Skerlić*, p. 43.

20 Miroslav Đorđević, "O Svetozarevom članku 'Srpske obmane'" ("On Svetozar's Article 'Serbia Defrauded'"), *Književnost*, I, 1946, no. 9, p. 147. Đorđević quotes from the unpublished diary of Kosta Mihailović.

21 *DANRS*, Ministarstvo Prosvete F v, 1122/870. The Serbian State Archives have mistakenly attributed this letter from Marković to Matić to the year 1870; the content clearly indicates that it belongs to 1869.

22 *Ibid.*, correspondence between Marković and Matić.

Marković state whether or not he had written the article in question.[23]

In what was coming to be typically flamboyant fashion, Marković responded with an "Open Letter to Mr. Matić" in *Zastava*.[24] Foolishly directing the brunt of his attack at Matić personally, Marković accused the Minister of Education of persecuting him. He admitted writing the article on the constitution, and stated that but for the harassment to which he had been subjected he would not add another word. But Živojin Žujović had been deprived of his scholarship for writing in *Sovremennik*, Marković claimed, and it was obvious that the same fate was in store for him; it was a challenge he was unable to ignore.

The Serbian government, he argued, granted its scholarships for the study of a specific discipline. If a student pursued his studies in good faith, what further obligation did he have to the government? Why should a student be prohibited from engaging in political discussion, a right ostensibly guaranteed to every Serbian citizen? Having chosen a public forum for his answer to the government, Marković was determined to obtain maximum propaganda advantage from the situation; he went on to discuss political developments in Serbia since the revolution. He pointed out that class distinctions, which were slowly but perceptibly growing in Serbia, were entirely artificial; fifty years ago, he wrote, there was only one class in Serbia: "We are all sons or grandsons of peasants."[25]

In the pristine peasant society which had existed after the winning of autonomy there had been an unparalleled

23 *Ibid.*

24 *Sabrani spisi*, I, pp. 187-201. When the "open letter" was printed in *Zastava* the newspaper noted in a foreword that only Svetozar Miletić had known the identity of the author of "Serbia Defrauded." *Zastava* stated that it had been reluctant to print the "open letter" because of the "harm" that would come to Marković; he had, however, insisted that it be published in full. *Zastava*, no. 8, January 21, 1870.

25 *Sabrani spisi*, I, p. 191.

opportunity for a wise and benevolent government to ensure that the state developed in accordance with the principles of freedom and justice. Had Serbia been in fact blessed with such government? On the contrary. A series of self-seeking governments, backed by the Obrenović dynasty (which he did not mention by name), had created a state system which in reality served only those who were in theory the servants of the state. Having created and absorbed an educated class and bureaucracy (Marković insisted that the two were practically synonymous in Serbia) to perpetuate the system, the governments of the past decade (i.e., since the fall of the Karađorđe dynasty) had reduced the Serbian people to a state of poverty and ignorance which for sheer degradation rivaled that of the *rayah* (helots) in Turkish-held Bosnia.[26]

Where was Serbia headed? Marković insisted that he cared not whether the Obrenović dynasty ended with the present ruler (Milan) or his son or grandson; what he wanted was a government which would give the Serbian people the opportunity to develop to the fullest their material and intellectual capabilities. When they eventually escaped from their present lowly state and no longer had need of any tutor (i.e., the enlightened intelligentsia), the natural consequence would be the establishment of a republic.[27]

Republican by admission and Karađorđevist by implication, Marković had driven a solid wedge between his radical movement and the ruling circles in Serbia. His action was deliberate; schooled in Russian revolutionary democracy, he realized that his movement would be fatally compromised by the slightest hint of cooperation with the established order or even the adoption of a lenient attitude toward it. Having seen the Russian and Serbian liberals abandon—at least in his view—liberalism to make peace

[26] *Ibid.*, p. 198.

[27] *Ibid.*, pp. 199-200.

with their governments, he was determined not to follow the same path.

There was never any doubt as to the action the Serbian government would take in response to Marković's articles. In the spring of 1869 it had removed his brother, Jevrem Marković, from a teaching post for alleged antigovernment statements;[28] now, in January of 1870, the Ministry of Education and Religion withdrew Svetozar Marković's scholarship on the grounds that he was being subsidized to study technology, not politics.[29]

THE LEAGUE OF PEACE AND FREEDOM

Marković's activities in the summer of 1869 had not been limited to the formation of his radical movement and his attacks on the Serbian ruling circles. After meeting with his fellow Serb students in Zürich to lay the foundations for his new party, Marković left for Lausanne to attend the congress of the League of Peace and Freedom; it will be recalled that Ivan Bochkarëv had attended the League's meeting the previous year.

The League of Peace and Freedom was founded in Switzerland in 1867 by a group of well-known liberals, bourgeois radicals, and republicans. Among its active supporters were Giuseppe Garibaldi, Jules Favre, Jules Ferry, Victor Hugo, Louis Blanc, John Stuart Mill, John Bright, Ludwig Büchner, Karl Vogt, and, of course, Michael Bakunin. The League was an outgrowth of earlier European "peace movements," and its program was essentially "an attempt to link the advocacy of peace to that of European union under republican government."[30] It was dominated by the "respectable left," but Bakunin led a small, vocifer-

28 *Ibid.*, pp. 136-137, 373-374.

29 *DANRS*, Ministarstvo Prosvete, F v, no. 1122, k 11/870.

30 G. D. H. Cole, *Marxism and Anarchism*, 1850-90, II of *A History of Socialist Thought*, London, 1957, p. 113.

ous wing which supported his own anarchist program. The 1869 congress of the League had three major topics on its agenda: the union of European states, the solution of the Polish and Eastern questions, and the elimination of class antagonisms.[31] Victor Hugo summed up the idealistic, sentimental aims of the congress in his formula, "society without kings, humanity without frontiers."[32]

When Marković arrived in Lausanne early in September he found the French republicans in the League holding a clear majority. The republicans were led by Victor Hugo, Jules Ferry, and Jules Barni, the noted philosopher and editor. These were the men, Marković noted, who had refused to accept Bakunin's "solution" to the "social problem" at the League's 1868 congress. Bakunin's program had called for a collectivism-anarchism, a "communism without a state," which Bakunin had contrasted with the statist communism of Marx and his followers. Calling for the total destruction of the state and the organization of property on a collective basis, Bakunin alienated not only the bourgeois radicals but also the Proudhonists and most of the German socialists.[33]

Marković commented favorably upon Bakunin's program, and his ex post facto support of it was largely determined by his attitude toward the Lausanne congress. He was by this time firmly committed to the cause of socialism, and he opposed both the liberalism and the middle-class democracy of the dominant wing of the League of Peace and Freedom. He supported the position of the socialist minority on all issues, displaying scant regard for the vast differences among the various socialist groups. He welcomed the proposals of some of the German Lassalleans, and at the same time praised the "wonderful speech" de-

[31] Marković, "Kongres Lige za mir i slobodu" ("The Congress of the League of Peace and Freedom"), *Sabrani spisi*, I, p. 144.

[32] Quoted in *Skerlić*, p. 33.

[33] Cole, *Marxism and Anarchism*, pp. 122-123.

livered by the Proudhonist Charles Longuet; Longuet advocated the establishment of a national bank (without a metallic backing) for the extension of free credit to the workers.[34] Marković also expressed his admiration for the Blanquist Swiss democrat Amand Goegg, who called for the tools of production—all machines and factories—to be turned over to the workers.[35] But the most constructive proposal to come out of the congress, Marković wrote, was the call for the solution of the Eastern Question on the basis of a "federal republic of free nations" in southeastern Europe.[36] Marković's later advocacy of a federal union in the Balkans owed much to the plan put forward at the League congress.

Despite the presence of liberals and pacifist republicans, Marković praised the Lausanne congress as a "congress of revolutionaries." In particular he singled out the French bourgeois radicals who, despite their hostility to socialism, were dedicated to the overthrow of Napoleon III. Under their influence Marković conceived an intense hatred for the French emperor and his liberal allies. He came to equate the Serbian dynasty, regency, and liberals with Napoleon and the Ollivieristes; much of his later criticism of the Serbian "national dynasty" (Ristić's term) reflected the views of the French radicals whom he met at Lausanne.

Marković attended the congress merely as an observer. His report on its work, published in *Zastava* in September of 1869, indicated that he had become an admirer of many socialist creeds, a firm adherent of none. Though never abandoning his faith in the teachings of Chernyshevsky, his short stay in Switzerland had already been marked by an increasing regard for the ideas of Marx, Proudhon, Lassalle, Blanqui, and Bakunin. In Marković's case it is no

[34] Longuet later became a Communard, went over to Marxism and the International, and married one of Marx's daughters.

[35] Marković, *Sabrani spisi*, I, p. 149.

[36] *Ibid.*, pp. 147-148.

easy matter to determine when eclecticism becomes dilettantism, particularly in the early stages of his career. Certainly while he was in Switzerland he was less interested in attaching himself to one of the feuding socialist factions than in determining which of their theories could be applied to Serbian conditions and which could not. But his attitude was frequently uncritical and his understanding often shallow, and he had still to attain the intellectual maturity necessary to equip him for serious work.

THE FIRST INTERNATIONAL

It was only natural that Marković should become associated with the organization which embodied the most *avant-garde* elements in the European socialist movement, the International Working Men's Association (First International). Through the Russian revolutionary *émigrés* in Zürich and Geneva[37] Marković became affiliated with the International, which had been founded in London in 1864 "primarily as a joint British-French Trade Union movement, in which it was hoped to secure the co-operation of like-minded groups in other countries."[38] Karl Marx, then living in London, managed to secure an invitation to the organizational meetings and quickly became a power within the movement.

From the outset a wide variety of groups were represented in the International. Mazzini sent his secretary to attend the sessions of the 1864 Inaugural Conference, but later the Italian republican-nationalist withdrew his followers from the organization. The French delegation to the

[37] Although the Smorgon Academy may have sent Marković to Switzerland to establish contacts with the *émigrés,* the lack of evidence has made it difficult to trace his relations with them; see E. N. Kusheva, "Iz russko-serbskikh revoliutsionnykh sviazei," pp. 350-351, and M. P. Sazhin, "Russkie v Tsiurikhe, 1870-73 gg." ("The Russians in Zürich, 1870-73"), *Katorga i ssylka,* vol. 95, no. 10, 1932, pp. 28-29.

[38] Cole, *Marxism and Anarchism,* p. 90.

Inaugural Conference was composed of three Proudhonists, one Trade Unionist, and one Marxist. The "British" delegation included several German *émigrés,* friends of Marx who had become prominent in the British Trade Union movement, and also the bona fide Trade Unionists George Howell, George Odger, and W. R. Cremer. Belgium and Switzerland were represented by a few individuals of uncertain persuasion, a Pole (Bobczynski) was strictly on his own, and Germany was not officially represented.

Once in a position of power, Karl Marx attempted to make the International a truly international organization; hence its membership was composed in each country of individuals who joined various sections or cells rather than of national parties.[39] Marx was well aware that any attempt to force the adoption of an extreme socialist position would be defeated by the Proudhonists and Trade Unionists; he therefore, in his inaugural address, gave his support to the cooperative movement which then (under the influence of Lassalle) dominated German socialism and to which the Proudhonists and Trade Unionists were not opposed.[40] Marx did, however, manage to secure the acceptance of the principle that "the emancipation of the working class must be the task of the working class itself."[41]

At the first two congresses of the International, at Geneva in 1866 and Lausanne in 1867, Marx's adherents clashed with the Proudhonists on the problem of private land ownership, a policy supported by the latter group. In the following two years the Marxists gradually overcame the followers of Proudhon, then turned their attention to the new and greater threat posed by the Bakuninists. After breaking with the League of Peace and Freedom in 1868,

39 *Ibid.*, p. 103.

40 Marx, "Inaugural Address of the Working Men's International Association," *Marx and Engels: Selected Works*, I, Moscow, 1958, p. 383.

41 Élie Halévy, *Histoire du socialisme européen*, 10th edition, Paris, 1948, pp. 150-151.

Michael Bakunin joined the International; the conflict between his followers and those of Marx led to the disintegration of the organization in the mid-1870's.[42]

The dispute centered around three main points. First, Marx insisted upon centralized control of the International; Bakunin, correctly identifying Marx as an authoritarian rather than a democratic centralist, demanded autonomy for the various affiliates down to the local level. Secondly, Marx held that the existing "police state" could only be replaced by a "peoples' state" under the control of the proletariat; Bakunin opposed the state in any form, and denounced Marx's "peoples' state" as the same old tyranny under a new name. Thirdly, although Marx condemned the liberals and socialists who cooperated with reactionary governments (the Ollivieristes in France, Lassalleans in Germany), he nevertheless held that socialists were obliged to work with the bourgeois radicals who sought by parliamentary means to improve the lot of the working class; Bakunin, after his break with the League of Peace and Freedom, resolutely opposed such cooperation, which in his view could only lead to disastrous consequences for the revolution and the working class.

Bakunin had earlier sought to merge the League with the International; had such a union taken place his supporters would have held a majority. The Brussels congress (1868) of the International had rejected the merger and had further stipulated that its members seek the liquidation of the League, whose individual members would be welcome to join the International. Bakunin thereupon withdrew from the League, joined the International, and formed his own Alliance of Social Democracy, through which he hoped to gain control of the International.[43]

[42] On the dispute see G. A. Brupbacher, *Marx und Bakunin*, Munich, 1913.

[43] Cole, *Marxism and Anarchism*, pp. 116-120.

In addition to the conflict on fundamental socialist issues Bakunin challenged the Marxists on the question of inheritance. At the 1869 congress in Basle, which he attended in person, Bakunin secured the support of a majority of the delegates for his proposal to make the abolition of the right of inheritance a principle of the International. He thus firmly established himself as a power to be reckoned with in the International; his support within the organization (especially among the Swiss and southern European members) grew steadily.

Svetozar Marković became affiliated with the International through its Russian Section, which was organized in the spring of 1870.[44] In the summer of 1868 Bakunin had

[44] The Russian Section, largely ignored by Western scholars, has received a fascinating variety of interpretations in the Soviet Union. First to examine the problem was V. A. Gorokhov, *I-i Internatsional i russkii sotsializm. "Narodnoe Delo"—Russkaia sektsiia internatsionala* (*The First International and Russian Socialism. The People's Cause and the Russian Section of the International*), Moscow, 1925. Gorokhov held that the work of the Section represented an attempt to fuse the revolutionary democracy of Chernyshevsky, Pisarev, and Dobroliubov with Marxism. E. Iaroslavskii, writing in *Istorik-Marksist* (1940, no. 10, pp. 54-80), noted only that the Section's "great historical service" was to popularize in Russia the ideas of the International (p. 69). R. Sh. Tagirov wrote a 1948 dissertation on the Section for the Kazan State Pedagogical Institute, and published a summary of his views in two articles in the *Uchënye Zapiski Kazanskogo Gosudarstvennogo Pedagogicheskogo Instituta*: "Russkaia sektsiia Mezhdunarodnogo Tovarishchestva rabochikh i Rossiia" ("The Russian Section of the First International and Russia"), vypusk VIII, 1949, pp. 113-132, and "Iz istorii Russkoi sektsii Mezhdunarodnogo Tovarishchestva Rabochikh (Russkaia sektsiia i evropeiskoe revoliutsionnoe dvizhenie)" ("From the History of the Russian Section of the First International [The Russian Section and the European Revolutionary Movement]"), vypusk II, part II, 1956, pp. 83-126. Tagirov does little beyond dividing the members of the Section into "mature" and "immature" Marxists, claiming that the latter were in the majority. N. K. Karataev repeated and updated Gorokhov's views in his "K voprosu ob ekonomicheskoi platforme russkoi sektsii I Internatsionala" ("On the Problem of the Economic Platform of the Russian Section of the First International"), *Uchënye Zapiski Moskovskogo Universiteta*, vypusk 130, 1949, pp. 86-114. Karataev amplified his argument (and viciously attacked B. P. Koz'min, who had recently died) in his commentaries in *Ekonomicheskaia platforma Russkoi sektsii I Internatsionala. Sbornik materialov* (*The Economic Platform of the Russian Section of the First*

been urged by a young revolutionary *émigré,* Nikolai Zhukovsky, to become coeditor of a newspaper. After some hesitation Bakunin accepted, and the first issue of *Narodnoe Delo* (*The People's Cause*), appeared in Geneva on September 1, 1868 (New Style). Bakunin wrote two of the articles in the first issue (Zhukovsky wrote the others), and in them called upon the Russian intelligentsia to renounce the trend toward positivism and utilitarianism which was, he maintained, leading to the creation of an intellectual elite isolated from the masses. Bakunin insisted upon the necessity for immediate, violent revolution; through such a program he hoped to unite the Russian revolutionaries in Switzerland and bring them, under his leadership, into the International.[45] Strong opposition to Bakunin, however, already existed among the Russian *émigrés.* One of

---

International. A Collection of Materials), Moscow, 1959; see esp. pp. 66ff., 76ff. D. A. Vvedenskii's 1954 dissertation on the Section for Moscow University was not made available to me, but it developed the argument that the work of the Section "paved the way for the liberation of the Russian proletariat, for its entrance into the historical arena." Vvedenskii's dissertation was followed by that of L. S. Bocharova, *Russkaia sektsiia I Internatsionala i eë sotsial'no-ekonomicheskaia platforma* (*The Russian Section of the First International and its Socio-Economic Platform*), unpublished Ph.D. dissertation, Moscow State University, 1955. Miss Bocharova wrote that the work of the Section was *not,* as Gorokhov and Karataev had insisted, an attempt to fuse revolutionary democracy with Marxism; rather, it was "a dialectical development of views, the *evolution* of the views of the Russian Section *from* the views of the revolutionary democrat Chernyshevsky *to* the principles of the Marxist wing of the First International" (pp. 164-165). She criticized B. P. Koz'min for identifying the Section with Russian populism, which in her view represented a "step backward" from the views of Chernyshevsky (pp. 199-200). Finally, the most extensive work on the Russian Section is that of B. P. Koz'min, *Russkaia sektsiia pervogo Internatsionala* (*The Russian Section of the First International*), Moscow, 1957. In this, his last major work, the dean of Soviet historians of the pre-1917 revolutionary movement presented an uncompromising Leninist concept of the Section. Subjecting all previous writers on the subject to vigorous criticism, Koz'min argued that not only were the members of the Section populists in the tradition of Chernyshevsky, they also had not the faintest understanding of Marxism.

[45] The first issue of *Narodnoe Delo* is analyzed in Gorokhov, *op. cit.,* pp. 17-25, and Venturi, *Roots of Revolution,* pp. 431-433.

the editors of *Narodnoe Delo* was Nikolai Utin, who like Zhukovsky had been in Switzerland since the early sixties. But, unlike Zhukovsky, Utin was no anarchist; before his departure from Russia he had been a member of one of the early populist revolutionary organizations (Land and Liberty) and in exile had become a disciple of Chernyshevsky. Utin's presence on the editorial board of *Narodnoe Delo* had been the cause of Bakunin's hesitation to join the group; after the first issue Bakunin found it impossible to work with Utin and severed his connection with the journal, whereupon Utin gained complete control of it. Utin published only three issues in 1869; in them he attempted to propagandize the views of Chernyshevsky. Since in his opinion those views conflicted in no way with the program of the First International, in November of 1869 he decided to form a Russian Section of the organization.[46]

A general strike of the Geneva construction workers erupted on November 11, 1869 (New Style). One of the leaders of the strike was the German exile Johann Philipp Becker, a friend of Marx and a key figure in the Geneva section of the International. Utin, who participated actively in the Geneva labor movement,[47] became acquainted with Becker at one of the meetings held by the strikers. The two men became friends, and under Becker's guidance Utin intensified the study of Marx's works which he had begun on his own. Becoming convinced that the Marxist wing of the International represented the vanguard of the labor movement in central and western Europe, Utin and the members of his *émigré* circle determined to join the organization in the hope of bringing the Russian revolu-

46 B. P. Koz'min, ed., *Sbornik materialov k izucheniiu istorii russkoi zhurnalistika*, vypusk iii (70-e gg. — seredina 90-kh gg. XIX v.) (*A Collection of Materials for the Study of the History of Russian Journalism*), Moscow, 1956, p. 152.

47 R. Sh. Tagirov, "Iz istorii russkoi sektsii," p. 84.

tionary movement into contact with its closest counterpart in the West.[48]

The Russian Section was formally organized in March of 1870; through Becker's influence it was quickly accepted into the International. On March 12 (New Style) Utin and two of his colleagues wrote Marx requesting that he represent the Russian Section on the General Council of the International.[49] The Section's main goal, the letter pointed out, was to propagandize the principles of the International among the Russian workers (all Chernyshevsky's disciples understood the term to include peasants) and to unite the workers in the name of the International. A second task was to expose Pan-Slavism and liberate the Russian youth from its grasp. In order to achieve its aims the Russian Section would, Utin and his colleagues told Marx, establish sections of the International in Russia and work to create firm ties between the working classes of Russia and western Europe.[50] The Russian *émigrés* welcomed Marx as an ally in their fight against the Pan-Slavs and Slavophils, and assured him that they had "nothing whatsoever in common with Bakunin and his few followers." "Brought up in the spirit of . . . Chernyshevsky's ideas," the Russians wrote, "we have joyfully welcomed your exposition of socialist principles and your criticism of the system of industrial feudalism."

Marx replied two weeks later, informing the Russian Section of its acceptance into the International. For his part, he wrote, he would be happy to represent the Section on the General Council. Urging the Russians to strive for the liquidation of the military régime in their country,

48 Koz'min, *Russkaia sektsiia*, pp. 73-81, 184-195.

49 Marx and Engels, *Perepiska K. Marksa i F. Engel'sa s russkimi politicheskimi deiateliami* (*The Correspondence of Marx and Engels with Russian Political Figures*), 2nd edition, Leningrad, 1951, pp. 36-39.

50 As Franco Venturi has pointed out (*op. cit.*, p. 443), the Utin program did not differ substantially from an earlier one drawn up by Bakunin.

Marx held that it was Russia's armed presence in Poland that had caused the rest of the continental states to establish similar military régimes. Praising the works of Chernyshevsky and the new book by N. Flerovsky (V. V. Bervi), *The Situation of the Working Class in Russia,*[51] Marx observed that such works indicated that Russia was beginning to take part in the general (working class) movement of the century.[52]

The establishment of the Russian Section of the International represented the first major attempt to link the Russian revolutionary movement with the socialist movement in the West. The Russian revolutionaries had long studied Western socialist theories and had striven to adapt them to Russian conditions, but until now no serious effort had been made to establish contact with Western socialists. Allying itself with Kark Marx, the Russian Section became identified with the most extreme elements among the Western socialists. Despite its diminished significance after 1871 and its manifestly imperfect understanding of Marx's theories, the work of the Section was of considerable importance in widening the path along which radical Western ideas flowed into Russia.

In its first letter to Marx the Russian Section informed him that it did not intend to limit its work to establishing ties between Russia and the West. Utin and his colleagues noted that they had already found adherents of the International among the Czechs, Poles, and Serbs, and that the latter had a flourishing organization, *Omladina,* through which they hoped to spread the ideas of the International among their countrymen. It was the first indication that Svetozar Marković and his tiny radical party had elected to make common cause with the members of the Russian

51 First published in 1869, Bervi's book was republished in Moscow in 1938: *Polozhenie rabochego klassa v Rossii.*

52 *Perepiska Marksa i Engel'sa,* pp. 38-39.

Section. Article 13 of the Regulations of the Section provided for the acceptance into the organization of "agents-correspondents" from all countries whose task would be to inform their countrymen of the work of the Section and the International; Svetozar Marković was the only individual ever to hold such a position in the Section.[53]

It is not known when Marković first came into contact with the Utin group. If the Smorgon Academy did indeed commission him to establish contact with the *émigrés*, it is probable that he did so not long after his arrival in Switzerland, but his movements in 1869 are virtually impossible to document. In February of 1870 Marković wrote to a friend of his intention to go to Geneva to "become better acquainted with European radical democracy,"[54] and it would seem likely that he knew Utin and his followers before this time. In any event, the Russian Section requested Marković to write an article dealing with the Serbian "working class," and he responded with an account which *Narodnoe Delo* published in May of 1870.[55]

Marković had obviously seen the letter to the Russian Section in which Marx had praised Flerovsky's (Bervi's) book; Marković titled his article "The Political and Economic Situation of the Working Class in Serbia" and adopted some of Flerovsky's terminology. Apparently in the attempt to impress Marx,[56] Marković hastened to claim the existence in Serbia of class distinctions: the workers (he noted that in Serbia the term meant "peasants") were the poorest and largest class, in between were the artisans and merchants, and "on top" were the bureaucrats. Hastily abandoning this rather questionable argument, Marković

[53] Koz'min, *Russkaia sektsiia*, pp. 206, 235.

[54] *Sabrani spisi*, I, pp. 208-210.

[55] *Narodnoe Delo*, nos. 2 and 3, May 1870.

[56] Utin surely sent copies of each number of *Narodnoe Delo* to Marx, and the latter, therefore, probably read Marković's article. Engels praised *Omladina* in a letter to Marx on March 27, 1870, but except for this indirect reference neither he nor Marx ever took any recorded notice of Marković.

switched to an attack on the Serbian liberals, whom he accused of attempting to convert *Omladina* into a tool of the government.[57] To thwart the liberals, a new radical party had been formed which had, Marković noted, the goal of seizing control of *Omladina*; he implied that the radicals would attempt to bring the organization into the International.

The remainder of Marković's article was a mixture of invective and random opinion. In a childish and distasteful display of spite he singled out the innocent Dimitrije Matić for special abuse among the bureaucrats; he went on to criticize the Serbian professors for never once having given a "revolutionary lecture," and sneered that Prince Miloš had been "no better than a Turk."[58] If Karl Marx read Marković's article it probably confirmed his less than enthusiastic opinion of the South Slavs. Certainly the editors of *Narodnoe Delo* were disappointed, for Marković was not asked again to write for the journal. Marković's article was denounced by many in Serbia as an attempt to split the ranks of the youth movement. Even the liberals who had opposed their party's *rapprochement* with the regency and dynasty called Marković a "charlatan and ignoramus" and his ideas the "products of an inflamed brain."[59] Marković's article on the Serbian "working class" was indeed a farrago of spiteful nonsense.

SERBIAN RADICALS VS. LIBERALS

His attack on the *Omladina* liberals, however, was a reflection of the struggle for control of that organization be-

57 The editors of *Narodnoe Delo* tampered with Marković's text and inserted a phrase making a ridiculous comparison between *Omladina* and the Fenian movement in Ireland; cf. the editor's note in *Markovich: Izbrannye sochineniia*, p. 124.

58 More succinct was Chernyshevsky's accurate characterization of Miloš as a "Christian pasha"; "Vozvrashchenie Kniazia Milosha Obrenovicha v Serbiiu" ("The Return of Prince Miloš Obrenović to Serbia"), *Polnoe sobranie sochineniia*, v, p. 628.

59 *Srbija*, Belgrade, no. 69, July 1, 1870.

tween Marković and Vladimir Jovanović. Jovanović had come to Zürich in the spring of 1870 and had participated in a series of political discussions with the Serbian students in the city, all of whom were to some extent under the influence of Marković.[60] Marković himself attended only a few of the sessions; he had developed a personal dislike for his former teacher and left Nikola Pašić and the others to debate with him.[61]

The Marković group condemned the compromise the liberals had made with the regency, insisting that the liberals had thereby forfeited the right to lead the youth movement (i.e., *Omladina*). Jovanović, although pointing out that he had been in prison and had not participated in the agreement, defended it on the grounds that the interests of the Serbian people and the dynasty were harmonious. By making a few concessions to the dynasty, he argued, the liberals ensured the eventual establishment of a constitutional monarchy. When the young radicals challenged Jovanović to defend the new liberal constitution, he replied that the major task confronting all Serbs was not that of introducing sweeping democratic reforms but rather that of achieving national unification and liberation, after which democracy would come in due course. The threat that the Turks would cede Bosnia-Hercegovina to Austria,[62] he noted, made it imperative for all Serbs to "unite under the national banner" in order to avoid being cut off forever from their brothers in the twin provinces. A Mazzinist devoid of republicanism, Jovanović held that only the principle of nationality could serve as the foundation for the progress and welfare of the Serbs.

[60] Jovanović, *Avtobiografija,* pp. 25-28.

[61] Marković, "Javan račun sa Vladimirom Jovanovićem" ("A Public Reckoning with Vladimir Jovanović"), *Pančevac,* no. 69, August 27, 1870.

[62] Such a possibility haunted the Belgrade government, which knew full well that Austria could take the province by force. The problem of Bosnia-Hercegovina led to worsened relations between Austria-Hungary and Serbia in the 1870's.

The principle of union on the basis of nationality alone was rejected out of hand by Marković and his followers. Their ideal, they told Jovanović, was a "union of free communes"; clearly they had accepted at least some of Bakunin's principles. The young radicals insisted that, in the struggle to create such a union, nothing was of greater importance than the maintaining of a resolute opposition to the Obrenović dynasty. They further held that Austria did not dare seize Bosnia-Hercegovina, for by so doing she would "call forth a movement of the Slavs . . . and extend the influence of the International, which would be even more dangerous for Austria than a Jugoslav movement."[63] Jovanović discussed Austrian policy at great length and insisted that the Viennese "Drang nach Osten" was far more dangerous—as indeed it proved to be in 1878—than the radicals were willing to admit.

Acknowledging their adherence to "the socialist cause," the Marković group pressed their attack on the liberals. Jovanović wryly observed that the newborn socialists seemed to feel that it was not they but the liberals who had renounced their principles. He demanded to know whether the radical-socialists, as they now styled themselves, were prepared to assume the leadership of Serbia. They were not, the socialists answered, because Serbia had no free press; they were not ready to admit that they as yet had no coherent program. Jovanović promised to support their demand for a free press, but he cautioned his radical young countrymen not to misuse it. They erred, he insisted, in equating the situation in capitalist Europe with that in backward, agrarian Serbia. The Serbian situation, in his view, demanded a Serbian solution best achieved through the cooperation of all political factions. He admitted that both the government and the dynasty had to some extent

[63] Jovanović, *Avtobiografija*, p. 26.

betrayed the liberal principles to which they had officially subscribed, but he argued that the overwhelming importance of national unification and liberation required a dynamic, flexible policy rather than slavish adherence to abstract political theory.

The socialists were adamant in their rejection of Jovanović's views, and insisted that the liberal party had forfeited its "progressive role." The leadership of the youth and the nation, they held, had now to pass to a "new generation of warriors," to the socialists. Frustrated in his attempt to secure the cooperation of the Zürich group, Jovanović uncharacteristically resorted to a bitter personal attack on Marković which served only to secure the latter's leadership of the young radicals.[64] The personal animosity between the two men became so intense that later in the spring of 1870 Marković refused to accept a position on the *Omladina* newspaper because of Jovanović's presence on the editorial board.[65] In a letter to Jovanović a few months after the Zürich discussions Marković reiterated his refusal to cooperate with the liberals: "You attack a government and a dynasty because they are not liberal, but I do not look for liberalism from the government or the dynasty; I do not want either the government or the dynasty. My goal is to ensure that the people know what is required, that is, a general *zadruga* [i.e., a state organized as one large commune], and instead of a government elected commissioners who will fulfill the national tasks in a manner prescribed by the people themselves. . . . You are a statesman, and I am a socialist, a man who denies the very foundation of the [contemporary] state. We differ in our fundamental concepts of the people, the state, and freedom."[66]

[64] *Pančevac*, no. 69, August 27, 1870.
[65] *C.d.*, II, pp. 171-195.
[66] Jovanović, *Autobiografija*, p. 28.

MARKOVIĆ'S PHILOSOPHY

Marković described some of his own "fundamental concepts" in his major philosophical treatise, "The Realist Direction in Science and Life," the first part of which he wrote in Switzerland.[67] His work showed that he had read deeply, if not always critically, in the works of the leaders of the *Materialismusstreit*; he was especially fond of the works of Ludwig Büchner,[68] and, if Hermann Wendel's information is correct, he rated Ernst Häckel's *Natürliche Schöpfungsgeschichte* above the works of Darwin himself.[69] He also knew Huxley's popularizations of Darwinism, and, as "The Realist Direction" indicated, he was now more familiar with the works of Marx. Marković's treatise was not completed until after his return to Serbia, but we shall consider it here as the unified exposition of his philosophical views he intended it to be.

Noting at the outset that his knowledge was too meager to set forth a philosophical system of his own, Marković stated a more modest goal: "to popularize the results of science, and especially to show the direction taken by science in recent times."[70] Marković used the term "science" in its true meaning of "systematized knowledge"; thus, like Chernyshevsky, he held it to include not only the natural sciences (which he preferred above all other disciplines) and mathematics, but also history, psychology, moral philosophy, and metaphysics.[71] He tended to use "science" (as well as "realism") as a synonym for "materialism," reflect-

67 "Realni pravac u nauci i životu," *Sabrani spisi,* I, pp. 225-361.

68 Part of his admiration for Büchner was no doubt due to the fact that the German scholar represented the Darmstadt workers in the International.

69 Wendel, *Aus dem südslawischen Risorgimento,* Gotha, 1921, pp. 149-150.

70 "Realni pravac," pp. 288-289.

71 Chernyshevsky, "Antropologicheskii printsip v filosofii" ("The Anthropological Principle in Philosophy"), *Polnoe sobranie sochinenii,* VII, p. 255.

ing his faith in the power of "science" to solve problems basically moral; in this instance he again followed the lead of Chernyshevsky, who had written that "the natural sciences have developed to such an extent that they provide a great deal of material for the precise solution of moral problems."[72] Marković accordingly conceived of "The Realist Direction" as an account of the development of materialist philosophy and a rationalization of its extension into all areas of human knowledge and activity.

In the first part of his study, subtitled "What is Realism?" Marković attempted to outline the conflict between "materialism-realism" (which he called "a scientific philosophy") and "idealism-dualism" ("unsuccessful, theological"). Like Chernyshevsky before him he ridiculed Comte and positivism,[73] but to a certain extent his analysis followed Comtian lines. The "theological phase" of intellectual development, he wrote, was the "childhood period of human thought"[74] from which mankind had still not wholly emerged. The Encyclopedists of the eighteenth century had dealt a deathblow to religion's hold on the minds of men, Marković claimed, and had prepared the ground for the French Revolution ("the greatest progress in European history"). The revolution, in turn, liberated science from the grasp of the middle and upper classes and made it the servant of all men.

[72] *Ibid.*, p. 258; as we shall see shortly, Chernyshevsky later modified his views.

[73] Marković frequently heaped scorn on Comte and cited Huxley's definition of positivism as "Catholicism without the Pope" ("Realni pravac," p. 290). Chernyshevsky wrote that, while he found "nothing wicked" in Comte's theories, he considered them comical; he regarded Comte's three-stage analysis of intellectual development as "rubbish." Chernyshevsky's break, or at least what he himself felt was his break, with positivism came only during his exile in Siberia; nevertheless, both he and Marković remained positivists to the extent that they denied the validity of pure speculation and metaphysics. See Chernyshevsky, *Polnoe sobranie sochinenii*, XIV, pp. 651-652.

[74] "Realni pravac," p. 229.

At this point Marković digressed into an account of the progress made in the natural sciences in the nineteenth century. Most of his data were from John William Draper's *History of the Intellectual Development of Europe*,[75] which he read in German translation. Although he accepted Draper's views concerning the historical development of the natural sciences, Marković was sharply critical of the American scholar's conclusions. He accused Draper of "charlatanism"[76] for asserting that, since matter and energy are eternal, they must therefore be creations of God, who rules nature according to eternal laws. Marković, by now a confirmed agnostic,[77] insisted that Charles Darwin had provided a "scientific foundation" for the explanation of all natural phenomena, thereby rendering the old theological view untenable.

Marković's criticism of Draper was the first step in his analysis of Darwinism; in that analysis he relied less on Darwin's own works than on those of his popularizers, Huxley, Büchner, and Häckel. His admiration for Häckel's interpretation of Darwin led him dangerously close to an extreme form of Social Darwinism and presented difficulties from which he did not wholly extricate himself. In his exposition of the Darwin-Häckel argument Marković wrote that science "teaches that between human races those which are more developed win the victory in the 'rivalry for the acquisition of the necessary means of existence.' It teaches that only through continuous perfection, through continuous activity, was man able to ascend to

[75] Draper's work was widely read among the Balkan intelligentsia. One of Marković's colleagues, Vasa Pelagić, asked the Moscow Slavic Committee to send him a copy of the work (Nikitin, *Slavianskie komitety*, pp. 101-102), and Liuben Karavelov often quoted Draper (*Izbrannye proizvedeniia bolgarskikh revoliutsionnykh demokratov* [*Selected Works of the Bulgarian Revolutionary Democrats*], pp. 157-158).

[76] Somewhat less damning was Engels' observation that Draper had an "anti-theoretical Yankee brain," *Marx and Engels, Selected Works*, II, p. 72.

[77] Cf. *Skerlić*, pp. 209-215.

such unattainable heights in relation to the other organisms, even in relation to the lower races of his own species. It consequently shows him that it [science] is the only way to victory in *further perfection*, and it guides him in the struggle."[78] Having pursued Social Darwinism (which he confused with Darwinism) to its logical conclusion, Marković suddenly realized its implications and attempted to qualify his argument; to do so he fell back on egalitarian socialist theory, and the result was an unsatisfactory syncretism. Despite the fact that natural selection has led to differing states of development among human races, he wrote, the establishment of a tyranny of the strong over the weak is not permissible: "Science preaches complete equality and brotherhood among people on the basis of the most concrete facts. Science shows that the single pride of man is his highly developed intellect, and therefore there cannot under any circumstances arise [a class of] 'nobles by blood.' "[79] Through his uncritical application of Darwinism to man and society, Marković fell into the Social Darwinist trap later eluded by Chernyshevsky, who rejected outright such an application.[80] Marković was here close to the Marxists and considerably removed from his Russian idol; as Thomas Masaryk has written, Chernyshevsky "more correctly diagnosed the aristocratic character of Darwin's teaching than the Darwinian Marxists who interpreted Darwinism democratically."[81] In any event Chernyshevsky avoided the intellectual confusion which plagued Marković; the latter, in the second half of his work, again contradicted his egalitarian beliefs when he wrote that the

78 "Realni pravac," p. 284.

79 *Ibid.*, p. 285.

80 Cf. Chernyshevsky, *Polnoe sobranie sochinenii*, x, pp. 745-770; xiv, pp. 539-542; xvi, pp. 479-503, 728-731. Chernyshevsky read the Russian translation of the *Origin of Species* during his imprisonment in 1862-64, but was unable publicly to comment on Darwinism until 1888. Marković thus could not have known his views.

81 *The Spirit of Russia*, ii, p. 29.

struggle for survival has made man *"physically and intellectually more perfect than woman."*[82]

Although Marković did not refer to him directly, Feuerbach exercised the strongest influence upon his concept of materialism. In the lengthy passage below on Darwinism, Feuerbachian materialism is clearly at the root of Marković's thought, although it is once again important to note that he has come to the Westerner Feuerbach only through the Russians Chernyshevsky and Pisarev. It is further clear that his interpretation of Darwinism places him more precisely in the naturalist, rather than the materialist, school:

"Science banishes from nature everything that is 'strange,' 'terrible,' and so forth; that is, everything that has held man in superstition and ignorance, in slavery. It says that man has no need of any rituals, ceremonies, or 'sacrificial offerings' in order to induce the forces of nature to help him or spare him evil. It says that natural forces act blindly, mechanically, that they can neither help man nor do him evil. It teaches man to recognize these forces and use them in order to increase his power a hundred and a thousand fold. If a man does not know the forces of nature he is a slave of nature . . . a savage. Only when he studies these forces does he become the master of nature, the summit of all creation. *Does science thus humble man by giving him the means to become the master of nature?*

"Science further teaches that all organisms are blood relatives—that they all rose one from the other as a result of continuous, gradual development. Science says that all organisms developed as a result of 'natural selection,' that is, that nature *selected* and let live those organisms which had some sort of advantage over similar organisms. Science

82 "Realni pravac," p. 322. Marković was a lifelong champion of the emancipation of women; clearly he did not recognize the implications of his remarks. Cf. Olga Arsenijević, "Svetozar Marković i pitanje oslobođenja ženskinja" ("Svetozar Marković and the Question of the Emancipation of Women"), *Letopis Matice Srpske*, vol. 358, 1946, pp. 207-212.

says that man is the *most developed* organism in nature, that he arose by the same law of 'natural selection,' and that his advantage over other organisms lies chiefly in the development of his intellectual capabilities. . . . It shows man the true meaning of his great strength—the intellect —with which he opens the laws of the universe.

"Science teaches that constant laws rule human activity and the activity of all society. It teaches that human morals depend upon the entire social structure and upon the position man occupies in society from the moment of birth. . . . Science teaches which conditions are necessary in order for man to be moral. It points out the laws of human society and of human necessity upon which depend human activity. In this science has a great advantage over any religion. Religions merely preach: 'be moral.' Science, on the other hand, teaches people *how they can become moral.*"[83]

This unbounded faith in "science" stemmed largely from the Russian interpretations of Darwinism and materialism, but Marković on some points diverged from his teachers among the Russian revolutionary democrats. Unlike many of the latter (especially Pisarev), Marković, who was less strongly influenced by positivism, did not question the validity of the social sciences (excluding metaphysics and pure speculation). He held that it was the failure of the social sciences to keep pace with the more precise disciplines which had repeatedly led to revolution. Europe in the 1870's, he wrote, is again on the verge of revolution because the development of applied science— i.e., technology—has far outstripped man's knowledge of society.[84] Now, Marković was here much closer to Karl Marx's theories than his modern Marxist critics, who insist that he was unable to "ascend" to historical material-

83 "Realni pravac," pp. 284-285.
84 *Ibid.*, p. 291.

ism, have been willing to admit.[85] Both Marković and Marx believed the basic factor in human progress to be man's control over the physical world, a control that had increased steadily since the dawn of civilization. Thus the substitution of "advances in man's control over the physical world" for Marx's "changes in economic conditions" and Marković's "development of science" brings us closer to the essence of both men's thought. This is not, to be sure, a ridiculous attempt to equate the two men, but rather an indication that Marković understood Marx much better than he has been credited.

Technological advances, Marković held with Marx, unlock the secrets of nature and point the way to progress. But Marx argued that the fruits of technology are appropriated by the exploiting classes at the expense of the lower classes—a situation which thus germinates class warfare. Marković, a product of a society in which "we are all sons or grandsons of peasants," had no genuine class theory. He did argue that society was becoming divided into two classes—capitalists and proletariat—but he did not clearly define either term and he refused to accept (though he did understand) the concept of universal "class struggle." He did not believe that the proletariat was the possessor of any particular "mission," and certainly he did not consider it the duty of the proletariat to liquidate the *bourgeoisie*. Further, Marković held that, while revolution was *perhaps* inevitable, its inevitability lay in the failure of human reason (the inability of the social sciences to keep pace with technology) rather than in inexorable historical laws. Marković remained convinced that the revolution could be avoided if only men would be reasonable, if only they would extend and apply to society what "science" had taught them of the physical world. Finally, under the in-

85 For the best example of severe Soviet Marxist criticism of Marković on Marxism see Karasëv, *Svetozar Markovich*, pp. 324ff.

fluence of the Russian revolutionary democrats, especially Pisarev and Tkachëv, Marković placed more emphasis than did Marx upon the role of the individual as a creative agent, as the exploiter of natural forces. He held to his view (which, it will be remembered, his Russian teachers had derived in large measure from Blanqui) that society would be led to the millennium by an intellectual elite.

Marković devoted the remainder of the first half of "The Realist Direction" to a discussion of his theory of knowledge. It was a theory which owed much to John Locke, although (as in the case of Feuerbachian materialism) he did not mention Locke's name. Marković developed his theory from Chernyshevsky, J. S. Mill, T. H. Huxley, and the leaders of the *Materialismusstreit,* all of whom were profoundly influenced by Locke.

Innate ideas, Marković wrote, do not exist; thought is a product of sense perception. There is no knowledge outside nature, and likewise no force outside nature: "Science has irrefutably proved that man has no knowledge other than the knowledge of natural laws and that there are no forces in the world other than the natural."[86] Insisting that all ideas have a material origin, with some zest Marković quoted one of his teachers: "There is no force on earth which could give the lie to Moleschott's famous truth: 'There is no thought without phosphorous'!"[87] This bit of bombast reflected the teachings of the school of Huxley, Moleschott, and others, which held that, not only does being precede consciousness, but consciousness itself, in relation to the neuro-chemical processes (i.e., being) which determine it, is but an epiphenomenon.

Continuing in this vein, Marković reduced the will itself to a material entity. The exercise of the will, he

[86] "Realni pravac," pp. 282-283.

[87] *Ibid.*, p. 283. The less dogmatic Chernyshevsky had been unable to decide whether phosphorous or sulphur activated the will; "Antropologicheskii printsip," p. 262.

wrote, produces motion; since motion is matter, it therefore follows that the will is material, "for only motion can produce motion."[88] But if "science" provided the answer to the "how" of the will, what could explain the "why"?

It was a problem Chernyshevsky also struggled with. If I ask a man, he wrote, "Why did you do that?" he will reply, "Because I wanted to." And in answer to "But why did you want to?" he will say only, "Simply because I wanted to." Utterly unsatisfactory, concluded Chernyshevsky, and modified his earlier view: "There are some theoretical problems to which science still does not provide precise solutions."[89] Writing a decade after Chernyshevsky, Marković attempted to solve the problem by attributing the stimulation of the will to reflex; this was of course the solution advanced by Wilhelm Max Wundt, one of the founders of experimental psychology. "*According to the theory of reflexes,*" Marković wrote, "*each thought is a reflex . . . motion in the brain in consequence of all past and present impressions.*"[90] Obviously, the "why" of the will remained without answer.

"The Realist Direction" was not the first exposition of materialist philosophy among the South Slavs. The works of Vogt, Liebig, Moleschott, and others were widely discussed in student circles in the latter half of the sixties, and in 1867 the outstanding Serbian journal *Letopis Matice Srpske* published a series of articles dealing with new theories in the natural sciences. Parts of Büchner's *Kraft und Stoff* were translated into Serbo-Croatian in 1869, and in the following decade many Serbian journals regularly published translations and discussions of Darwinist and materialist views. Marković thus did not introduce the new

[88] "Realni pravac," p. 276.

[89] "Antropologicheskii printsip," pp. 261-263.

[90] "Realni pravac," pp. 276-277. Marković was perhaps influenced also by Marx's activist criticism of "truth," on which see Bertrand Russell, *A History of Western Philosophy*, New York, 1945, pp. 783-784.

concepts to his countrymen when the *Letopis Matice Srpske* published his work in 1871 and 1872, but his was a major role in securing their wide dissemination among the educated class.[91]

In the second half of his work Marković's first concern was the concept of morality. On the basis of his reading (in German translation) of Lecky, he rejected both the intuitive and the utilitarian views of morality and turned instead to Darwinism, "which provides the basis for a correct theory of morals." Darwin proved, Marković claimed, that the basis of morality is man's natural instinct for the company of man, an instinct which operates "*without the participation of the human will.*" Morality is thus egoism, since man clearly foresees some advantage to himself in his associations with others of his kind: the social contract is not based upon altruism. Man's love for society is *normally* a reflection of his egoism, Marković agreed, but there are exceptions. Morality, like all phenomena, has a material basis; like everything else morality must therefore be in a constant state of development and perfection. Thus altruism may indeed be found in a few exceptional individuals: among the most moral (i.e., altruistic) of men, Marković noted, were Robert Owen, Jan Hus, and Jesus Christ.[92]

Marković objected to the lengths to which Mill had carried his utilitarian concept of morality. The "greatest happiness," he insisted, is a goal rather than a principle; realist theory had shown that *any* action based upon social in-

[91] Consult Uroš Džonić, "Darwin u srpskoj nauci i književnosti" ("Darwin in Serbian Science and Literature"), *Srpski književni glasnik*, XXII, 1909, pp. 293-297. On Marković and the introduction of materialist philosophy into Serbia see *Skerlić*, pp. 199-204, and Dragutin Ilić, "Dah materijalizma u srpskoj književnosti" ("A Breath of Materialism in Serbian Literature"), *Brankovo kolo*, Belgrade, II, 1896, pp. 1071-1080. See also K. A. Koperzhinskii, "Serbskie deiateli 60-kh godov i peredovaia russkaia literatura."

[92] "Realni pravac," pp. 292-305. The order is Marković's.

stincts is moral.[93] Marković thus challenged the teachings not only of Mill but also of Chernyshevsky, who likewise subscribed to a utilitarian theory of enlightened egoism.[94]

The institutions of the family and marriage next occupied Marković's attention. The modern concept of the family, according to Marković, holds that a man owns his wife as an object of private property, and the emancipation of women from this state of slavery inevitably leads to the destruction not only of marriage but also of the family. Contradicting his sources (the *Communist Manifesto* and Chernyshevsky's *What is to be Done?*), Marković insisted that such emancipation did not, however, necessarily mean the "communism of women." Those who drew such a conclusion were guilty, Marković maintained, of failing to understand the difference between marriage and matrimony. Matrimony, he wrote, "is a natural—physical and moral—relation between man and woman which is based upon mutual inclination and is accomplished by the free will of two persons." Marriage, on the other hand, is "a social—religious or civil—institution, by which matrimony is sanctified and strengthened." When society has progressed to the point where *all* matrimony is based upon the free will of the participants, there will be no need for marriage.[95]

In his concluding remarks Marković arrived at his central thesis. A careful study of science, he wrote, had convinced him that the only just, moral, and free social organization was one based upon communism.

Private property, he argued, did not exist in primitive society. The origin of private property was the family; when a man began to regard a woman and children as "his

93 *Ibid.*, pp. 305-316.

94 Chernyshevsky, "Antropologicheskii printsip," pp. 282-284; Masaryk, *The Spirit of Russia*, II, pp. 8-17.

95 "Realni pravac," pp. 320-331. There scarcely seems a need for a discussion of this admittedly interesting bit of logic.

own," the concept of private property came into being and was gradually extended to tools, weapons, caves, and so forth. Only later did the concept spread to include land, and even in "modern, cultured nations" such as Russia and India, he noted, land is still held in communal ownership. In Russia the land is regularly reapportioned among the members of the commune,[96] none of whom have the right to alienate their allotments; a "similar situation," Marković observed, had until recently existed in Serbia.[97] The experience of Russia, India, and Serbia had, he claimed, proved that communal land is worked better and more efficiently than private land.[98]

The disintegration of communal landownership, Marković held, was the result not of the development of better agricultural methods but of the centralization of power in the hands of one or a few members of the commune and of the consequent growth of inequality among men—of the growth of capitalism. When society legalized capitalism, it legalized inequality. Men were enslaved by the profit motive; all morality was abandoned in the pursuit of personal gain. Capitalism thus represented a denial of the most perfect principle upon which society can be based, equality. Only through equality in rights and property, Marković maintained, do men have freedom: "The fullest development of freedom in society with regard to private property is *communism,* that is, that condition in society where every member of society is free to use for his own purposes each and every item of the common property."[99]

[96] Marković erred in giving the impression that *all* communal land in Russia was periodically repartitioned; some of the communes held land in hereditary household tenure.

[97] It is unclear what Marković meant by a "similar situation"; the *zadruga* never practiced periodic repartition, and most of the arable land was individually owned.

[98] "Realni pravac," pp. 335-338.

[99] *Ibid.,* p. 350.

It is not true, he insisted, that communism means the destruction of personal freedoms; on the contrary, "communism in the realm of property means *the destruction of personal right* [*to something*] *as a result of the extreme development of personal freedom.*" Marković's "extreme development of personal freedom" clearly bordered on anarchy; despite his protests and his avowed renunciation of Bakunin's principles, Marković never completely freed himself from the influence of the Russian revolutionary-anarchist. Marković would certainly have denied that he was an anarchist, however, and would have cited his belief that society would reach its ideal state (communism) only when men reached a state of perfect morality. Thus there would be no question of anarchy, since enlightened egoism would lead man to do good (more precisely, to refrain from doing evil) to society since he sees his own interests in those of society.

Turning to the economic foundations of the "perfect society," Marković first noted his belief that "*that which a man produces* belongs to him and to no one else." The means of production belong to the producers (again a Blanquist doctrine Marković derived partly from Marx's interpretation, partly from that of some of the Russian revolutionary democrats). Furthermore, natural resources, which are not produced by man, belong to society and cannot be appropriated by any individual. Capitalist society, Marković observed, is the very antithesis of communism for in it the few exploit the many through interest and rent (coming back now to the Ricardian socialism he had begun to study in Russia). But actually the capitalist system is wholly justified, Marković derisively noted, in giving the individual the right to give himself to another individual for a certain length of time and for a certain "equivalent": such is the case with prostitutes, servants, and the working class. Capitalism, he charged, gives the individual the right to choose to be a slave.[100]

The inequality of capitalist society creates the conditions necessary for revolution; as he had noted earlier, socio-economic relationships had not kept pace with the advance of technology. Force is the foundation of capitalist society, for only by forcible means can the majority be kept in a state of inequality. There is no inequality under communism, he claimed, for all large agricultural and industrial enterprises are the property of society; and "society," he implied, could not abuse itself.

Consumer goods under a communist system would, Marković held, remain in the realm of private property. Goods would exchange according to their labor value; although there would initially be differences in the quality of labor, as society progressed labor would become equal qualitatively as well as quantitatively. But there can be no firm, detailed blueprint for the new society, he observed, because "the development of the social organization in all its complexity and diversity must be unlimited. Therefore it is nonsense to invent some sort of ideal organization as a pattern for all societies."[101]

On such an uncertain note Marković concluded "The Realist Direction in Science and Life." What had started as an exposition of materialist philosophy ended as a communist *profession de foi.* That Marković had indeed become a communist is obvious, but it is equally true that he belonged to no readily recognizable school of communist thought. His argument contained many elements of Marxism, but ignored the proletariat, deplored the "class struggle," and adopted a vague and ambiguous attitude toward Marx's historical determinism. Some of his views stemmed from Auguste Blanqui through the Russians Peter Tkachëv and Dimitry Pisarev, but unlike all three of those in-

[100] *Ibid.*, p. 354.

[101] *Ibid.*, pp. 357-358.

dividuals he had no clearly defined formula (having rejected the path of social revolution) for the acquisition of power by the "enlightened intelligentsia" (a term Marković consistently used but never satisfactorily defined). His refusal to commit himself to any blueprint for the society of the future was, however, clearly in the tradition of Blanqui and Tkachëv. Finally, Marković often hovered on the brink of Bakuninist anarchism, yet for him it was an anarchism of logical implication rather than of conscious design.

MARKOVIĆ AND SOCIALISM

Marković continued his discussion of some of Marx's theories in the final work of his stay in Switzerland. His article, published in the republican newspaper *Pančevac*,[102] set forth some Marxist arguments but drew from them conclusions based upon the teachings of the Russian revolutionary democrats. He presented a brief history of the economic development of Europe, using data largely drawn from the first volume of *Das Kapital*.[103] He discussed the various stages of that development and pointed out the "contradictions" in each which, according to Marx, had led to its destruction. He went on to analyze briefly the Ricardian and Marxian theories of value, insisting that only labor is productive (i.e., creates capital), since capital is merely "stored-up human labor." He had first expressed such views in Russia, and now, two years later, he displayed a firmer grasp of Marx's theory of surplus value. He agreed with Marx that the capitalist exploits the worker by taking from him most of the fruits of his labor, and maintained that that exploitation (again the failure of the social sci-

102 *C.d.*, III, pp. 51-116.

103 *Ibid.*, pp. 84-85. Marković recommended *Das Kapital* to his readers as the best exposition of the principles of "scientific socialism," but he also urged them to consult the works of K. Marlo, F. A. Lange, Lassalle, and Chernyshevsky!

ences to keep pace with technology) had led Europe to the verge of a great social revolution.[104]

Analyzing the background of the European revolutionary movement, Marković singled out the French Revolution of 1848 for special attention and based his findings largely on Marx's "The Class Struggles in France" and "The Eighteenth Brumaire of Louis Bonaparte."[105] His discussion of the revolution was patterned almost exclusively upon Marx's works, but when he came to the causes for its failure his conclusions were in the spirit of Chernyshevsky and Bakunin. The revolution in France had failed, he said, because it was limited to the large urban centers, did not attract the peasants, and lacked the guiding force of a unified socialist movement.[106] Certainly he constructed a sound case for his views, which had much to recommend them, but in slighting the role of the proletariat he swung sharply away from the Marxist argument he had presented in the first part of his essay.

Continuing what became virtually a headlong flight from Marx, Marković adopted the rather confusing position that revolution and class struggle are inevitable but that Serbia must find a way to avoid them. He attempted to get back to Marx by claiming that "scientific socialism" and the program of the International provided the blueprint for the new Europe which would arise from the revolutionary chaos; he followed this, however, with the comment that the solution for Serbia lay (as his colleagues had earlier told Vladimir Jovanović) in the establishment of a society based upon "free peasant associations."[107] It now appeared that he relied not only upon Chernyshevsky and Bakunin for guidance, but also, to a lesser extent, upon Eugen Dühring.

104 *Ibid.*, pp. 79ff.
105 *Ibid.*, pp. 100ff.
106 *Ibid.*, pp. 108ff.
107 *Ibid.*, pp. 110ff.

So far as Serbia itself was concerned, Marković never seriously considered any program other than that of an agrarian socialism based primarily upon the teachings of Chernyshevsky, with admixtures of Bakunin, Dühring, and others. He was enormously impressed by what he considered the profound complexity of Marxian theory and by the extent of Marx's influence in the International; the very name of the International was of enormous significance to Marković, who was beginning in 1870 to see himself as part of a European-wide movement for social justice. As we shall see in the following chapter, Marković at one point went so far as to sound Marx's cry for the workers of the world to unite, but unlike Marx he understood the slogan in a humanitarian and sentimental sense. As Slobodan Jovanović has observed, Marković under the influence of Chernyshevsky, "conceived of socialism not as an economic doctrine but as a new philosophical view of man and life."[108] Marx's socialism was primarily a philosophy of history; the socialism of Chernyshevsky and Marković was primarily a system of ethics.

But to the ethical socialism of Chernyshevsky Marković added an element of eclecticism which frequently led him into theoretical mazes. In the last part of his article on European socialism he noted that the scientific socialism of Karl Marx proceeded from the premise that all social and political relations are determined by the relations between capital and labor; so long as the means of production remain the monopoly of one class, Marković held, the revolution would continue until the working class overthrew the "kings and Rothschilds"[109] and their armies ("which in-

[108] "Svetozar Marković," p. 70.

[109] Marković frequently singled out the Rothschilds for abuse, indicating not only his dislike of capitalists but also a certain anti-Semitism which most investigators have overlooked. He often used words like "yid" and "kike" (cf., for example, *Radenik*, no. 1, June 1, 1871), and his excoriation of the Serbian merchants (many of whom were Jews) likewise

fect entire nations with syphilis"). But Marković added to the Marxist argument an important codicil of his own which Marx would never have allowed: "local conditions," Marković insisted, will determine the nature of the new society which the working class will establish in each country. Peasant and worker associations would everywhere be the basic social unit, but their exact nature would depend upon the historical and economic conditions in each country.[110]

Thus Marković's ethical, eclectic socialism had led him to a point somewhere between Marx and Chernyshevsky but undoubtedly closer to the latter. Much of Marković's terminology was derived from Marx, but to that terminology he gave his own special meanings (for example, his insistence that, in Serbia, "worker" was synonymous with "peasant"). He remained an agrarian socialist on the model of Chernyshevsky, but he had over his Russian teacher the advantage of direct contact with the socialist movement in the West; his was a broader if simultaneously less profound concept of that movement.

By the summer of 1870 Svetozar Marković was ready to return to Serbia, there to lead in person the struggle of his young radical movement to wrest control of *Omladina* from the liberals and capture the allegiance of the young generation of Serbs. His brother was willing to continue to support him in Zürich, but Marković had made up his mind to return home.[111]

Despite the immaturity displayed in his writings in 1869-70, Marković had accomplished a great deal during his fourteen months in Switzerland. He had founded the radical party, and counted among his few associates some

---

reflected a measure of animosity toward the Jews. His was certainly not, however, a rabid anti-Semitism, and in fact was considerably milder than that of many of his fellow Serbs.

110 *C.d.*, III, pp. 110ff.

111 *Skerlić*, pp. 37-39.

extremely capable young men, notably Nikola Pašić and Đura Ljočić. He had been accepted into the ranks of the Russian revolutionary *émigrés,* and through them had become affiliated with the First International. Now widely known in Serbia due to the furor over his criticism of the government and the withdrawal of his state scholarship, Marković seemed likely to become a public figure of importance: "Friend of Russian revolutionaries, a man who had studied socialism in Switzerland, and, finally, a student who had hurled his scholarship in the face of the government when it had dared to meddle in his convictions—all this, together with the preceding short but energetic activity of Liuben Karavelov, guaranteed to Marković the role of spiritual leader of the generation."[112]

[112] Viktorov-Toporov, "Svetozar Markovich," p. 43.

CHAPTER IV

Socialism in the Balkans

SERVED only by the Danube and poor roads, the Belgrade to which Svetozar Marković returned in the summer of 1870 was difficult to reach, and due to the climate and lack of amenities was singularly uninviting when one got there. Belgrade was the seat of the government and the official capital of the principality, though the National Assembly met in the interior town of Kragujevac. In addition to its governmental functions Belgrade was the chief trading center of Serbia. Through the city passed nearly all Serbian imports and exports, the origin and destination of which was the Habsburg Empire.[1]

A Russian visitor to Serbia in the late 1860's was impressed by the backwardness of Belgrade in comparison with the rest of the country. The capital, he wrote, was representative neither of Serbia nor of Western civilization; on the contrary it "represented a rebuff" to both. The reason for Belgrade's lag behind the remainder of the principality lay in the "cunning policy" of the government, which used the city as a "highly reliable brake" to dangerous political currents. For a population of less than 25,000 the government maintained nearly 500 gendarmes in the city, one for every fifty inhabitants.

SERBIAN POLITICS

Until the compromise between the liberals and the regency, even the most moderate members of the liberal

[1] Vladislav Milenković, *Ekonomska istorija Beograda* (*The Economic History of Belgrade*), Belgrade, 1932. See also Mijo Mirković, *Ekonomska historija Jugoslavije*, and B. N. Gavrilović (and others), *Beograd*, Belgrade, 1940.

party were looked upon with great suspicion in Belgrade, and fists and clubs were frequently used on liberal candidates during elections. The political life of the city, the Russian traveler observed, was dominated by the new class of merchants, "who do not understand any goal but exploitation," and by the bureaucracy, that "blind tool of the government." The Belgrade ethic, which the ruling circles wanted to spread throughout the country, was one of "speculation, of coarse materialism, of insolent rebuff to progress, of lack of respect for ideas and of implacable conservatism. It is strange and sad to recall how many educated and well-meaning people of Serbia tremble for some sort of Serbian principles, fearing they will give way to Western civilization. Can it be that all this is an indispensable trait of the Serbian character?"[2]

Although the political atmosphere in Belgrade was indeed conservative in 1870 it was less repressive than the above report would indicate. The harsh months following the assassination of Prince Michael in 1868 were followed by the liberal-regency compromise in 1869, an event which marked the beginning of modern party politics in Serbia.[3] Disagreement among themselves prevented the regents from establishing a dictatorial triumvirate in the years before Prince Milan Obrenović reached his majority, and none of the three was strong enough to establish a personal régime. Jovan Gavrilović, the weakest of the regents, was an elderly gentleman with no political following. Milivoje Blaznavac, an army colonel and formerly a Karađorđevist, had little support outside the army and the small conservative party, and his ardent Austrophilism won him the active dislike of the majority of his countrymen. Jovan

[2] Rovinsky, "Belgrad," part I, p. 572; see parts I and II, *passim*. Svetozar Marković was impressed by what he considered the accuracy of Rovinsky's analysis; cf. *C.d.*, VII, p. 103.

[3] Cf. Vasa Čubrilović, *Istorija političke misli u Srbiji XIX veka*, pp. 320-328. See also below, pp. 254-255.

Ristić, the third regent, was not sufficiently anti-Austrian for the taste of many Serbs, but he collaborated with the liberals in pursuing a "Great Serbia" foreign policy and was the dominant figure in Serbian politics.[4]

The power maneuvers of Blaznavac and Ristić led to the crystallization of the political system which prevailed in Serbia until the First World War. Blaznavac represented the conservatives, in whose ranks were found the most prosperous merchants and landowners, many of the higher bureaucrats, and an important segment of the military leadership. The conservatives favored a pliable monarchy, a laissez-faire economy, and a cautiously expansionist foreign policy under the tutelage of Austria and at the expense of Turkey. Ristić and the liberals represented the bulk of the merchant and professional classes, a minority of the intellectuals, and nearly all the lesser civil servants. United in support of a constitutional monarchy, Ristić and the liberals also favored a laissez-faire economy but above all they pursued a bellicose foreign policy, setting the pattern for almost every government in Serbia in the years 1869-1914. It was the foreign policy established by the liberals and pursued by most other parties (most notably Nikola Pašić's Radicals) which led the country into one war after another, culminating in the final catastrophic conflict of 1914-18 which produced, at a tragically high cost, a united Yugoslavia under Serbian domination.

When Svetozar Marković returned to Serbia he was convinced that he could (as the Russian Section of the International had told Marx) build a strong radical-socialist movement on the foundation of *Omladina*, the Serbian youth organization. He had, however, underestimated the strength of Vladimir Jovanović and the liberals.

The summer of 1870 saw the struggle between Marković and Jovanović for the leadership of the young generation

[4] *Vlada Milana*, I, pp. 1-30, 78-155.

take on an increasingly bitter, personal character. Marković had foreseen a break with Jovanović as early as December of 1868, when he wrote that Jovanović, the "most intelligent, honest and bold" of the liberals, was nevertheless certain to oppose any attempt to establish a radical-socialist party in Serbia.[5] Despite the fact that Jovanović had not been a party to the liberal-regency compromise, Marković regarded him as having betrayed liberalism; Jovanović in his turn looked upon Marković as a reckless young radical.

When Jovanović left Zürich in the spring of 1870 he told Marković's friends who accompanied him to the railway station that he would publish his views on the radical-socialist movement; that, he observed, would "destroy or save" Marković. Upon his return to Serbia, however, he was persuaded by Svetozar Miletić to refrain from attacking Marković in print; Miletić held that a polemic between the two men would only weaken *Omladina* at a time when the organization seemed destined to play an important role in Serbian politics. For his part Marković also agreed to suspend his quarrel with Jovanović; for the moment he had another problem to contend with.[6]

Dragiša Stanojević, a republican and former professor at the *Velika Škola*,[7] published (in August of 1870) a lengthy critique of the ideas expressed by Marković in his last article written in Switzerland.[8] He attacked Marković's "Marxian socialism" and insisted that it was incompatible with individual freedom and with decentralized socialism based upon the commune. Stanojević further maintained that Marković erred in attacking the republicans: "a true

[5] *Skerlić*, p. 42.

[6] *Pančevac*, no. 69, August 27, 1870. [7] See above, pp. 63-64.

[8] *Pančevac*, nos. 55-57, 1870. On Stanojević see Andrija Radenić, "Dragiša Stanojević—život, rad, i ideje" ("Dragiša Stanojević—His Life, Work and Ideas"), *Istoriski časopis*, VII, 1957, pp. 145-212; Kosta Milutinović, "Prvi socijalisti u Beogradu" ("The First Socialists in Belgrade"), *Godišnjak Muzeja grada Beograda*, I, 1954, pp. 237-254. The latter article analyzes the work of Stanojević and Živojin Žujović.

republican cannot possibly be an enemy of socialism." Marković, who had gone to Karlovac (in Croatia) for a rest cure, felt compelled to defend both himself and Karl Marx. He responded with a biting, sarcastic assault out of all proportion to Stanojević's criticism. His defense of Marx, however, was of considerable interest.

Deriding Stanojević's Lassallean reformism, Marković wrote that "Marx was the first to show that the proletarian seeks not mercy but a reckoning with the capitalist."[9] Marx had shown the "reactionary nature" of the "parlor socialists" who in their desire to please everyone appeal to the "heart and pocket" of the capitalists. Only the bourgeois socialists, Marković maintained, expect anything from the state; Marx's "true socialism" rejected such an approach and placed its faith in the proletariat. The followers of Marx, Marković boasted erroneously, are now in the majority in the International. Marx's greatest service, he claimed, was in showing the proletariat that the solution of the "social problem" lay in the union of the proletariat of all countries into a single party; coming from a man who had previously neglected the proletariat, it was a strange and unexpected argument.

The remainder of Marković's reply was in rather poor taste, in view of the fact that he and Stanojević had earlier planned to found a republican-socialist newspaper,[10] and that both men were solidly opposed to the existing régime in Belgrade. Calling Stanojević "liar," "dishonest," and "ignorant," Marković revealed a petty and almost vicious side of his nature. He was unable to tolerate opposition of even the most constructive variety; his friends might well ask with Molière,

> "What dire fate attends
> Your enemies, if thus you treat
> Your friends?"

[9] *Pančevac*, no. 64, 1870; Marković's full reply is in nos. 60-65.
[10] Radenić, "Dragiša Stanojević," p. 152.

Understandably rather surprised by the intensity of Marković's assault, Stanojević nevertheless responded in conciliatory fashion. Admitting that perhaps he had not understood Marković clearly, he apologized for his error and said that he valued Marković's discussions of socialism "higher than anything I have read in the Serbian language." Stanojević generously ascribed Marković's abusive language to his poor health, and insisted that there could be no real quarrel between them: "I cannot bear antipathy toward a man who has the fate of the proletarian at heart."[11] Then in forced exile because of his alleged complicity in the assassination of Prince Michael, Stanojević later abandoned his Lassallean socialism and became one of Marković's most devoted followers.

MARKOVIĆ AND OMLADINA

Thus the brief polemic with Stanojević ended amicably, with Marković the ideological if not the personal victor. Such was not the case with the dispute which followed. Marković broke the truce with Vladimir Jovanović in mid-August of 1870, on the eve of the fifth *Omladina* congress, timing his action to secure support for the radical-socialist program he intended to present. Writing in *Pančevac,* the left republican Serbian newspaper published in the Hungarian Banat, Marković assailed the liberals and Jovanović personally for "prostituting" their liberalism in return for the privilege of sharing power with the regency. Endeavoring to maneuver Jovanović into a public debate prior to the *Omladina* congress, Marković challenged him to submit his "program" to a jury of twelve *Omladina* members for comparison with the program of the radical-socialists. Jovanović refused, preferring to lay his dispute with Marković before the full congress, where the liberals were certain of a majority.[12]

11 *Pančevac,* 1870, no. 69; Stanojević's full reply is in nos. 66-69.
12 *Ibid.,* nos. 68-69, August 23 and 27, 1870.

The *Omladina* congress met in Novi Sad late in August of 1870 with several hundred delegates in attendance. Marković and his followers immediately offered for consideration a lengthy resolution calling for:

1. The solution of the nationality problem in Austria-Hungary, and the Eastern Question, on the principle of "free humanity."
2. The organization of the state on the basis of a community of individuals with equal legal rights. The form of the state is the *opština* [commune] and the state is considered a collection of free *opštinas*.
3. A law establishing direct popular voting, with the executors of the laws being responsible before the regular courts.
4. The material independence of each member of the community. Without material independence there can be neither honesty, order, nor freedom in the nation.
5. The right to work and the right to an education for both women and men.
6. Special schools for workers in addition to general education; schools for agriculture, the trades, industry, and commerce.
7. The union of the people without consideration of religious differences. The aim of *Omladina* is to unite the Serbian people on the basis of science—on the basis of conscience, and in this regard religion stands outside the circle of *Omladina's* work.[13]

In opposition to the democratic, rather vaguely socialist program of the Marković group, the liberals presented their own program, the central feature of which was a call for an aggressive foreign policy. The only problem facing *Omladina*, they held, was that of the swift unification of the South Slavs (excluding the Bulgarians and Croatians!) under the aegis of Serbia. The liberals, convinced of the overriding importance of unification, refused to commit themselves to any domestic program. Even when pressed on the

[13] Radenić, "Dragiša Stanojević," pp. 180-181. Stanojević gave the radical-socialist program his full support.

problem of land reform Jovanović and his group declined to take a stand; thus by implication they allied themselves with the ruling circles in Belgrade, and the fundamental dichotomy between the two factions struggling for the leadership of the young generation was clearly revealed.[14]

In the end neither program was adopted. In the interests of unity the majority of the delegates voted to accept a contradictory and meaningless compromise calling for both a decentralized form of government and an expansionist foreign policy.

After the congress Marković denounced the "narrow patriotism" of the liberals and compared them to the Russian Slavophils, who "glorified everything that was 'of the people': foolishness and superstition, Orthodoxy and the Tsar."[15] Commenting on the differences between the radical-socialists and the liberals, Marković observed that the former party "wants the nation freed by popular initiative, goes to the people and works along with them. The other group [the liberals] wants to free the nation and command it—they demand the dynasty and ministerial posts. You [liberals] need a clique to form a cabinet of ministers; our place is in the workshop or the village hut—where therefore is the solidarity between us?"[16]

For his part Vladimir Jovanović warned that Serbia was haunted by the "red spectre of Panslavism." In an attempt to counter Marković's growing influence by linking him with Russian imperialism, Jovanović had earlier in the year produced a perceptive study of the Eastern Question which was in part a strong criticism of the radical-socialists. The Balkan Christians, Jovanović wrote, would perhaps prefer Muscovite tsarism to the false liberalism of Austria-

14 V. N. Kondrat'eva, "Novye arkhivnye materialy po istorii Ob'edinennoi serbskoi omladiny" ("New Archival Materials on the History of Omladina"), *UZIS*, xx, 1960, p. 308.

15 Božidar Kovačević, "Život Svetozara Markovića" ("The Life of Svetozar Marković"), *Književnost*, I, 1946, p. 121.

16 *Skerlić*, p. 42.

Hungary or the barbarism of the Turks, but they were determined not to abandon their right to liberty and national independence for Russian domination. Russian policy, he charged, was to encourage a bloody struggle between the Balkan Christians and the Turks which would leave both exhausted and unable to oppose a Russian seizure of Constantinople and the Straits: "This is what Russian diplomacy means by 'emancipation of the Eastern Christians.'" Serbia could not rely, Jovanović declared, on Russia, the International, or any other outside power to aid her in the struggle against the Turks. In order to remain free herself and liberate the Serbs still under foreign oppression, Serbia must follow the example of the first revolution and take up arms herself.[17]

Svetozar Marković won only two minor victories at the *Omladina* congress. One of his adherents, the priest Vasa Pelagić, was named to lead the *Omladina* organization in Bosnia, and Marković and Đura Ljočić were elected to the Belgrade council of the organization.

Upon their return to Serbia Marković and Ljočić attempted to infuse new vigor into the Serbian wing of *Omladina*. They laid plans to form committees of the organization throughout the principality, and conducted a spirited campaign to win new members who would, they hoped, support the radical-socialists.[18] The liberals on the Belgrade council blocked Marković and Ljočić at every turn. They refused to participate in organizational work, and early in the winter summoned the two radical-socialists and informed them that they had decided to support Vladimir Jovanović for the editorship of the *Omladina* newspaper. Marković threatened to withdraw from the Belgrade council if Jovanović were elected, and when the liberals reported to Ristić that he was plotting to overthrow

[17] Vladimir Jovanović, *Les Serbes*, pp. 280-283, 297-300.
[18] Simić, "Prilozi za građu," pp. 110-111.

the government, he made good his threat. In a letter to the parent organization announcing their resignation, Marković and Ljočić wrote that their original mistake "was in agreeing to work with people to whom we are not bound by mutual convictions." Henceforth, they warned, the radical-socialists would not hesitate to work outside *Omladina*, although they hoped eventually to change the policy of the organization.[19]

Despite his desire to capture control of *Omladina* Marković had never placed all his hopes in the organization. Realizing that he had to conduct his socialist campaign on the widest possible front, he had earlier become a regular contributor to the republican *Pančevac*, through which he had introduced the Serbs to the theories of Karl Marx. He also wrote a series of articles, beginning with a discussion of the Franco-Prussian War, for *Narodni Prijatelj* (*The People's Friend*), another republican newspaper which published for a few months in Zemun, a small town in Hungarian territory across the Sava from Belgrade.[20]

Also during the period 1870-71 Marković became an unofficial counselor of the *Velika Škola* student society *Pobratimstvo* (Brotherhood), where he continued the work begun by Liuben Karavelov in 1867-68. Marković guided the members of the society in the study of the works of the *Materialismusstreit* and the Russian radicals. Intoxicated with the doctrines expounded by Marković, the Belgrade students became zealous crusaders for social reform. They began to call for a new *Realschule* educational system to replace the prevailing classicism. A demand for the opening of an agricultural school was presented to the National Assembly, and one of Marković's more enthusi-

19 *Markovich: Izbrannye sochineniia*, pp. 814-816.

20 *Narodni prijatelj*, nos. 2 and 3, July 12 and 19, 1870. See also Andrija Radenić, "Nekoliko podataka o štampi u Zemunu sedamdesetih godina XIX veka" ("Some Information on the Zemun Press in the Seventies of the 19th Century"), *Istoriski glasnik*, 1955, no. 1.

astic admirers proposed that the government close the *Velika Škola* ("this breeding-ground of bureaucrats") and open in its stead a new independent and coeducational school based on "social-democratic principles."[21]

The Serbian government not unnaturally began to take an interest in the activities of *Pobratimstvo*, which had been founded in 1867 as a literary and debating society. When one of Herzen's more inflammatory political articles was read during one of the meetings of the society, the rector of the *Velika Škola* was ordered to censor its programs. The students protested vigorously, and the government considered closing the society. Late in February of 1871 a particularly vociferous and violent outburst followed the appointment of an incompetent, conservative government lawyer as professor of criminal law at the *Velika Škola*. The students refused to accept the appointment, and in the demonstrations that followed several gendarmes were injured. The government retaliated by expelling the second- and fourth-year law students and ordering the dissolution of *Pobratimstvo*.[22] An order was issued forbidding all discussion in the press of the expulsions and the closing of *Pobratimstvo*. Marković, however, was able to print a full account in *Pančevac*, which was published not in Serbia but in the Hungarian Banat.[23]

THE COOPERATIVE MOVEMENT

Especially noteworthy among Svetozar Marković's activities during the first year after his return to Serbia was his attempt to establish a cooperative movement. Cooperatives were necessary, he wrote, for three reasons.[24] First, the population increase and the consequent increase in demand in

21 *Skerlić*, p. 59.

22 *Ibid.*, p. 60.

23 "Zakonitost u Velikoj školi u Srbiji" ("Legality in the Serbian Velika Škola"), *Pančevac*, no. 20, March 7, 1871.

24 *C.d.*, III, pp. 6-8.

the market place had led to a steep rise in prices, which threatened to pauperize the vast majority of the population; cooperatives would give the lower classes the economic power necessary to force prices down. Secondly, cooperatives were necessary to break the strangle hold of capital on labor. Only those with capital were able to purchase raw materials and, following the bourgeois motto "Buy as cheap as possible, sell as dear as possible," the capitalists were increasing their wealth at a geometrical rate at the expense of the lower classes. Lastly, Marković wrote, cooperatives would provide the Serbian artisans with the means to meet the competition of foreign manufactured goods. He admitted that the latter had a qualitative as well as a quantitative advantage over the products of Serbian cottage industry, and he did not minimize the difficulties facing the artisans. We not only have no capital, he told the artisans, but we likewise do not have the workers required by modern large-scale industry. It will be the task of the cooperatives, he noted, to train workers in the methods of modern production; recognizing the advantages of large-scale production, he insisted that the artisan cooperatives would be but a transitional step toward the development of modern industry. If the cooperative movement were to succeed, Marković predicted, then "later, when the Balkan Peninsula is liberated from the rule of the savage horde [i.e., the Turks], when all the resources of this rich peninsula . . . are in the hands of its inhabitants, we would have skilled hands, qualified specialists and perfected organization, and we would not fear that foreigners would seize all our industry and our natural riches, as we fear today in 'free' Serbia."[25]

Svetozar Marković's concept of cooperativism was a highly individual one. It derived in part from the artels he had seen in Russia and those described in Chernyshevsky's

[25] *Ibid.*, p. 49.

What is to be Done? and in part from his observations of the Swiss cooperative movement. He was also schooled in the theories of Owen, Fourier, St.-Simon, Blanc, Lassalle, and Dühring, all of whom (especially Blanc) influenced his work in the cooperative field. And certainly Karl Marx's praise of the cooperative movement was not lost on Marković who was, however, apparently unaware of its political significance.

It was true that the average Serbian consumer was adversely affected by steadily rising prices after about the middle of the nineteenth century, and Marković had a certain practical foundation for his call for the establishment of consumer cooperatives. He erred, however, in claiming that many Serbian trades and handicrafts faced extinction due to the influx of foreign manufactured goods. Some relatively insignificant handicrafts were indeed disappearing: the makers of the Turkish fez lost the market for their product after the revolution, and the potters were driven out of business by the import of factory-made dishware from the Habsburg Empire. But on the whole the number of individuals employed in the trades and handicrafts grew steadily in the second half of the nineteenth century.[26] Socialist theory played a larger role in Marković's establishment of producer cooperatives than pressing economic necessity.

Early in 1870 Đura Ljočić, acting on Marković's instructions, participated in the founding of a cabinetmakers' cooperative in Belgrade, the first such organization in Serbia and one of the most successful. When Marković returned to Serbia later in the year he immediately began to organize producer associations in various other trades; by the spring of 1871 he had established cooperatives among the Belgrade cobblers, tailors, and farriers.[27] Simi-

[26] Vladimir Jovanović, *Statističan pregled*, pp. 219ff.

[27] *Jedinstvo*, Belgrade, no. 137, July 6, 1871, commented on the con-

lar organizations were established under his direction in several provincial towns; the most successful were in Šabac, Smederevo, and Požarevac.[28]

The cooperatives were organized along strictly democratic lines. Each was governed by an elected committee, the powers of which were clearly defined. The committee members ordinarily received no remuneration for their administrative services. Such a system worked well when the entire operation was under one roof, but Marković admitted that it would not be feasible for large-scale enterprises. Characteristically, however, he left unanswered the problem of cooperative organization under conditions of large-scale production.[29]

The most controversial of Marković's ventures into the cooperative field was the consumers' cooperative which he and Ljočić established in Belgrade in 1870. According to the recently discovered statutes of the organization, its goal was the "mutual supply of all consumer goods, at the most favorable price possible, offering members the possibility of a cash savings."[30] Members were required to buy a minimum of one share of stock at one Austrian ducat per share. The maximum number of shares which could be owned by an individual was not clearly specified, but no member could have more than one vote in the organization regardless of the number of shares he owned. All citizens were eligible to buy from the cooperative but only the members were to share in the profits.

During the first year of its operation the Belgrade consumers' cooperative was highly successful. Marković, a member of the governing committee, had originally envisioned a cautious and gradual expansion; so popular was

---

siderable number of cooperatives that had been established in Belgrade. See also *Zadružni Leksikon FNRJ*, II, Zagreb, 1957, cols. 1228-1229.

28 *Vidov Dan*, Belgrade, no. 93, May 1, 1871; Marković, *C.d.*, III, pp. 4-5.

29 *C.d.*, III, pp. 22-23.

30 *Zadružni Leksikon FNRJ*, II, col. 1229.

the enterprise, however, that within a few months two new stores were opened as branches of the original store on the Terazije, the main street in Belgrade.[31] At the end of its first year the consumers' cooperative declared a net profit amounting to the equivalent of about 3,300 French francs.[32]

Despite the apparent success of Marković's cooperatives the movement was short-lived. A wide variety of internal and external pressures combined to destroy the movement, and by the middle of the 1870's only the cabinetmakers' cooperative remained in existence in Belgrade. A few of the producer cooperatives survived in provincial towns until the end of the century, and through them the co-operative movement retained a faint measure of life.[33]

Internal conflicts destroyed most of the producer co-operatives. Marković held that many were ruined by their tendency to become capitalist organizations; after initial success the leaders of a cooperative would hire workers to operate their establishment and would themselves refuse to work. Others engaged in "cutthroat competition" with similar cooperatives in provincial towns and the Vojvodina and the Banat, where Marković had also established the movement. Still others collapsed, Marković noted, because of their failure to establish a just wage policy. In those where wages were paid on a piecework basis, the skilled workers earned far more than the less skilled; in those where all workers were paid the same regardless of production (the policy favored by Marković), there was a tendency toward laziness and shoddy workmanship.[34]

A final reason for the failure of the producer coopera-

31 *Radenik,* Belgrade, nos. 16 and 17, July 6 and 8, 1871; *Skerlić,* p. 64.

32 *Radenik,* no. 16, July 6, 1871, printed the year-end financial report of the consumers' cooperative.

33 *Obshchestvenno-politicheskie i kul'turnye sviazi narodov SSSR i Iugoslavii,* pp. 144-145.

34 *Zastava,* Novi Sad, nos. 18-19, 1872.

tives was the hostile attitude of the government. When one of the organizations established a school for its apprentices, in which they were to be instructed not only in the trade but also in elementary school subjects, the government ordered the school closed on the grounds that no private school could be established without the permission of the Ministry of Education.[35] Government opposition to the cooperatives was directed in no small measure at Marković personally. It was scarcely surprising that the ruling circles should regard with something less than enthusiasm any project undertaken by a man who had publicly proclaimed himself a communist,[36] a republican, an adherent of the First International, an opponent of the dynasty, and (as we shall see shortly) an ardent supporter of the Paris Commune.

The consumers' cooperative was the most bitterly condemned of all Marković's organizations. The Belgrade shopkeepers complained that it presented unfair competition, and even many of the peasants grumbled about the low prices paid by the cooperative for their produce. The government taxed the organization heavily; the grocers' guild[37] combined with some of the peasant suppliers in a vicious campaign against the cooperative, and by the spring of 1872 it was forced to declare bankruptcy.[38]

Marković refused to abandon his faith in the cooperatives despite the almost complete disintegration of the movement in Serbia. He insisted that the producer and consumer associations could still become the foundation

35 *Ibid.*, no. 19.

36 Marković declared himself a communist in a speech at the sixth *Omladina* congress in 1871; *Skerlić*, p. 55. At that time the second half of his "Realist Direction in Science and Life" had not yet been published.

37 The guild system was established by law in 1847. By the 1870's the guilds had lost much of their economic power though they still formed a significant political pressure group; cf. Karasëv, *Svetozar Markovich*, p. 76, and *Skerlić*, p. 65.

38 *Jedinstvo*, no. 89, April 26, 1872.

upon which to modernize the Serbian economy. Pondering his failure, Marković demanded government action to assist the cooperatives. In a speech in Novi Sad he called for the establishment of a Ministry of Labor in Vienna to promote the welfare of the associations in the Vojvodina and the Banat;[39] it was a suggestion unlikely to appeal to the Habsburg authorities. For Serbia he proposed a comprehensive legislative program; he urged the National Assembly to pass laws which would:

1. Establish the legal regulations for the forming of cooperatives, specify their professional and social functions, provide for the families of deceased members.
2. Liquidate the guilds.
3. Provide for the establishment of trade-grammar schools within the cooperatives.
4. Enable foreign artisans to obtain Serbian citizenship with a minimum of delay.
5. Establish district savings banks for the extension of low-cost credit to the cooperatives.[40]

No amount of legislation, Marković admitted, would of itself establish the cooperative movement on a sound foundation. The associations had to reform themselves from within. To thwart the tendency of the cooperatives to become capitalist enterprises, he proposed that the organizations renounce their exclusive character which had led them to limit the number of members, and above all that they refrain from hiring any more than a minimum of nonmember workers. The cooperatives must be open to all, he insisted, and the members must abandon the "boss psychology" which had in many cases led them to exploit their hired workers.[41] The cooperatives were formed, he noted, to prevent the development in Serbia of a "moneyed aristocracy." When stored-up human labor (capital) begins to rule contemporary labor, Marković warned, the

39 *Zastava*, no. 19, 1872. 40 *C.d.*, III, pp. 47-49. 41 *Ibid.*, pp. 18-21.

worker cannot be the master of his own labor; a class of proletarians appears, and there inevitably follows a social revolution. The cooperatives, he observed with some irony, were intended to forestall rather than foster such a situation.[42]

Concerning the problem of wages, Marković maintained that the cooperatives which had deviated from his policy of equal remuneration for all workers had struck at the very principles of cooperativism. There must of course be checks against laziness and poor workmanship (he proposed fines), but the basic principle of wage equality must be maintained, regardless of differences in skill: "*If each member of the association really works according to his conscience and with all his might for the benefit of the association, and if he fulfills the work assigned to him, then he is completely fulfilling the conditions demanded of a member of the association. He must be compensated the same as every other member of the association.* If one member is more capable than another and can with *equal* diligence bring the association more benefit, then his reward is already present in the fact that he is rewarded by nature itself."[43]

There were any number of objections to such a plan, and Marković admitted that the ignoble character of some of the cooperative members presented grave problems.[44] But the moral foundation of the associations, he maintained, was "brotherly love and solidarity among the members,"[45] and if the principle was honored chiefly in the breach it was merely due to a lack of education. Through education, he insisted, men would gain an understanding of their "true interests," which lay in the interests of society; never was he closer to the noble, sentimental idealism of Robert Owen, whom, it will be remembered, he had

[42] *Ibid.*, pp. 36-37.

[43] *Zastava*, no. 19, 1872.

[44] *C.d.*, III, p. 12.

[45] *Ibid.*, p. 15.

praised (along with Jan Hus and Christ) as one of the three "most moral" men of all time.[46]

In addition to the hostility of the government and the merchants Marković blamed internal dissension and the lack of capable, dedicated organizers for the failure of the cooperatives.[47] He was only partially correct. His biographer has pointed out that the cooperative movement was exclusively (the hired workers' not being members of the cooperatives) one of the artisan-small proprietor class, of the petty *bourgeoisie*.[48] These individuals joined Marković's cooperatives not out of "brotherly love" but rather because of a simple, straightforward desire for personal profit. When it seemed that the establishment of cooperatives might lead to lower costs and increased profits, they supported the movement. When their hopes were not fulfilled, or when insoluble disputes arose over the division of income, the dissatisfied members left the organizations. Marković was never able to reconcile himself to the fact that the highest principle subscribed to by most members of his cooperatives was greed.[49]

Strangely enough for a disciple of Chernyshevsky, Marković largely ignored the peasants in his cooperative movement. He made no attempt to organize the associations among the peasantry, but it is doubtful that he would have enjoyed a great deal of success had he done so. Agricultural cooperation has traditionally enjoyed its greatest successes among a literate peasantry having a highly developed individual agriculture, the expansion of which is limited by both lack of investment capital and geography. The Serbian peasants certainly lacked investment capital, but they were illiterate and uninformed, and their agriculture remained relatively backward despite some improvement in the nineteenth century. And the weakness of the

[46] See above, p. 114.
[47] *Skerlić*, p. 65.
[48] *Ibid.*, pp. 62-63.
[49] Cf. *Radenik*, no. 17, July 8, 1871.

zadruga "spirit" of cooperation, in which Marković placed so much faith, was reflected in the ever-increasing rate of disintegration among the *zadrugas*.

SOCIALIST JOURNALISM

Marković's activities in the first two years after his return to Serbia were largely directed toward the urban population and the intelligentsia, and it was in order to win the support of these groups that he founded the first socialist newspaper in the Balkans. The project for a socialist newspaper was conceived by Marković and his colleagues during their debates with Vladimir Jovanović in Zürich.[50] The young radical-socialists had complained that freedom of the press did not exist in Serbia; they pointed out that the reaction which followed Prince Michael's assassination had led to the suppression of liberal newspapers, and one of their number later wrote that after the assassination "the political field was manured by *Jedinstvo* and *Vidov Dan*, from whom it was not possible to hear a sincere and wise word."[51]

Jedinstvo (*Unity*) was a triweekly Belgrade newspaper edited by Ristić's protégé Vukašin Petrović, who later occupied high ministerial posts in several governments between 1875 and 1900. A well-written and generally well-informed newspaper, *Jedinstvo* pursued a militantly nationalist political line; it became genuinely "liberal" only in 1872 when it changed its editorial policy in the attempt to win the followers of Svetozar Marković to the liberal party.

Vidov Dan (*St. Vitus' Day*), a right-wing conservative

50 Jovanović, *Avtobiografija*, p. 25.

51 *Rad*, Belgrade, no. 9, March 1, 1875. *Rad* claimed that the newspapers *Srbija* and *Mlada Srbadija* were suppressed after the assassination. In reality *Srbija* continued to publish until 1870, and *Mlada Srbadija*, the *Omladina* journal published in Novi Sad, was founded only in 1870 and continued to publish until 1872.

triweekly, may have been subsidized by Budapest.[52] Under the editorship of Miloš Popović, who before founding *Vidov Dan* had edited the official journal of the Serbian government, the newspaper pursued a policy that was frequently more reactionary than conservative (*Vidov Dan* had led the press campaign against the liberals after the assassination of Michael). Although able to provide its readers with timely news from its correspondents in several European capitals, *Vidov Dan* was on the whole less reliable than *Jedinstvo* because of its extremely tendentious editorial policy.

There were several other newspapers available to the Belgrade and Serbian public during the early 1870's, although the average life of the journals was short (*Vidov Dan*'s fifteen years was unusually long) and the journalistic scene constantly shifting. The journal of the Belgrade business community, *Trgovački Glasnik* (*The Commercial Herald*), carried political news only occasionally (it published the Marković-Ljočić letter of resignation from the Belgrade council of *Omladina*). In 1870 the government forced the suspension of two opposition liberal newspapers, *Srbija* (*Serbia*) and *Govornica* (*The Tribune*), and the principality was temporarily without a domestic opposition newspaper.[53]

There was no lack of journalistic opposition to the Serbian government, however, for newspapers in Serbo-Croatian printed outside the principality regularly reached Belgrade, where they had a small but enthusiastic audience. *Zastava*, Svetozar Miletić's outstanding Novi Sad journal, was highly respected among the Serbian intelligentsia as an articulate champion of liberalism and democracy. The radical republican *Pančevac*, published in Pančevo by Jo-

[52] Andrija Radenić, "Vojvođanska štampa prema Namesništvu, 1868-1872" ("The Attitude of the Vojvodina Press toward the Regency, 1868-1872"), *Istoriski časopis*, VI, 1956, p. 72.

[53] *Jedinstvo*, no. 89, April 26, 1872.

van Pavlović, carried Marković's discussions of Marxism and printed the first Serbo-Croatian translation of the *Communist Manifesto*. *Narodni Prijatelj*, as we have seen earlier, was a republican newspaper published in Zemun whose editorial policy was similar to that of *Pančevac*. All three newspapers *Zastava*, *Pančevac* and *Narodni Prijatelj* —were tolerated by the Hungarian authorities in the Vojvodina and the Banat so long as their opposition was directed toward Belgrade rather than Budapest.

Another newspaper regularly read in Serbia was *Svoboda* (*Freedom*), which the Bulgarian revolutionaries Liuben Karavelov and Vasil Levsky published in Bucharest. Through his activities in *Omladina* and *Pobratimstvo* Karavelov had a wide following among the young Serbian intellectuals, who valued his journal highly. *Svoboda* was highly critical of the Serbian government, accusing it of compromising with the Turks at the expense of South Slav liberation and unity.[54] All of the newspapers which Svetozar Marković published maintained close ties with Bulgarian revolutionaries in Rumania.

The Serbian press laws were subject to a variety of interpretations, most of them unfavorable to journalists unwilling to support the government and the dynasty. While professing to uphold the freedom of the press, the laws provided fines and imprisonment for "irresponsible" criticism of the dynasty or government. The police were empowered to "maintain surveillance" over potentially hostile newspapers; all Belgrade journals had to be printed at the government printing press (not entirely a disadvantage, since the costs were relatively low), and a copy of each issue had to be presented for police inspection at least one hour before planned distribution.[55]

[54] *Ibid.*, no. 44, February 27, 1871; see also Konstantinov, *Vođi bugarskog narodnog pokreta*, pp. 139-143.

[55] *Vlada Milana*, I, pp. 69-70.

In April of 1871, a month and a half before he began to publish his newspaper, Marković announced its program in a brochure which Jovan Pavlović printed at the *Pančevac* printing press in Pančevo.[56] The program was remarkable chiefly for its ambiguity. Marković censured the National Assembly for its subservience to the government, and proposed to remedy the weaknesses of the legislative process with a plan calling for pure democracy. Concerning the economic philosophy of his forthcoming journal Marković wrote that the problem in Serbia was not the distribution but rather the creation of wealth: "Our goal must be to create *educated workers, workers with capital, to create collective capital and collective production.*" Toward this end the program he outlined promised to work for the development of the "*free zadruga,* an association for production, exchange, credit." Marković admitted that the old family *zadruga,* which had a multitude of shortcomings and which was already fast disappearing, was not the final solution to the economic problems of Serbia. It was on the contrary even in a modernized form to be only a model, a "first step," and simultaneously a check to those "who would appropriate the fruits of another's labor."

In the field of foreign affairs Marković's program was perhaps equally vague but far more portentous in some of its implications. Marković again criticized the liberals and repeated his unwavering hostility to their "Great Serbia." But it was clear that some sort of Serbian union would eventually come; what form should it take? Marković be-

[56] *Jedinstvo* (no. 89, April 26, 1872) accused Marković of not having the courage to publish his program in Belgrade; in view of the editorial policy of *Radenik* the charge was clearly unfounded. Marković maintained close ties with *Pančevac* and may have made the translation of the *Communist Manifesto* which the journal published in nos. 28-42, April-May 1871; cf. M. Panić-Surep, "Manifest Komunističke partije iz 1871 godine" ("The Communist Party Manifesto in 1871"), *Bibliotekar,* 1948-49, 1, pp. 19-21.

gan by insisting that Serbia had to reform her internal institutions before she could be considered fit to participate in, let alone lead, the movement for Serbian liberation: "We want *unity* through *freedom*, and not the other way around." Forced to face the problem of leadership, Marković equivocated but left himself open to the charge of being excessively fond of Montenegro: "The Serbian people in free Montenegro maintain their freedom by their own strength. The Serbian people in Serbia were liberated when they rose 'with axes and pitchforks' against *dahi* outrages. Since that time, when the Serbs in Serbia retired [the principle of] self-government, and let the magnates worry about our liberation, forty years have passed and our liberation creeps along at a snail's pace. . . . Those to whom the present situation guarantees power consider the question of national liberation and union a question of 'the political situation' and not of the life and death of the nation."[57]

Jedinstvo later called Marković a "traitor" because he would have not "Great Serbia" but "Great Montenegro."[58] It is extremely doubtful that Marković ever favored such a policy, but his praise of Montenegro reinforced Vladimir Jovanović's attempt to link him with Russian imperialism. The Russian government had been opposed to the election of Milan Obrenović to succeed his cousin Michael, and had attempted to maneuver the election of Prince Nikola of Montenegro. Failing in its efforts, St. Petersburg then tried to engineer a regency headed by Jovan Marinović and Ilija Garašanin who would, it was believed, be more tractable than Ristić and Blaznavac.[59] The clumsy Russian attempts to intervene in Serbian politics created an un-

[57] Marković's program is reproduced by Slobodan Komadinić in his article "Prvi socijalistički program" ("The First Socialist Program"), *Savremenik*, Belgrade, May 1955, pp. 588-597.

[58] *Jedinstvo*, no. 109, May 20, 1872.

[59] *Vlada Milana*, I, pp. 110-111.

favorable impression in the principality, and the charge that Marković was in the service not only of Prince Nikola but also of Tsar Alexander II was to play a major role in efforts of the Serbian government to suppress the radical-socialist movement.

Despite the difficulties confronting him, Marković was able to launch the first socialist newspaper in the Balkans on June 1, 1871. Vladimir Jovanović, his hostility toward the socialists notwithstanding, had promised to use his influence to help secure permission for the venture,[60] and it was probably he who induced the government to grant its consent. Đura Ljočić was chosen by Marković to serve as editor and publisher of the newspaper; in addition to being Marković's closest collaborator in this period, Ljočić was also a man of some means who was able to provide considerable financial support to the radical-socialist movement.

Marković chose the name *Radenik* (*The Worker*)[61] for his newspaper. Like his defense of Marx's concept of the proletariat in the polemic with Dragiša Stanojević, it was an abrupt and seemingly discordant departure. Serbia had no industrial proletariat, and Marković, convinced that the country did not have to pass through a capitalist stage, was far from wanting to create one. Why, then, should he name his newspaper *The Worker*? Several considerations influenced him; not the least of these was his unfortunate tendency to preach loudest the theories freshest in his mind. More importantly, however, Marković saw himself part of a European revolutionary movement, whose leaders were, in his view, Chernyshevsky in the Slav lands and Marx in the West. And whereas the revolution was still

[60] Jovanović, *Avtobiografija*, p. 25.

[61] In 1872 the spelling was changed to *Radnik*, but I have retained the original throughout. Also on the staff of the journal at its founding were: Nikola Pašić, Jevrem Marković, Stevan Popović-Beli, Pavle Mijajlović, Dimitrije Cenić, Jovan Alavantić, Anastasije Vučković, and Anta Aleksić.

decades away in Russia, there were real accomplishments in the West: the International itself, labor agitation, reform (which Marković tended to confuse with revolution) in Britain, and, finally, the Paris Commune. This latter tragic episode in French history had an enormous influence upon Marković and was the largest single factor in his decision to pursue a Marxist direction in the early months of *Radenik.*

Simultaneously with his brochure outlining the *Radenik* program Marković had published an article on the Paris Commune,[62] and his defense of the Commune was a recurrent theme in the newspaper itself in the summer of 1871. The militancy of Marković's articles on the French uprising contrasted sharply with the ambiguous program he had outlined for his journal. The Commune might be destroyed, he wrote, but its principles would live on until their eventual triumph.[63]

Late in June of 1871 Marković received a copy of "The Civil War in France," a collection of Marx's speeches which Engels had published, and immediately began to serialize the work in *Radenik.*[64] Marx's correspondence with the London *Daily News* dealing with the International was also published.[65] Marković regularly received the journal of Marx's Leipzig followers, *Volksstaat,* and frequently quoted from it in the columns of *Radenik.* Marx's works (especially *Das Kapital* and the *Communist Manifesto*) were frequently cited in the Serbian socialist journal, which in March of 1872 began to serialize Chapter Ten ("The Working Day") of *Das Kapital.*[66]

62 Cf. Komadinić, "Prvi socijalistički program."

63 See especially Marković's articles "Pogibija Pariske komune" ("The Fall of the Paris Commune"), *Radenik,* no. 1, June 1, 1871, and "Beli Teror" ("The White Terror"), *ibid.,* nos. 17-21, July 8-17, 1871.

64 *Ibid.,* nos. 20-25, July 15-29, 1871, nos. 35-39. August 24-September 2, 1871.

65 *Ibid.,* no. 15, July 3, 1871.

66 *Ibid.,* nos. 26-35, March 7-31, 1872.

Marković's own articles on the Paris Commune in the summer of 1871 followed Marx's analysis closely and drew their factual data almost exclusively from "The Civil War in France." *Vidov Dan* and *Jedinstvo*, having begun a vigorous campaign against the Commune before the appearance of *Radenik*, now intensified their condemnation of the socialist uprising. Following the lead of the majority of the European press, the two newspapers sought to link the Commune with the International.[67] *Vidov Dan* declined to enter into a polemic with *Radenik*, refusing even to acknowledge the existence of such a newspaper.[68] It continued, however, to denounce the outrages of the "Paris madmen" and censured those in Serbia who supported them.

Jedinstvo willingly accepted the challenge presented by Marković and devoted a series of penetrating and reasonably objective articles to the Commune and the International. The newspaper of the government liberals refused to moderate its condemnation of the Commune, but made the rather surprising concession that the principles of the International contained some merit: "It must be acknowledged that the principles of this organization are reasonable and vigorous."[69] But *Jedinstvo* quickly qualified its statement: while the economic and political theories of the International might contain some abstract merit, its social principles were barbaric and inadmissible. The liberal newspaper joined with *Vidov Dan* in excoriating the International and socialists in general for proposing "incest, the abolition of marriage, and the eradication of religion."[70]

Marković, delighted with the opportunity given him by

67 *Vidov Dan* and *Jedinstvo* for May, June, July 1871.

68 In its only reference to *Radenik*, *Vidov Dan* announced that journal's demise in its issue of May 23, 1872.

69 *Jedinstvo*, no. 128, June 23, 1871.

70 *Ibid.*, nos. 126-138, June 20-July 7, 1871; see also *Vidov Dan* for the same period, and *Radenik*, no. 17, July 8, 1871.

the respectable Belgrade press, revealed himself a skilled polemicist. Employing a formidable mixture of fact, oversimplification, half-truth, sarcasm, ridicule, and occasionally profanity, he produced in the first issues of *Radenik* a forceful attack on the Serbian liberals and conservatives which was simultaneously a spirited profession of faith in communism. The success of his campaign was indicated by the numerous cries it produced for Serbia to abandon freedom of the press.[71]

He began by ridiculing "the entire 'civilized' world, from *The Times* to the Serbian press," for its condemnation of the Commune. That "civilized world," he wrote, was composed of "rich Englishmen, Brussels ministers and their deputies (the representatives of the capitalists), the European rulers and their marshals, generals, and other magnates, Viennese kikes and Belgrade journalists,"[72] none of whom had any sympathy for the working class. Responding to the criticism of the violence of the Commune, Marković discussed the problem of terror. Terror could, he admitted, be either "red" or "white," i.e., the tool of the lower as well as the upper classes. But he maintained that the "white terror" was the greater enemy of mankind, and he identified it with capitalism, monarchism, and reaction. The "white terror" had existed in Serbia since the assassination of Prince Michael, he maintained, and the Belgrade press acted as its lackey. It was in order to intensify the terror, he claimed, that *Vidov Dan* was spreading the rumor that members of the International had established operations on the lower Danube and were taking the names of well-to-do citizens to give to the Gen-

71 *Radenik*, no. 17, July 8, 1871; *DANRS*, Narodna Skupština, 1871, k2, Interpelacija no. 26.

72 *Radenik*, no. 1, June 1, 1871; on Marković's epithet for Jews see above, p. 121. In his discussion of the problem of terror Marković obviously referred to Marx's exhortation to the Hungarian revolutionaries of 1848 to meet the "white terror" with the "red terror."

eral Council (of the International) for reference at the outbreak of the revolution.[73]

Marković switched abruptly from humor to bitter denunciation in accusing *Vidov Dan* of "combining Jesuit cunning[74] with Asiatic cruelty" in its attempt to discredit the International and the Commune. He vowed that *Radenik* would fight all such "charlatans and terrorists" and would prove that socialists "are not cannibals." Taunting his adversaries for their ignorance, Marković noted that the upper classes had always "screamed like lunatics" when they heard the words "Commune" and "communism," yet they were unaware that there was a vast difference between the two. The Commune "was merely a political entity," while communism "is an economic system whereby people unite their labor and property, in order that the products of their labor be the property not of any individual but of the community." And in the realm of morality "*the Christian ethic itself, as it is set forth in the gospel, is fundamentally communist.*"[75] He scoffed at the "lurid tales" spread by the opponents of the Commune and the International, and, quoting from the first Serbo-Croatian edition of the *Communist Manifesto,* insisted that communist family ties would be based upon love and not, "as in bourgeois society, upon financial considerations."[76]

The reception given *Radenik* was remarkable. In a country with a five per cent literacy rate it could scarcely have been foreseen that a socialist journal would have

[73] *Ibid.,* no. 17, July 8, 1871.

[74] Marković was opposed to all religions, but he singled out the Roman Catholic Church for special abuse, probably because of its condemnation of the Commune. Early in 1872 (*Radenik,* no. 2, January 8) he wrote that one of the major events of the previous year was the "obvious decline" of Roman Catholicism, which had become "a religion *without moral principles and without spiritual* organization."

[75] *Radenik,* nos. 18-19, July 10 and 13, 1871.

[76] *Ibid.,* no. 21, July 17, 1871.

more than a very few readers, yet within one week after it began publication *Radenik* announced that it would not be able to fill any more requests for copies of the first issue. According to a socialist source the newspaper soon had a circulation of 1,500, an unprecedented figure in a city where the average journal printed no more than six to eight hundred copies of each issue.[77] *Radenik* was read throughout Serbia. It regularly printed notices asking subscribers in Smederevo, Šabac, Požarevac, Kragujevac, Negotin, Užice, and other provincial towns to make their payments to the local *Radenik* agent. "Correspondents" from various parts of Serbia sent in items of local interest, and their reports were invariably challenged in *Jedinstvo* by that newspaper's "correspondents" in the same towns.

With success came a certain amount of the bourgeois respectability that Marković professed to loathe. The Belgrade citizenry began to use *Radenik*'s columns for personal notices of name days, deaths, quarrels (chiefly disinheritances), and services; even bureaucrats occasionally used the socialist journal, rather than one of its more officially acceptable competitors, for such purposes.[78] *Vidov Dan* and *Jedinstvo* carried some of the advertising for the cooperatives, but by far the greater amount was published in Marković's newspaper. By the beginning of 1872 *Radenik*'s four-page folio format regularly printed one or two large advertisements, often with illustrations, for private business firms. Small notices from tradesmen appeared in every issue, and on occasion a Viennese insurance firm purchased considerable advertising space.

RADENIK AND ITS FOLLOWING

A wide variety of personality and opinion was reflected in the audience which *Radenik* quickly attracted. In the

[77] *Rad*, no. 9, March 1, 1875, p. 133.
[78] Cf., for example, *Radenik*, no. 85, December 23, 1871.

vanguard was the alienated intelligentsia—those intellectuals who were outside society, could not be used by society, and who therefore wanted to reform it. In this *omnium gatherum* were *Velika Škola* students who had first come into contact with the radical-socialist movement through *Pobratimstvo* and *Omladina*; writers who were in rebellion against the dominant romantic vein in Serbian literature; and students who had returned from abroad unable to adjust to the humdrum life of backward Serbia. In addition to the intelligentsia, which we shall discuss in a moment, there were other groups that welcomed the appearance of *Radenik*. Nikola Pašić noted in 1882 that Marković's journal had received considerable support from the opposition liberals.[79] Dissatisfied with their party's compromise with the regency, the opposition liberals looked to Svetozar Miletić and *Zastava* for leadership, but Marković and *Radenik* provided a more immediate tribune of legal opposition to the government. The socialist movement was moreover a vehicle which could be abandoned at any moment; few of the dissident liberals joined the socialists, though they delighted in their attacks on the government. A small but significant number of junior army officers supported *Radenik* and its program. Some, like Jevrem Marković and Sava Grujić, were genuine adherents of the socialist movement; others, like Đorđe Vlajković, who had received a Habsburg commission in 1847 and who later led the Serbian volunteers in the uprising in Bosnia-Hercegovina in 1875, lent their support as a form of protest against the cautious foreign policy of the Serbian government. Although *Radenik* enjoyed the support of some members of the cooperatives, the majority of such individuals cared little for ideology and

[79] Cf. Pašić's comments in *Rad prve glavne Skupštine Narodne Radikalne Stranke* (*The Work of the First General Assembly of the Popular Radical Party*), Belgrade, 1882, pp. 17-19.

were indifferent to the journal. In the Vojvodina, however, where the cooperative movement had a somewhat greater intellectual content, the members long remained a major source of strength for the radical-socialist movement.

The radical-socialists drew further support from two unusual sources, the young conservatives and a group of young Orthodox priests. The former were led by Aćim Čumić, who later (1874-75) served brief terms as foreign minister and prime minister in conservative governments; he also became a bitter enemy of Svetozar Marković and was held responsible by the socialists for his death.[80] Like the socialists, the young conservatives were opposed to the "Great Serbia" foreign policy of the liberals, and they also shared with the socialists an aversion to the "administrative despotism" created by the liberals. In August of 1871 Čumić joined with several of the socialists (Svetozar Marković not among them) and a few opposition liberals in producing a political program advocating a government so decentralized as to be virtually powerless at the national level.[81]

One of the signatories of the 1871 program was Vasa Pelagić, a young Bosnian priest. Pelagić had studied in Russia under the auspices of the Moscow Slavic Committee, and had come under the influence of Chernyshevsky and Pisarev. Upon his return to Serbia he had been instrumental in the founding of *Omladina* and in 1870 was elected chief of the organization's Bosnian wing. He be-

[80] *Rad*, no. 9, March 1, 1875, p. 134.

[81] The original program is in *DANRS*, PO 25/209, 1871. Slobodan Jovanović, who apparently had not seen the program, wrote that no conservative had signed it (*Vlada Milana*, I, p. 129). Two authors, apparently mistaking Jevrem Marković's signature, have written that Svetozar Marković signed the program (Simić, "Prilozi za građu," p. 579, and Slobodan Komadinić, "Prvi socijalistički program"). Both the latter writers were attacked for their slipshod scholarship by Radoslav Perović in his "Povodom jednog izdanja prvog srpskog socijalističkog programa" ("On the Occasion of an Edition of the First Serbian Socialist Program"), published in brochure form in Belgrade, 1955.

came one of Marković's most capable lieutenants, and brought with him into the radical-socialist movement several young seminary students and priests.[82]

Of the various groups which were attracted to *Radenik* and the radical-socialist movement, none was more significant than that band of *avant-garde* literati, led by Đura Jakšić and Milovan Glišić, which in the 1870's created a new realist current in Serbian literature. Svetozar Marković had preached the cause of literary realism since the middle year of his stay in St. Petersburg, and upon his return to Serbia he became the guiding spirit of a literary circle which included many of the finest Serbian writers of the latter half of the century.[83] The outstanding regular member of the group was Đura Jakšić (1832-78).[84] Jakšić had come of age during the revolutions of 1848-49, and was a devotee of the Hungarian poet and patriot Sandor Petöfi. Although his writing prior to the 1870's had been wholly in the romantic vein, Jakšić, under the influence of Svetozar Marković, developed a realist approach which colored but did not obscure his essential romanticism; Jovan Skerlić has aptly described him as the Heine of the Serbian youth.[85] Jakšić's prestige was of enormous value to Marković and his cause, and it was chiefly through him that many of the young writers became affiliated with the radical-socialist movement.

Another important figure in the literary circle which gathered around Marković was the dramatist Milovan Glišić (1847-1908).[86] Glišić was one of the most gifted real-

[82] Cf. Nikitin, *Slavianskie komitety*, pp. 101-102; Nikitin refers to Risto Besarović, *Vaso Pelagić*, Belgrade, 1953, which I have not consulted.

[83] See above, p. 72.

[84] Skerlić, *Istorija nove srpske književnosti*, pp. 295-304; Momčilo Miletić, "Svetozar Marković i Đura Jakšić."

[85] Skerlić, *Istorija nove srpske književnosti*, p. 301.

[86] *Ibid.*, pp. 356-361; Miroslav Đorđević, "Glišićev realizam i društvena stvarnost Srbije njegovog doba" ("Glišić's Realism and the Social Reality of the Serbia of his Day"), *Književnost*, IV, no. 2, 1949, pp. 68-90.

ist writers guided into intellectual maturity by Svetozar Marković. A talented translator as well as writer, Glišić rendered superb Serbo-Croatian translations of Russian and French classics.

The greatest Serbian writer of the period was Jovan Jovanović-Zmaj (1833-1904).[87] Though himself a democrat and liberal of the Svetozar Miletić school, Zmaj held Marković and his radical-socialist movement in high regard. Deeply moved by Marković's emotional defense of the Paris Commune in *Radenik*, Zmaj produced a splendidly romantic, sentimental work ("At the Grave of the Slain Communists") in honor of the socialist uprising. Marković defended Zmaj against those of the radical-socialists who criticized his liberalism and romanticism; such noble and honest men, Marković wrote, "are always champions of truth and justice, whether with pen or sword in hand."[88]

The talent of several of the young literati who became adherents of the radical-socialist movement exceeded their fame. Danilo Medić, a brilliant, neurotic poet, was after Zmaj and Jakšić perhaps the outstanding Serbian writer of the period. Sima Popović, poet and political figure, edited the republican *Narodni Prijatelj* before entering the service of Prince Nikola of Montenegro. Among the later realist writers who carried on the tradition inspired by Svetozar Marković were Janko Veselinović, novelist and short-story writer; Laza Lazarević, military doctor and writer who rendered one of the Serbo-Croatian translations of Chernyshevsky's *What is to be Done?*; Vladimir M. Jovanović (no relation to the liberal leader), writer of socialist poetry; and Jaša Tomić, a prolific writer and historian who served for a time as the Serbian correspondent for the Leipzig *Volksstaat*.

[87] Skerlić, *Istorija*, pp. 284-295. From 1864 until 1871 Jovanović edited a Serbo-Croatian journal, *Zmaj* (*The Dragon*) in Budapest; hence the hyphenated nickname by which he is known.

[88] Quoted in *Skerlić*, p. 194.

The "angry young men" among the Serbian writers of the 1870's were attracted to *Radenik* primarily because it was the one Serbian journal which attempted to express their opposition to the "establishment," i.e., the government, class structure (these writers became champions of the peasant), literature, religion, and mores. Though they occasionally differed with *Radenik* on specific issues (few of them, for example, had much admiration for Marković's denial of aesthetics), the writers valued the socialist journal as an effective voice of protest. Most of them accepted Marković's precept that the writer must inspire the people, must "live life as the people live it, express the feelings and aspirations of the people."[89]

A partial explanation of *Radenik*'s immediate popularity among the writers and the alienated intelligentsia at large was its commencement coincidentally with the suppression of Liuben Karavelov's *Svoboda*. Heeding the warning from Constantinople that *Svoboda*'s "extreme views" were "dangerous to the existing situation in the Empire," the Rumanian government was obliged in the summer of 1871 to order the journal to cease publication.[90] *Radenik* maintained close contact with Karavelov and his associates. During the suspension of *Svoboda* Marković's journal carried a proclamation written by Karavelov and issued by the Bulgarian Revolutionary Central Committee;[91] the proclamation embodied a call to the Bulgarian people for an uprising against the Turks.[92] When Karavelov resumed publication of *Svoboda* in December of 1871, *Radenik* announced that it would act as the journal's subscription

89 Quoted in Jovan Popović, "Svetozareva buktinja nad našom knjizevnošću," p. 21.

90 *Radenik*, no. 6, June 12, 1871.

91 On the committee see Aleksand'r Burmov, *B'lgarski revoliutsionen tsentralen komitet (1868-1877)* (*The Bulgarian Revolutionary Central Committee [1868-1877]*), 2nd edition, Sofia, 1950. See also Konstantinov, *Vođi, passim.*

92 *Radenik*, no. 26, July 31, 1871.

agent in Serbia.[93] Karavelov managed to continue publication at irregular intervals throughout 1872; at the end of that year, however, *Svoboda* quietly expired.

VRAGOLAN

The examples of *Svoboda* and *Radenik* emboldened the young Serbian literati to found their own journal. *Radenik* did not publish Serbian literature, and a forum was needed for those writers who felt restricted by the journals which, as Marković said, by and large ignored everything that had happened since the fourteenth century.[94] Such a vehicle was created in the late summer of 1871 when Mihailo Niketić, a close friend of Marković, founded *Vragolan* (*Little Imp*). As some of *Radenik*'s sharpest attacks on the Serbian government were superficially concealed in its articles on the Paris Commune, so *Vragolan*, with its brilliant satires on bygone ages and fictitious characters, criticized what one Marxist writer has unfairly called the "still-born scholastic aesthetics"[95] of the Serbian literature of the period. Đura Jakšić and Milovan Glišić were the chief contributors to the journal, and both Marković and Karavelov occasionally published short articles.[96]

The weekly issues of *Vragolan* created a sensation among the Belgrade reading public, and the journal quickly became as popular as *Radenik*. Success led its writers to disregard caution and discretion, and their criticism not only of the older romantic writers but also of individuals in the government (especially Ristić) became increasingly virulent. The Serbian government, already un-

93 *Ibid.*, nos. 79-80, December 9 and 11, 1871.

94 *C.d.*, VIII, pp. 55-71.

95 Jovan Popović, "Svetozareva buktinja," p. 18.

96 Some investigators (among them Jovan Skerlić) have held that Karavelov wrote the articles in *Vragolan* signed "Hadži Voštac"; in 1908, however, Mihailo Niketić recalled that Glišić and Jakšić had used that pseudonym. See Todor Marković, "Ljuben Karavelov u srpskoj književnosti," p. 443.

der attack from *Radenik* but unable to prosecute because the journal stayed just within the bounds of legality, was in no mood to tolerate a new opposition journal, particularly not one so well written as *Vragolan*. Incensed by a series of satires in November and December, the government suppressed *Vragolan* and arrested Niketić (the author of the satires was not known, but under the law the editor was responsible for all that appeared in the journal).[97]

The Serbian press was forbidden to publish the news of the suppression of *Vragolan* and the arrest of Niketić. *Radenik*, however, announced in February of 1872 that the journal had ceased publication "because the subscribers failed to pay on time." And, obeying the letter of the law, *Radenik* did not inform its readers that Niketić had been arrested: it merely noted that he had been released after spending two months in jail.[98]

Despite the efforts of Marković, Niketić, and the literati, it proved impossible to revive *Vragolan*. Several journals of its type followed in the 1870's, but none was able to attain the prominence of Niketić's short-lived journal.[99]

RADENIK AND SERBIAN OFFICIALDOM

Throughout the latter half of 1871 *Radenik* itself lived a precarious existence. Despite its attempts to be merely reformist at home while praising revolution abroad, *Radenik* and its staff were under constant threat of government intervention. The journal continued on its course, however, and became if anything more militantly socialist. It was therefore to be expected that *Radenik* would infuriate and appall official, respectable Belgrade as much as it delighted the rebellious young intellectuals. The Rus-

[97] In a play on the pseudonym "Hadži Voštac" (see the preceding footnote) *Jedinstvo* (no. 199, September 19, 1872) noted that *Vragolan* had ceased to "wax" (*voštiti*).

[98] *Radenik*, nos. 13, 15, February 4 and 9, 1872.

[99] Cf. Skerlić, *Istorija nove srpske književnosti*, p. 339.

sian consul, Shishkin, summarized not only his own reaction but also that of the Serbian conservatives and government liberals in a dispatch to his government a few weeks after the appearance of the socialist journal: "At the end of May of this year there appeared in Belgrade the newspaper *Radenik,* which is not satisfied with justifying all the violence of the Commune but which also tries to spread the social-democratic theories of the International Association of Workers in the Serbian nation. The editor-publisher of this newspaper, Dzhuro L'ochich, and the couple of dozen young people who serve as his collaborators do not conceal the fact that a number of them belong to the International Association, and, disclaiming all the ancient laws and customs which serve as the foundation of the social and political system, strive for the introduction into Serbia of that order of things which proved as perilous as it was bankrupt in Paris."[100]

Marković and his journal were bitterly condemned in the Serbian National Assembly. In the brochure outlining *Radenik*'s program Marković had accused the Assembly of being a mere rubber-stamp body which had never rejected a single important paragraph of any law proposed by the government.[101] His criticism outraged many deputies, and *Radenik*'s defense of the European socialist movement did little to soothe their anger. In October of 1871 fourteen prominent deputies addressed an interpellation to the minister of internal affairs, stating that the journal *Radenik* preached communism and the doctrines of the International, thus striking at the very foundations of the state: faith, morals, and property.[102] Noting their extreme concern with the dangers presented by the "atheistic and

100 Quoted from the Russian archives in Kusheva, "Iz russko-serbskikh revoliutsionnykh sviazei," p. 351.

101 Komadinić, "Prvi socijalistički program."

102 *DANRS,* Narodna Skupština, 1871 k2, Interpelacija no. 26, October 11, 1871.

immoral" newspaper, the deputies demanded to know whether there were laws to protect the state against such pernicious doctrines; they further asked how the government proposed to go about "strangling this embryonic communism" and whether it would take steps to prevent journals similar to *Radenik* from coming into the country.[103]

Another interpellation concerning *Radenik* was directed to the government in the same month. A deputy from a provincial town noted that the editor of the socialist newspaper had sent him an excerpt from a *Radenik* article on the railroad question. While admitting that there was nothing punishable in the article, the deputy asked if there were not some law prohibiting such "irresponsible journalism."[104]

Radenik had joined with the opposition liberals in opposing the government's plans to begin railway construction in Serbia. The radical-socialists were not at this time represented in the National Assembly, where the case against the railroads was presented by Ljubomir Kaljević, leader of the liberal opposition and later (1875-76) prime minister. Kaljević's position, which *Radenik* strongly endorsed, was that railroads were wholly unnecessary in agricultural Serbia. The building of a system of railroads, he argued, would only benefit Serbia's enemies: in time of war the Turks could quickly transport troops to the principality, and Austria-Hungary could use the railroads to force Serbia into total economic subservience. Further, the enormous cost of construction would make it financially impossible for the country to undertake any "wars of liberation." *Radenik* sharply disagreed with Kaljević on

103 There were indeed laws providing severe penalties for criticizing the National Assembly and spreading "pernicious doctrines," and they were later used against Marković; see below, chap. VI.

104 *DANRS*, Narodna Skupština, 1871 k2, Interpelacija no. 24, October 9, 1871.

this latter point, remaining firm in its opposition to "Great Serbia." The socialist journal took the lead, however, in predicting (citing the example of Rumania)[105] the dire consequences of the influx of foreign capital, without which it would be impossible to build railroads in Serbia.[106]

The position of the government was that, if the Serbian economy were to be developed beyond its existing primitive state, railroads were a vital necessity. Furthermore, since it had already been decided to link Vienna and Constantinople by rail,[107] it behooved Serbia to ensure that the line crossed her territory.[108] *Vidov Dan* and *Jedinstvo* supported the government position. After an intensely bitter parliamentary and press debate (one issue of *Radenik* was confiscated)[109] the government easily passed the necessary legislation.

It proved easier to establish a policy than to begin construction. Hampered by lack of capital, Serbia was unable to lay a single rail (although much surveying was done in the early seventies) until 1878, when work was finally begun on the first line in the country, that linking Belgrade and Aleksinac. By that time both radical-socialists and the former opposition liberals had dropped their manifestly unreasonable objections; Kaljević attempted to start the construction of the lines during his term as prime minister, and Nikola Pašić was the leading Serbian railway construction engineer in the late seventies.

105 A German firm had gone bankrupt in the attempt to build a railway system in Rumania, and Rumanian investors lost heavily.

106 *Radenik*, nos. 41-72, September 7-November 23, 1871.

107 Construction of a line from Constantinople to the Austrian border through Sarajevo (thus by-passing Serbia) was begun in 1872.

108 Slobodan Jovanović discusses the railway debate in *Vlada Milana*, I, pp. 107-108.

109 No. 50, which should have appeared on September 30, 1871, was seized by the police. In the following issue (no. 51, October 2) *Radenik* announced that no. 50 had been "held up" pending a court decision. No further reference was made to the matter, and no copy of the offending issue has survived.

Marković himself did not contribute to the lengthy discussion of the railroad question, although *Radenik* published little else in the autumn of 1871. His last major article for the journal in 1871 was one in August devoted to the Russian revolutionary movement. Prompted by what he considered a tendentious article in *Vidov Dan*[110] linking the erratic Jacobin Sergei Nechaev with the main currents of revolutionary activity in Russia, and the Russian revolutionaries in general with the International, Marković replied with what was at once a defense of the Russian revolutionary democrats and a periphrastic attack on his opponents in Serbia.[111]

MARKOVIĆ ON RUSSIAN REVOLUTIONARY DEMOCRACY

He began his article with a brief discussion of the Great Reforms in Russia. The experiences of the Crimean War, he wrote, had dramatized the urgent need for reforms,[112] but the government was determined to introduce only those "reforms" which would "strengthen the state order . . . and the ruling dynasty." He went on to note that the mainstay of the tsarist government was the gentry, which occupied its position "not only by virtue of its wealth and power over the common people, but also because it occupied all the most important posts in the bureaucracy." The government had the interests of the gentry at heart when it freed the serfs: "The government wished to free the peasant juridically from the power of the landlord while economically enslaving him more than ever. The

110 *Vidov Dan*, no. 162, July 29, 1871.

111 Marković, "Ruski revolucionari i Nečajev" ("The Russian Revolutionaries and Nechaev"), *Radenik*, nos. 29-31, 37, August 9-28, 1871.

112 Marković's discussion of the responsibility for Russia's defeat recalled none too subtly his earlier statement that Serbia's greatest need was "the destruction of the bureaucratic system": "This terrible corruption of the bureaucracy was the main reason why the Crimean War turned out so unsuccessfully for Russia. The bureaucrats left the army without food, without uniforms, without ammunition in the most difficult and decisive moments."

Russian government saw, just as the governments of the West had also seen, that the capitalists are more reliable as the basis of the Imperial state order than the gentry, and therefore it intended to turn its gentry-landholders into . . . capitalists."

Marković was bitterly contemptuous of the Russian reforms and what he insisted were their English models, and he mocked Herzen's praise of the tsar. There were only a few people in Russia, he wrote, who understood what the reforms really signified, "who knew that it is not possible for the sheep to be intact and the wolves satisfied, that a Mongol-Byzantine despotic empire and popular self-government cannot co-exist, that it is impossible to reconcile the workers and the gentry, freedom and domination." These enlightened few were led by Chernyshevsky and Dobroliubov, both "men of the people, men with strong intellect and erudition . . . with character as strong as steel . . . pure as gold." Of Chernyshevsky Marković wrote: "In the 19th century there has not been a single reformer who so deeply and universally planned social reorganization and who possessed such erudition and experience in the exposition of his science, as did Chernyshevsky. His reform embraced all men and all society: the family, the commune, the state, all fundamental concepts of morality, religion, property, education, politics, nationality, etc.: in a word: in the form of an orderly system he scientifically set forth the fundamental principles for a radical social reorganization in Russia." Marković's praise of his teacher was also a statement of his own aspirations; with scant regard for accuracy (or, for that matter, consistency), he wrote that the force and logic of Chernyshevsky's theories had *obliged* the Russian government to introduce reforms.

Marković finally came to the main points in his discussion. He denied *Vidov Dan*'s allegation that there existed close ideological ties between the Russian revolutionary movement and the International: "The revolutionary movement in Russia has its history, which is very old, much older than the history of the International. . . . The revolutionary principles in Russia are . . . older and more radical than the principles of the International." The International, he insisted, concerned itself primarily with economic and political affairs, while the Russian revolutionary movement struck deep at the social organization of the state.

Although he was obviously not familiar with all the details of the Nechaev case, Marković dismissed the Russian Jacobin as a "simple *loud-mouth and swindler*." In his writings Nechaev had produced "much fuss, many childish and foolish threats, but *no principles whatsoever*."

Vidov Dan had clearly intended its article on Nechaev and the International as an attack on the Serbian radical-socialists, and Marković met the challenge directly: "The development of thought cannot be stopped by any kind of force. Governmental tyranny only accelerates the existing popular revolution, since every hour demonstrates to the people the necessity of realizing as quickly as possible the principles that are preached to them, if they wish to be delivered from tyranny. The popular revolution always arises out of the inescapable needs of the people themselves."

Marković's answer to *Vidov Dan*, with its glorification of the Russian revolutionary democrats, demonstrated the continuing conflict in his thinking between their views of socialism and those of the Commune, the International, and Karl Marx. Throughout the life of *Radenik* Marković praised *avant-garde* Western socialism, yet it became clear that he did not seek to introduce that kind of socialism into Serbia. He valued Marx as the most profound critic of the social and economic development of the industrialized West, but he revered Chernyshevsky. Marković's entire career embodied a search for a method of reconciling Western and "Russian" socialism, and he never recognized the quixotic nature of his quest. The "Russian" socialism he so stoutly defended was but a loose-jointed synthesis of pre-Marxian Western socialism; Marković's efforts to add a touch of Marxism to this jumble served only to confuse him (as well it might), as indeed it confused some of his Russian contemporaries. The real issue was not Western vs. "Russian" socialism but Western visionary reformism vs. Marxism.

Of Marković's personal life after his return to Serbia little is known. His health apparently gave him little trouble, and he devoted all his time to his work. He published few articles in *Radenik* after August of 1871; he was occupied with the writing of his book *Serbia in the East*,[113] excerpts from which *Radenik* published early in 1872. He was apparently supported by his brother, a fact his enemies did not let him forget: "You returned to the homeland not having learned anything with which you could *earn your bread*, but full of an ungovernable determination to rush headlong into the political struggle. . . . You who wanted to create a labor party were not ashamed to live off the charity of your brother or more precisely off the property of his wife (for you perhaps do not wish to show me that one can live off literary work in Serbia?)."[114]

THE END OF RADENIK

Foreshadowing the approaching suppression of *Radenik*, the attacks on Marković became more severe and personal in the spring of 1872. In the absence of Vladimir Jovanović, a new spokesman for the government liberals appeared to direct the final assault. Vladan Đorđević, a young phy-

[113] *Radenik*, nos. 4-19, January 13-February 18, 1872.
[114] *Jedinstvo*, no. 89, April 26, 1872; see also above, p. 74.

sician[115] who had studied in Vienna and who later became one of Serbia's most prominent citizens,[116] was to launch his political career by acting as the unofficial prosecutor of *Radenik* and its staff.

When Đorđević began his attack, Marković was already in exile in Novi Sad. Early in 1872 the Serbian government had abandoned its relatively lenient attitude toward the radical-socialist movement to undertake a series of repressive measures. Two small brochures containing some of Marković's articles were banned, and unusually severe prison sentences (thirteen months in one case) were meted out to those persons found in possession of them. Vasa Pelagić, the Bosnian priest, was expelled from Serbia as a vagrant. In March of 1872 the government decided to strike at the heart of the radical-socialist movement and issued an order for Marković's arrest. Somehow Marković received warning, and at dawn on the day he was to be arrested he was rowed across the Sava to Hungarian territory by one of his colleagues.[117]

The quarrel between Marković and Đorđević which led to the suppression of *Radenik* had its beginnings in November of 1871, when Đorđević announced in the socialist journal that he planned to convert his office into a hospital

115 *Vidov Dan*, no. 79, April 16, 1872, printed a letter from a Serb whose wife had recently undergone an operation at the hands of Vladan Đorđević; the husband wrote that he was completely satisfied with the results (he did not elaborate) and advised his countrymen that, so long as Belgrade had doctors of Đorđević's caliber, they had no need to go to Vienna or Budapest for medical treatment.

116 On Đorđević see V. Subotić, *Dr. Vladan Đorđević*, Belgrade, 1910. In 1873 he became one of Prince Milan's personal physicians; he founded the Serbian Red Cross, served as ambassador to Greece and Turkey, and was prime minister and foreign minister in the last three years of the century. He edited an intellectual journal, wrote a four-volume history of Serbian military medicine and a series of historical novels.

117 *Skerlić*, p. 68. Skerlić's biography is the only source for Marković's departure from Serbia, but it should be remembered that, writing in 1910 (the date of the first edition), he had access to many documents which have since been lost.

where the poor could receive free medical care.[118] A few months later *Radenik* published an article, signed "A worker," which viciously attacked Đorđević; among other things it accused him of being a "money-grabbing bourgeois" who had no intention of helping the poor or the "workers."[119] The article was actually written by one of Marković's coworkers, Dimitrije Cenić, but the outraged Đorđević assumed that "A worker" could only be Marković himself.

Đorđević was not given to moderation. His honor had been called into question, and he intended simultaneously to vindicate himself and destroy his opponent. The severity of his attack on Marković indicated that the government, determined to discredit the socialists, gave Đorđević its wholehearted support and supplied him with information to use against the movement and its leader. In a letter to *Radenik* Đorđević maintained that "A worker" (he ridiculed the author's failure to sign his name) condemned his hospital "only because it did not emanate from the decisions of a 'worker assembly.' " Lampooning Marković's connections with the Western socialist movement, Đorđević observed that "he has heard that in other countries there are thousands of workers who suffer at the hands of the capitalists, and he saw what great roles the defenders of these poor workers play, and immediately he sees capitalists and a poor working class in Serbia, and he —noble knight from La Manche—rises up to do battle with the dragon which is perhaps only a windmill. . . ."[120] Đorđević derided the collapse of Marković's cooperatives. Everything connected with the "labor movement," he in-

[118] *Radenik,* no. 64, November 4, 1871; the advertisement was thrice repeated.

[119] *Ibid.,* no. 35, March 31, 1872.

[120] *Ibid.,* no. 36, March 31, 1872; this issue as apparently misdated, for no. 35 appeared on March 31 and no. 37 on April 5. No 36 ordinarily would have been dated April 3.

sisted, was the result not of "worker initiative" but of Marković's own handiwork; he had deluded uneducated people and made them believe that everything *he* did was a product of *their* mind and will. Finally, the Serbian "labor problem," Đorđević claimed, was merely a problem of poverty.

Despite the fact that he had not written the article on Đorđević's hospital, Marković, from his exile in Novi Sad, willingly accepted the challenge to debate the Serbian "labor problem." In an incomplete article which *Radenik* published in three parts in April and May,[121] he developed a theme he had begun the previous summer in a debate with *Jedinstvo*: "A worker is a man who earns his bread by his own labor, and in Serbia such people are in the overwhelming majority."[122] He challenged Đorđević's claim that the only problem in Serbia was one of poverty; the ills of the country, he maintained, could not be cured by the distribution of alms. Far from being a problem of poverty, the "labor problem" was one of organizing the "national labor" on a strong and equitable basis in order to ensure to each member of society the right to live in comfort from the fruits of his own labor: "This is the real *labor problem* as it is conceived by all reasonable people in Europe and as *Radenik* too has always understood and presented it." The "labor problem," Marković insisted, embraced more than the relations between workers and capitalists; he noted that the "labor party" in Germany had been obliged to reject Lassalle's program in favor of the much wider socio-economic reforms of the International.

Marković went on to discuss "productive" and "unproductive" labor. The peasants and manual laborers obviously engaged in productive labor, but he implied that

[121] *Ibid.*, nos. 44, 49, 51, April 23, May 5 and 17, 1872.
[122] *Ibid.*, no. 21, July 17, 1871.

the only productive nonphysical labor was that concerned with education; bureaucrats, the military, merchants, and salesmen were all, he maintained, engaged in unproductive labor. Furthermore, by importing foreign luxuries to satisfy the tastes their high salaries had spawned, such individuals destroyed part of the useful labor of the peasants, whose products were exchanged for such luxuries. The unproductive members of society thus were themselves a luxury; by liquidating (he did not specify a means) these two "luxuries," the unproductive class and the unnecessary imports, Serbia could increase her national capital enormously in the space of a few years. Marković did not discuss any other possible consequences of the liquidation of the army and the bureaucracy.

In the last part of the article which *Radenik* was able to publish Marković lashed out at the bureaucrats, whose only goal was to stay in office, and the businessmen, who were motivated by a desire for profits rather than a concern for the national welfare. The Serbian businessmen, he claimed, refused to invest their money in agricultural or industrial enterprises, preferring instead to import high-profit luxury items and loan money to the peasants at usurious rates of interest.

Jedinstvo joined the attack on Marković late in April with an article on "our political flappers associated with *Radenik*."[123] The liberal newspaper scoffed at *Radenik*'s "feeble efforts" to introduce an alien philosophy into Serbia; as soon as that journal's policy became clear, *Jedinstvo* claimed, three hundred individuals cancelled their subscriptions. Ominously, the article predicted that *Radenik* would soon expire. In its next issue *Jedinstvo* referred sarcastically to the "unweaned Svetozar Marković," that

123 *Jedinstvo*, no. 86-87, April 23, 1872.

"puffed-up frog," and his "organized army" of "student loafers."[124]

Vladan Đorđević struck the final blows in a letter to *Zastava* in which he stated that Svetozar Miletić, the editor of that newspaper, had in his possession a letter from "the communist and republican Svetozar Marković" in which Marković indicated his intention to seek the election of Prince Nikola of Montenegro to rule Serbia.[125] *Zastava* categorically denied that Miletić had ever possessed or seen such a letter,[126] but the damage had been done. Marković's own words had left him open to such a charge,[127] and, coming from the responsible, respected Dr. Đorđević, the accusation carried considerable weight. In an attempt further to discredit Marković, Đorđević published an "Open Letter to Mr. Svetozar Marković" in *Jedinstvo,* in which he pictured the radical-socialist leader as a misguided visionary: "I hold that for the development of civil freedom in Serbia and for the economic salvation of our homeland it is a colossal misfortune that such a gifted man as you laid the foundations of your education in a land of the most terrible contrasts. You went there [to Russia] with a soul thirsty to drink its fill of pure science . . . but instead your primary intellectual sustenance was socialism, which in the circumstances in which Chernyshevsky and Pisarev and so on lived had to become a *caricature.*"[128]

The campaign of the government liberals against Marković and his associates was carefully planned. In an attempt to make their policies more attractive to the young Serbs who had flocked to Marković's banner, the liberals "liberalized" many of their views. The semiofficial *Jedinstvo* serialized one of Pisarev's works during the first three

[124] *Ibid.,* no. 88, April 25, 1872.

[125] *Zastava,* no. 50, April 28, 1872; *Jedinstvo* reprinted Đorđević's letter in no. 109, May 20, 1872, three days after the death of *Radenik.*

[126] *Zastava,* no. 51, April 30, 1872.

[127] See above, p. 147.

[128] *Jedinstvo,* no. 89, April 26, 1872.

months of 1872 and conducted a battle of words with the conservative-reactionary *Vidov Dan* over the foreign policy of the government. *Jedinstvo* published a sympathetic obituary of Mazzini in March, referring to the Italian hero as one of the "greatest representatives of European liberalism."[129] Late in the year the liberal newspaper welcomed the appearance of a new journal edited by Mihailo Niketić, close friend of Marković and former editor of *Vragolan*.[130]

Although Marković had already left Serbia, the government remained determined to crush the radical-socialist movement. On March 31 Đura Ljočić, the official editor of *Radenik*, published a strange notice to the effect that he had "lost a yellow ruler on Thursday evening,"[131] and in the following issue *Radenik* announced that Stevan Milićević had succeeded Ljočić as editor.[132] In view of Marković's training in Russian revolutionary circles and his lifelong delight in conspiracy, Ljočić's notice would seem to have been an attempt to warn him of the intensification of government pressure. The change in editors, *Radenik* promised, would not be accompanied by a change in editorial policy. The journal was as good as its word. It continued to print news of the International, and published most of Marković's reply to Vladan Đorđević. The socialist newspaper likewise continued to gibe at *Vidov Dan* and *Jedinstvo* for their ignorance of Western socialism and for their attempts to portray Karl Marx as the "evil genius" behind the International.[133]

The days of *Radenik*, however, were clearly numbered.

129 *Ibid.*, no. 52, March 5, 1872. *Vidov Dan* likewise praised Mazzini (no. 48, March 5, 1872); in its own obituary *Radenik* lauded Mazzini and belittled the treatment accorded him by the other Belgrade newspapers.

130 *Jedinstvo*, no. 199, September 19, 1872.

131 *Radenik*, no. 36, March 31 (April 3), 1872.

132 *Ibid.*, no. 37, April 5, 1872.

133 *Ibid.*, no. 49, May 5, 1872. *Radenik* jeered at its competitors, but Marković himself had in an early issue of his journal (no. 4, June 8, 1871) referred to Marx as a "well-to-do man."

Early in April one of the journal's writers and chief financial mainstays, Đoka Mijatović, referred to Christ (in a series of articles dealing with the International) as a "socialist, communist and revolutionary."[134] Five weeks later Editor Milićević, apparently under pressure, published an apology for Mijatović's "intemperate words," but the issue which carried his statement was the last published by *Radenik*.[135] The government had the excuse it desired; Marković's "treason" (the last issue of *Radenik* carried his denial of the charge) and Mijatović's "blasphemy" were crimes punishable by law. *Radenik* was ordered to cease publication.[136]

None of the *Radenik* staff was imprisoned (Mijatović soon went into exile with Marković) and Marković himself was of course beyond the jurisdiction of the Serbian government,[137] but the radical-socialist movement had seemingly suffered irreparable damage. All of the most important cooperatives had collapsed and the few that remained were soon, with very few exceptions, to expire. *Pobratimstvo* had been proscribed after Marković had won most of its members to his cause, and *Omladina*, which disintegrated after its 1871 congress, had at least been kept out of radical-socialist hands. *Vragolan* had quickly been extinguished, and now the pernicious *Radenik* was dead, its editor in exile and branded as a traitor. No radical-socialist deputies sat in the National Assembly.[138]

134 *Ibid.*, nos. 34-39, March 29-April 9, 1872; the offending statement was in no. 39. Mijatović used excessively offensive language; Marković had not been harassed for his own statement that the Christian ethic was basically communist. Mijatović was the son of a wealthy landowner, and had studied law in Budapest and Paris, agronomy in Boston and New York; see Andrija Radenić, "Vojvođanska štampa," p. 71.

135 *Radenik*, no. 51, May 17, 1872. 136 *Skerlić*, p. 69.

137 The Serbian government had had little difficulty in persuading the Hungarian authorities to arrest Vladimir Jovanović after the assassination of Prince Michael, but apparently it made no representations concerning Svetozar Marković.

138 Jevrem Marković was elected to the National Assembly in the au-

Svetozar Marković's failure seemed complete; yet in some degree he had achieved all his goals. His activities in *Omladina* and *Pobratimstvo* had won a large number of young Serbs to the radical-socialist cause; many eventually dropped away, but those who remained formed the core of a small but significant Serbian socialist movement. The cooperatives had failed, but the idea of cooperation survived and became identified with a nonpartisan attempt to preserve the *zadrugas*. Further, Marković's influence was a major factor in the creation of a strong realist current in Serbian literature. *Radenik* itself represented a remarkable achievement; the establishment of a flourishing socialist newspaper in a country where ninety-five per cent of the population was illiterate was one of the more surprising successes which the European socialist movement had enjoyed up to that time.

But there was also a negative side of Marković's work. By rejecting the slightest compromise with the government liberals, and by preaching an extreme materialism and an attenuated Marxism, Svetozar Marković completed the alienation of the Serbian intelligentsia. An increasing number of young Serbs, educated beyond both their status and their prospects for satisfactory employment, had become discontented with the slow-moving, backward society in which they were obliged to live. Marković's dramatic return to Serbia had united these alienated intellectuals, and his leadership had given their hostility to society a measure of purpose. But the net effect of his activity was to drive still deeper the wedge between the alienated intelligentsia and society; still worse, the ambiguity of

tumn of 1871, but his election was nullified on a technicality and a conservative candidate won an apparently corrupt second contest; see *Radenik*, no. 30, August 12, 1871, and no. 49, September 28, 1871; Jaša M. Prodanović, *Istorija političkih stranaka i struja u Srbiji* (*The History of Political Parties and Currents in Serbia*), book 1, Belgrade, 1947, p. 335.

Marković's program militated against the creation of a genuinely effective opposition. Unable to decide whether he himself was "Russian socialist," Marxist, or cooperativist, Marković stimulated but did not fulfill the hopes of malcontent intellectuals in search of an alternative to contemporary society.

Marković's exile in Novi Sad was to give him time to reflect upon his failures and decide the course for the second phase of his struggle to establish a coherent socialist program.

CHAPTER V

Reorganization of the Revolution

NOVI SAD, the chief city of the Hungarian-ruled Vojvodina, was an ideal base for Marković during his enforced exile. The town had long been a major center of Serbian intellectual and cultural life and remained so in 1872, despite the continuing growth of an autonomous Serbia. Originally a Magyar village (Vásárosvárad), during centuries of war between the Ottoman and Habsburg Empires Novi Sad became a heterogeneous town of Serbs, Magyars, Germans, Slovaks, Slovenes, Jews, and Russians. By the middle of the nineteenth century there were about 12,000 Serbs and 9,000 Magyars in the town, with the remaining ethnic groups totaling perhaps another three or four thousand.

From Roman times until the eighteenth century Novi Sad owed its prominence to its strategic location; together with the fortress of Petrovaradin on the south bank of the river, it dominated a vital section of the Danube. With the gradual retreat of the Turks the town became, especially in the eighteenth century, both an important agricultural center and a focal point of Serbian nationalism. Its citizens played an important role in the Serbian Revolution, and many of them streamed into the principality after the winning of autonomy to form the bureaucratic and intellectual cadres.

The vigorous intellectual life of the Vojvodina Serbs was at its peak in the 1870's. A few years previously the famous Serbian literary society, *Matica Srpska*, had transferred its headquarters from Budapest to Novi Sad; most of the literati in all the Serb lands maintained contact with the society and endeavored to publish their works through it. *Omladina* had its permanent headquarters in Novi Sad, where it published its journal. Svetozar Miletić's *Zastava* was one of the finest newspapers in the Balkans; its articulate liberalism made it, and Novi Sad, a focal point of the liberal opposition to the Serbian government.[1]

Marković received a warm reception in Novi Sad. Despite their rejection of his socialist views, Svetozar Miletić and the Vojvodina liberals welcomed Marković as a victim and fellow opponent of the ruling circles in Belgrade. *Matica Srpska* had recently published Marković's "The Realist Direction in Science and Life," and the work had caused a sensation among the Novi Sad intellectuals; its author was a prized addition to the groups which met regularly to discuss philosophy and politics.

The Novi Sad artisans were delighted at Marković's arrival. He has been instrumental in the founding of cooperatives in the Vojvodina, and his popularity as a fiery champion of artisan interests knew few bounds. Early in April of 1872 the Novi Sad Union of Serbian Artisans (*Zadruga srba zanatlija*) announced that Marković and Đoka Mijatović, "great friends of labor and the artisans," had agreed to write for its recently founded newspaper.[2] Marković wrote a few minor articles for the journal during his exile, and worked closely with the Union. He advised it in its efforts to establish branches throughout the Vojvodina, regularly lectured at its meetings, and established in its ranks the nucleus of the Vojvodina socialist movement. Because of Marković's association with the organization the Union was dissolved by the Magyar authorities in 1873.[3]

1 Cf. *Skerlić*, p. 69; Skerlić perhaps stretches a point when he compares the role of Novi Sad with that of Brussels in the French opposition to Louis Napoleon.

2 *Radenik*, no. 36, March 31 (April 3), 1872; *Glas Zanatlija* (*The Voice of the Artisans*) published in Novi Sad in 1872-1873.

3 Triva Krstonošić, "Svetozar Marković i njegove veze sa zadružnim

Đoka Mijatović left Serbia a few weeks after Marković. He came to Novi Sad with plans to publish a socialist newspaper and a "socialist-scientific" monthly journal with Marković's editorial assistance, but neither his nature nor his convictions permitted serious work. Both projects were abandoned after the appearance of the first issue of the newspaper early in June. In the summer of 1872 Mijatović accompanied Marković to Zürich; he remained in the city and eventually earned a medical degree, but died in 1878 at the age of thirty.[4]

REVOLUTIONARY CONSPIRACY

During the first three months of his stay in Novi Sad Marković was occupied primarily with preparations for a revolt in Bosnia-Hercegovina. The extent of Marković's participation in the revolutionary movement has only recently, with the publication of certain Russian documents and the discovery of Marković's letters, become a relatively well-documented matter of historical record. After the sixth and last *Omladina* congress in August of 1871, there was an inevitable split of the organization into several factions; the two most important were the liberals who supported the Serbian government (Vladimir Jovanović's group) and the revolutionaries.[5] The latter included socialists, opposition liberals, and a few conservatives.[6] The

organizacijama u Vojvodini" ("Svetozar Marković and the Vojvodina Zadruga Organizations"), *Zadružni arhiv*, I, 1953, pp. 91-114. See also *Zadružni Leksikon FNRJ*, II, 1450, and Vasa Stajić "Svetozar Marković i socijalisti u Novom Sadu, 1872-1880" ("Svetozar Marković and the Socialists in Novi Sad, 1872-1880"), *Letopis Matice Srpske*, v. 358, 1946, pp. 105-125.

[4] Kosta Milutinović, "Agrarna problematika prvih srpskih socijalista," pp. 80-81.

[5] The disintegration of *Omladina* was due both to the hostile attitudes of the Serbian and Magyar authorities and to the disruptive influence of the socialists within the organization; cf. *Vlada Milana* I, pp. 134-5, 145-6.

[6] The conservatives who signed the 1871 near-anarchist political program joined the revolutionaries; see above, p. 155.

leaders of the revolutionaries were Svetozar and Jevrem Marković, Vasa Pelagić, Sava Grujić, and Đorđe Vlajković (who later led the Serbian volunteers in the uprising of 1875 in Hercegovina). After a bitter debate in which Vasa Pelagić denounced several of his colleagues, in December of 1871 the revolutionaries delegated Jevrem Marković to meet secretly with the Serbian government to solicit its support for an uprising against the Turks in Bosnia-Hercegovina.[7]

Securing an interview with Colonel Blaznavac, Jevrem Marković revealed the plans of the revolutionary group. The Slavic Committees of Moscow and Odessa, he said, had promised financial assistance, and certain "Balkan sources" (which he did not identify) would also lend their support. Arms and ammunition were being collected, and the uprising was planned for February of 1872. Blaznavac, after consulting with his coregent Jovan Ristić and Prime Minister Milojković, bluntly informed Marković that the Serbian government would under no circumstances lend its support. The revolt had virtually no hope of success, he insisted, in part because the "assistance" from the Slavic Committees was insignificant. Blaznavac did not reveal that the decision not to support the project was influenced more by the hostile attitude of official Russia than by the prospect of failure; informed of the plans for the revolt, the Russian consul, Shishkin, stated his government's unequivocal opposition.[8] The fact that Shishkin was consulted, however, indicated that Belgrade was far from disinterested in Jevrem Marković's proposal.

Although refusing to support the revolutionaries, Blaznavac, unquestionably surprised that the government's fiercest critics should suddenly seek its cooperation, coun-

[7] Kusheva, "Iz russko-serbskikh revoliutsionnykh sviazei," pp. 351-352.

[8] *Ibid.* This was certainly not the only case in which the policies of the Slavic Committees and those of the Russian government failed to harmonize; see Nikitin, *Slavianskie komitety*, pp. 66-67, 93ff.

tered with his own proposal. He observed that the cause of Serbian liberation and unification would be greatly advanced if *Radenik, Zastava,* and the followers of those journals would abandon their socialism, cancel their plans for an immediate revolt, and pursue a policy of nationalism and support for the Obrenović dynasty. Jevrem Marković, whose political acumen left something to be desired, agreed to urge his colleagues to call off the scheduled revolt and promised to discuss Blaznavac's suggestions with his brother and Svetozar Miletić, who had joined the revolutionaries.[9]

According to recently discovered evidence,[10] Svetozar Marković himself exchanged letters with Blaznavac early in 1872, discussing the possibility of cooperation between the revolutionaries and the government. The whole affair was an incredible departure for Svetozar, if not for his brother, and can only be explained by the presumption that he hoped to secure concessions in the form of a cessation of government activity against the radical-socialist movement. To the consternation of many of his associates, however, it appeared that Marković, who had denounced both Russian and Serbian liberals for concluding a *rapprochement* with a repressive régime, had attempted to do precisely the same thing. In any event, Blaznavac offered to consider the possibility of cooperation; he suggested that Marković discuss the problem with Miletić, and for his own part promised to consult Ristić. Miletić was not unreceptive, but Ristić adamantly refused to deal with the socialists and forced Marković to flee Serbia.[11]

[9] Kondrat'eva, "Novye arkhivnye materialy," pp. 319-324. Jevrem Marković remained more nationalist than socialist throughout his life, and differed with his brother on the relative priority of national liberation and internal reform; cf. Kusheva, "Iz russko-serbskikh revoliutsionnykh sviazei," p. 352.

[10] Čubrilović, *Istorija političke misli,* pp. 337-338.

[11] Marković made this clear in *Srbija na istoku,* p. 1.

The negotiations with Blaznavac were distasteful to many of the radical-socialists. Vasa Pelagić, leader of the Bosnian wing of the revolutionary organization and a staunch socialist, objected violently to the secret talks and accused Jevrem Marković of being in the pay of the Serbian government. For a time the hostility between Pelagić and the elder Marković brother threatened to destroy the harmony of both radical-socialist and revolutionary movements; Svetozar Marković, however, managed to retain Pelagić's confidence, and the quarrel was eventually smoothed over.[12]

Blaznavac's ostensibly gratuitous linking of the liberal *Zastava* with the socialist *Radenik* had ample foundation. Miletić and his colleagues on *Zastava* joined with the radical-socialists late in 1871 to create a secret revolutionary organization, the Society for Serbian Liberation and Unification (*Družina za oslobođenje i ujedinjenje srpsko*).[13] Although the origins of the society remain mysterious, it is obvious that Miletić and Svetozar Marković were instrumental in its founding; associated with them were representatives of all the Serb lands.[14] Liuben Karavelov was in close touch with the society, and promised to launch a revolt in Bulgaria simultaneously with that in Bosnia-Hercegovina.[15]

Svetozar Marković quickly emerged as the leader of the revolutionary movement. In a letter to his brother outlining the situation, Marković wrote that for the moment he would remain "in waiting" in Novi Sad. Ever the conspirator, he would immediately write Nikola Pašić and Pera Velimirović, who had left Serbia, directing them to

12 *IAB*, Svetozar to Jevrem Marković, n.p. (but Novi Sad), n.d., letter no. 8.

13 Čubrilović, *Istorija političke misli*, pp. 333-338.

14 Pelagić represented Bosnia; Đorđe Vlajković, Serbia; Pera Matanović, Montenegro; Kosta Ugrinić, Slavonia.

15 *IAB*, Svetozar to Jevrem Marković, letter no. 8.

return to the principality to "prepare surgeons" for the "operation" in Hercegovina. Pašić and Velimirović would send money to two fellow conspirators (identified only as Dreč and Filipović), who would then return to a town in Dalmatia (Metković) near their "base" (Mostar) in Hercegovina. He had discussed his plans with Miletić, Svetozar told his brother, and they agreed that the central revolutionary organization (i.e., the society) had to be strengthened in the Vojvodina. Miletić had also advised the printing of revolutionary leaflets for distribution throughout the Serb lands on the eve of the uprising; Marković concurred, noting only that it would be better to have them printed at the "Zürich press"[16] rather than in Novi Sad or Belgrade. Finally, in connection with the plans for the revolt, Marković asked his brother to meet him (if possible with Sava Grujić) in Zemun as soon as possible.[17]

Despite the aberration of his negotiations with Blaznavac, Svetozar Marković's participation in the revolutionary movement was in the service not of "Great Serbia" but in that of the older and wider concept of South Slav unity which had its immediate origins in the Illyrian movement of the first half of the century.[18] Marković did not, however, consider himself a part of the Illyrian movement, to which his known writings devote virtually no attention. Influenced more than he cared to admit by the Pan-Slavs, but most of all by the Russian revolutionary democrats, he saw the coming revolution in Bosnia-Herce-

[16] This was apparently a reference to Marković's Russian friends in Zürich, whose identity remains unknown. It could not have been the Russian Section of the International, whose press was in Geneva.

[17] *IAB*, Svetozar to Jevrem Marković, n.p. (but Novi Sad), n.d., letter no. 9; see also letters nos. 7 and 8, and *Rad* (Belgrade), no. 9, 1875, p. 133.

[18] Of the many works on the Illyrian movement the more important are listed in Stavrianos, *The Balkans since 1453*, pp. 897, 903-904; see also Ferdo Šišić's *Jugoslovenska misao* (*The Yugoslav Concept*), Belgrade, 1937, especially pp. 59-82, 209-211.

govina as the first step in a Balkan national-liberation movement which would eventually create, he hoped, a democratic, federative state embracing all the Balkan (i.e., South) Slavs. He regarded the differences between Serbs, Croats, and Bulgars as both accidental and superficial (he usually referred to the first two as the "Serbo-Croatian people"[19]), and insisted that if the concept of nationality were regarded in a "progressive" rather than a "reactionary" light there would be in the South Slav lands, "as in Switzerland and America," a total absence of a "nationality problem."[20]

SERBIA IN THE EAST

Some of Marković's early writings had seemed to his opponents to equivocate concerning Serbia's role in the national-liberation movement.[21] He attempted to clarify his views in his *Serbia in the East,* which he published in book form in Novi Sad in June of 1872.[22] The work was conceived by Marković both as a manifesto of the revolutionary movement and a reply to Vladimir Jovanović's book on Serbia's "mission" in the East, which two years previously had outlined the foreign policy of the Serbian liberals.[23] The Serbian Revolution, Marković wrote, had never been properly evaluated.[24] It was more than a mere change of governments; it was the "eradication of an entire unproductive class of people, who lived a completely different life, spoke a different language, worshipped another faith, and regarded the Serbian people as its prop-

19 *Radenik,* no. 5, January 15, 1872.

20 *Ibid.,* no. 20, February 20, 1872; for Marković's views on the Swiss solution of the nationality problem see Prodanović, *Shvatanje Svetozara Markovića o državi,* pp. 12-15.

21 *Jedinstvo,* no. 89, April 26, 1872.

22 Cf. Marković's announcement in *Radenik,* no. 35, March 31, 1872.

23 *Les Serbes et la Mission de la Serbie dans l'Europe d'Orient.*

24 Marković knew the works of Ranke, Nil Popov and Vuk Karadžić, all of whom he criticized for their "shallow understanding" of the problem.

erty."[25] At a stroke the Serbs became free, but their freedom, based upon the ancient social and political institutions of the *zadruga* and the *opština*, was quickly curbed by the development of a centralized, bureaucratic despotism.[26] Chiefly responsible for the stifling of Serbian freedom, Marković maintained, were the Obrenović dynasty and its supporters. As soon as the Obrenovićes were returned to power in 1858, he noted, they quickly reestablished their despotic rule in Serbia, then began to cast about for a means to extend their rule beyond the borders of the principality. Thus in the reign of Prince Michael there was born the "Great Serbia" policy which saw bureaucratic, undemocratic, and monarchical Serbia seek to build a South Slav empire.[27]

Once again Marković contrasted Serbia's policy with that of Montenegro. The latter, he maintained, also sought to liberate all the Serb lands, but, unlike Serbia, Montenegro looked forward to the creation of an independent, free society and not to the strengthening of its dynasty.[28]

According to Marković, Serbia had to revamp her thinking if she was to deserve the leadership of the national-liberation movement. The government had to realize that its powers derived from the Serbian people, who would not permit the establishment of the Obrenović-liberal "Great Serbia." The revolution against the Turks, he insisted, had to be followed by the complete liberation of all the oppressed Balkan Slavs and their union on the basis of democratic federalism; "Great Serbia" would merely exchange one set of masters for another.[29] Mazzini had been wrong, Marković maintained, in his claim that "it is all the same, king or president, what matters is unity."[30] "Great Serbia," he later observed, was a dan-

[25] *Srbija na istoku*, p. 27.
[26] *Ibid.*, pp. 13-23, 36-50.
[27] Cf. Čubrilović, *Istorija političke misli*, p. 301.
[28] *Srbija na istoku*, pp. 108-113.
[29] *Ibid.*, pp. 113-116.
[30] *Radenik*, no. 31, March 19, 1872.

gerous policy which would bring the Serbs into conflict with the Bulgars, Croats, and Rumanians, and would if realized be nothing but a "Magyar despotism." Democratic union on a federal basis was the only way to ensure freedom in the Balkans.[31]

Serbia in the East (coupled with Marković's later amplification of his views on Balkan federation)[32] was a landmark in the history of the national-liberation movement among the Balkan Slavs. As Professor Vasa Čubrilović has pointed out, Marković was the first Serb to perceive the dangers inherent in the attempt to reconcile Serb nationalism with the concept of South Slav unity.[33] Marković clearly diagnosed the imperialism inherent in Prince Michael's scheme for Balkan cooperation against the Turks, a scheme which the liberals had expanded into the "Great Serbia" policy. He rejected outright the liberal view that the Serbs had somehow earned the right to exclusive South Slav leadership. Marković's greatest contribution to the revolutionary national-liberation movement was his attempt to subdue the separate nationalisms of the Balkan Slavs in favor of democratic federalism.[34]

The uprising in Bosnia-Hercegovina did not actually take place until July of 1875, a few months after Marković's death. His influence had, however, contributed greatly to the launching of the revolt, and many of his associates took an active part in it.[35]

31 *Rad*, nos. 21-22, 1874.

32 Cf. *ibid.*, where Marković considers the possibility of including the non-Slavs in a Balkan union.

33 *Istorija političke misli*, p. 303.

34 Marković's program was clearly not, as one enthusiastic observer has written, a "deep and farsighted Marxist solution of both the problem of national liberation and the socialist revolution." Dušan Nedeljković, *Naša filozofija u borbi za socijalizam* (*Our Philosophy in the Struggle for Socialism*), Belgrade, 1952, pp. 64-65.

35 On the uprising see Vasa Čubrilović, *Bosanski ustanak, 1875-78* (*The Bosnian Uprising, 1875-78*), Belgrade, 1930; other sources are listed in Stavrianos, *op. cit.*, pp. 915-916.

MARKOVIĆ AND BAKUNIN

Immediately after the publication of *Serbia in the East* Marković and Đoka Mijatović left for Zürich. An agent of the Russian Third Section (political police) in that city notified his superiors that Marković had come to discuss plans for a revolution in Bosnia-Hercegovina with Michael Bakunin. The agent had earlier informed St. Petersburg that the revolt would begin on August 20, 1872; Marković's arrival, he now wrote, would have the effect of delaying its start because he and Bakunin had decided to work out a more precise socialist program for the uprising. Sergei Nechaev ("another conspirator"), the agent noted, had decided to postpone his departure from Zürich pending the negotiations with Marković.[36] The Russian agent's report was correct only in that Marković had indeed come to Zürich to meet with Bakunin. No date had been set for the revolt, with which Bakunin had no known connection, and Marković was decidedly hostile toward Nechaev, whom he apparently did not see in Switzerland. Bakunin, on the verge of success in his struggle to seize control of the International (if necessary by wrecking it),[37] founded a "Slav Section" of that organization upon his arrival in Zürich in the spring of 1872. He then organized within the section a "Slav Brotherhood," which had as its major source of support the Serbian students in the city. Lacking decisive influence among the Russian *émigrés*, Bakunin attempted to strengthen his personal organization in the International by winning the allegiance of the Western and Southern Slav students, and to this end he summoned a "Serbian socialist congress" to meet in Zürich.[38]

[36] Kusheva, "Iz russko-serbskikh revoliutsionnykh sviazei," pp. 352-353.

[37] The International was for all practical purposes destroyed at the Hague Congress later in 1872.

[38] Meijer, *Knowledge and Revolution*, pp. 89-90, 94-95.

There is no evidence to indicate the extent of Svetozar Marković's contacts with the Russian revolutionaries (other than Bakunin) in the summer of 1872. Though the Russian Section of the International was still in existence in Geneva, Marković apparently did not visit his former colleagues. Circumstantial evidence would seem to indicate that he did meet some of Lavrov's followers in Zürich; according to three wholly independent sources, Marković, in rejecting Bakunin's program, emphasized his solidarity with Lavrov.[39] Lavrov himself did not arrive in Zürich until November of 1872, but his friends in the city had earlier in the year founded a press, probably the one Marković had suggested for the printing of revolutionary leaflets.[40] Marković adopted a Lavrovian, anti-Bakuninist stand at the Serbian socialist congress, and after 1872 there existed a certain parallelism between the thought of the two men.

Marković had earlier condemned Bakunin as the representative of "extreme decentralization" in the International and had given his support to Karl Marx.[41] But his own ideas concerning the limitation of the central state power and the delegation of the widest possible autonomy to the lowest administrative units were in many respects not far removed from those of Bakunin, and indeed in November of 1870 Marković had sent one of his colleagues to Locarno to discuss with Bakunin the possibility of joint revolutionary action.[42] Nothing came of the project, but it did indicate Marković's agreement with Bakunin on many points.

The Serbian socialist congress in Zürich developed into

[39] Viktorov-Toporov, "Svetozar Markovich," p. 42; Wendel, *Aus dem südslawischen Risorgimento*, p. 153; Koz'min, *Russkaia sektsiia*, pp. 233-244.

[40] Meijer, *op. cit.*, pp. 117-139; Venturi, *Roots of Revolution*, pp. 457-468; Yarmolinsky, *Road to Revolution*, pp. 183-184.

[41] *Pančevac*, no. 62, August 2, 1870.

[42] *Skerlić*, pp. 78-79.

a rather uneven contest between the followers of Marković and those of Bakunin, the latter being in the majority.[43] Bakunin was, as Jovan Skerlić has pointed out,[44] the only Slav before Tolstoy to enjoy a European reputation, and it was to him that the majority of the young Serbs in Switzerland now gravitated. It is not known how many Serbs were then in Zürich, but the number could scarcely have been less than twenty; only four of them supported Marković, who was denounced by one of Bakunin's adherents as a Marxist.[45] Because of the large majority against him, Marković decided against a fruitless assault on the Bakuninists and remained in the background throughout the congress. He later wrote to Pašić that his greatest error had been his failure to draw the Bakuninists back to Serbia, where he was certain of a majority in any gathering of socialists; he also made a mistake, he noted, "in not taking a decisive stand against Bakunin immediately, and in not telling him to keep out of Serbian affairs, of which he knew nothing."[46]

During the last week in July Marković and Bakunin met four times; Bakunin noted a "discussion décisive" in his diary on July 29, and on the following day "dernière explication avec Marković."[47] Marković refused to be swayed by the dynamic anarchist and declined to accept the two programs which the congress had agreed upon in sessions he had not attended.

The fact that there were two programs indicated the lack of solidarity among the Serbian Bakuninists themselves. The programs have been carefully analyzed by the Dutch scholar J. M. Meijer;[48] suffice it here to point out only

[43] Jovan M. Žujović, *Uticaj Svetozara Markovića na školsku omladinu* (*Svetozar Marković's Influence on the Student Youth*), Belgrade, 1925, pp. 7-10; Žujović was one of the Bakuninists in Zürich in 1872; see also *Skerlić*, p. 75.

[44] *Skerlić*, p. 76. [45] *Ibid.*, p. 81. [46] *Ibid.*, p. 85.

[47] Quoted in Meijer, *op. cit.*, p. 96. [48] *Ibid.*, pp. 95-96.

that Article 6 of the "practical part" of both programs called for a "to the people" movement of the intelligentsia, anticipating a development soon to take shape in Russia.[49]

Immediately after the congress the Serbian Bakuninists split into two factions. One continued to follow Bakunin, while the others gravitated to the Jacobin Sergei Nechaev and his Polish counterpart Gaspar Turski; in 1873 the young Serbs of the latter persuasion formed a "Cercle slave" in Zürich and Paris.[50]

The Serbs who remained with Bakunin were infuriated at Marković's refusal to commit his prestige as the leading Serbian socialist to their cause. Đoka Mijatović, Marković's former collaborator, went over to Bakunin in Zürich and contributed funds for the founding of a press for the printing of anarchist, anti-Marković literature. In a gesture which had no practical significance Marković was formally expelled from the "socialist party," as the Zürich Bakuninists pompously styled their tiny organization.[51]

A fierce battle of words ensued in which Marković was clearly the victor. The Bakuninists had no effective support in Serbia, while Marković was widely known not only in the principality but also in Bosnia-Hercegovina and the Vojvodina. The embittered anarchists were soon reduced to writing to one another of the perfidy of Marković and his followers, to whom they referred as "dead men"; one of their letters was intercepted by the Russian Third Section, which expelled two female Serbian anarchists from Russia for "correspondence with foreign agitators."[52] Marković wrote to Pašić that "not one of the Zürich Serbs understands Bakuninist theory," and that they did not "see clearly the elementary principles of socialism and the

49 On the "to the people" movement in Russia see Venturi, *Roots of Revolution*, pp. 469-506.

50 Kusheva, "Iz russko-serbskikh revoliutsionnykh sviazei," pp. 354-355.

51 *Skerlić*, p. 87.

52 Kusheva, *op. cit.*, pp. 353-354.

socialist revolution."[53] And later in the year he wrote that "it is absurd to regard the dregs of society . . . as socialist material, as Bakunin in his revolutionary zeal does."[54]

NOVI SAD AGAIN

Marković returned to Novi Sad in August of 1872 with Milica and Anka Ninković, who had attended the socialist congress with him, representing half his total support. The daughters of a retired professor, the Ninković sisters had become acquainted with Marković in the spring of 1872 and had quickly come under his influence. He saw in them not only genuine friendship (whether love or not remains a mystery) but also an opportunity to give a practical meaning to his beliefs in female emancipation. Marković adopted a protective, rather paternal attitude toward the girls and guided them in their education. He tutored them in mathematics and Russian, introduced them to the works of Chernyshevsky, and converted them to socialism.[55]

Marković lived in the Ninković home upon his return to Novi Sad. In the autumn of 1872 he induced Mrs. Ninković to take her daughters back to Zürich to continue their education. Milica and Anka Ninković studied in Switzerland for two years, returning in 1874 to found a school in Kragujevac.[56]

The Novi Sad school system had earlier come under attack from Marković, who considered it unfit to educate the Ninković sisters or anyone else. In an article written

[53] *Skerlić*, pp. 85-86.

[54] *Izbrannye Sochineniia*, p. 828.

[55] Milan Bogdanović, "Milica Ninković," *Književnost*, I, 1946, pp. 149-152; Vidosava Obradović, "Svetozar Marković i sestre Ninković" ("Svetozar Marković and the Ninković Sisters"), *Žena danas* (Belgrade), 1939, no. 20, pp. 7-8; Dragoslav Ilić, *Prve žene socijalisti u Srbiji* (*The First Women Socialists in Serbia*), Belgrade, 1956, pp. 17-36.

[56] Savić, "Svetozar Marković u emigraciji"; on the school founded by the Ninković sisters see *Oslobođenje* (Kragujevac), no. 1, January 1, 1875.

in the spring of 1872 he had condemned the emphasis upon classicism and religion in the schools, and had called for more study of the natural and physical sciences. The local teachers resented his criticism and ostracized him socially.[57]

Further problems arose for Marković in connection with his activities among the Novi Sad students. When he arrived in Novi Sad in March of 1872 he had taken a room in the home of a carpenter whose sons attended the *gimnazija.* The young men were immediately attracted to Marković, who sympathized with their rebellion against the curriculum and attempted to turn their youthful discontent to his own advantage. Through them Marković met other students, and soon created an informal discussion group into which he infused his *avant-garde* theories of society and education. Several of the students became vociferous in their rebellion against curriculum and teachers, and were punished harshly for their disrespectful attitude toward both teachers and parents. Marković was denounced by the respectable citizens of the town, and was forced to move to the home of the freethinker Petar Ninković and his two attractive daughters.[58]

Shortly after Marković's return from Zürich he was involved in still another unpleasant incident which for a time left a cloud of suspicion over him. Anxious to return to Serbia, he wrote Blaznavac (who had just become prime minister) asking for permission. He insisted that he had no intention of inciting a revolt against the Serbian government; on the contrary he wanted merely to work through parliamentary channels to secure the acceptance of his program. Blaznavac refused the request and made public parts of Marković's letter, attempting by his editing to suggest that Marković had broken with his as-

[57] *IAB*, Svetozar to Ilka Marković, Novi Sad, May 1, 1872, letter no. 7.

[58] Vasa Stajić, "Svetozar Marković i socijalisti u Novom Sadu," pp. 107-108.

sociates, including his own brother. For a time many in Belgrade, including even Jevrem Marković, accepted Blaznavac's version of the letter; when Svetozar Marković's demands that the entire contents of the letter be made public went unheeded, however, Blaznavac was discredited and the incident soon forgotten.[59]

The Hungarian authorities were anything but indifferent to Marković's presence in Novi Sad. Such a revolutionary socialist could be tolerated, within limits, for his subversive value with respect to Serbia, but his activities among the Vojvodina artisans and students threatened to cancel the positive considerations. In October of 1872 the governor of the Vojvodina issued an order directing the Novi Sad authorities to maintain a close surveillance over Marković and all "foreign adventurers" in the town. The mayor of Novi Sad, Pavle Mačvanski, interpreted the order broadly, and Marković was hounded by the police.[60] The situation rapidly became intolerable, and Marković resolved to leave as soon as possible. He was in dire financial straits, occasionally being without enough money to buy food;[61] it would appear that his brother, because of the Blaznavac letter affair, had temporarily halted his financial support.

Marković was impatient to return to Serbia and resume active leadership of the socialist movement. His health had begun to bother him again, and he felt that only work would restore his vigor. Under virtual house arrest, cut off from his associates in Serbia, the winter of 1872-73 was the low point in Marković's career. He wrote to his friends that his return to Serbia would mean immediate imprison-

59 *Skerlić*, pp. 88-89.

60 Kosta Milutinović, "Proterivanje Svetozara Markovića iz Vojvodine" ("The Expulsion of Svetozar Marković from the Vojvodina"), *Istoriski časopis*, v, 1955, pp. 351-353.

61 *Oslobođenje*, no. 27, March 2, 1875.

ment, but he stressed his determination to end an exile which had become unbearable.[62]

The months in the Vojvodina had been a period of intense reflection for Marković. He came to realize that the doctrinaire, theoretical approach he had adopted in *Radenik* was unsuitable in Serbia; he had paid too much attention to theory and had neglected politics. In December of 1872 he wrote that "*all my work from the very beginning has been in error. Now a new foundation must be laid*, and for that work and more work is necessary."[63]

In March of 1873 Marković was ordered to leave Novi Sad. Outraged by the arbitrary order, Svetozar Miletić, formerly mayor and now member of the city council, demanded an explanation. Mayor Mačvanski claimed that Marković was being expelled for his connection with "Great Serbia propaganda" and for his communism. Marković certainly had no connection with "Great Serbia propaganda," though the second charge was without question valid; in any event the immediate excuse used by the authorities to expel Marković was his failure to remove his hat in the presence of a religious procession. Miletić was unable to obtain a reversal of the order, but he did influence the city council to pass a resolution criticizing the treatment of Marković and demanding that there be no such occurrences in the future. The resolution had moral rather than practical value.[64]

Marković left Novi Sad about March 20 and traveled to Sremski Karlovci, where he stayed for three weeks in the home of his friend Šandor Radovanović. Long chairman of the municipality, Radovanović was widely known in the Vojvodina as a successful farmer and vintner. Marković first visited him in the summer of 1872, and the two men

[62] *Rad*, no. 9, 1875, p. 133; *Skerlić*, p. 89.

[63] *Skerlić*, p. 91.

[64] Milutinović, "Proterivanje Svetozara Markovića," pp. 352-354; *Skerlić*, p. 90; Savić, "Svetozar Marković u emigraciji."

became firm friends. A contemporary reported that Radovanović wholeheartedly embraced Marković's principles and became a "fantastic socialist."[65] But Radovanović's friendship availed him little, and soon after Marković arrived in Sremski Karlovci the police ordered him to leave; he managed to prolong his stay until mid-April, then took a boat down the Danube to Belgrade.[66]

As he had foreseen, he was arrested as soon as he set foot on Serbian soil. However, the new prime minister, Jovan Ristić, almost immediately countermanded the order (issued by the minister of the interior) and within a few hours Marković was released.[67]

Ristić, who had earlier rejected the slightest compromise with the socialists, was not motivated wholly by selfless magnanimity. Late in March Blaznavac, who had been prime minister since August of 1872, had suddenly and unexpectedly died at the age of forty-eight.[68] Having attained his majority the previous summer, Prince Milan went against the advice of nearly every politician in Serbia and appointed Ristić to form a new government. Ristić had become unpopular with both liberals and conservatives because of his association with bureaucratic scandals.[69] Finding many of his former friends now opposed to him, Ristić hoped to forestall the addition of the socialists to the ranks of his enemies; hence his order for Marković's release.

After spending a few weeks in Belgrade, Marković

65 Savić, *loc. cit.* Radovanović had been one of the leaders of the Vojvodina liberals. He was arrested in 1868 along with Svetozar Miletić, Vladimir Jovanović, and Liuben Karavelov on suspicion of complicity in the assassination of Prince Michael. Cf. *Jedinstvo*, no. 207, September 29, 1872.

66 Milutinović, "Proterivanje Svetozara Markovića," pp. 354-356.

67 *Skerlić*, p. 92.

68 It was rumored in Serbia that Blaznavac died from poison administered by Prince Milan, but Slobodan Jovanović has blamed lack of proper medical attention; *Vlada Milana*, I, p. 164.

69 On the scandals see *Vlada Milana*, I, pp. 165ff., 193ff.

traveled to a mineral springs, Aranđelovac, in central Serbia for a rest cure. He remained at the resort until late in August of 1873, resting, conferring frequently with Nikola Pašić (who was working near by as a civil engineer), and carrying on an extensive correspondence.

SOCIALISM RECONSIDERED

Marković's letters in the spring and summer of 1873 reflected the changes that had taken place in his thinking during his exile. To his nephew Nikola Marković (who later founded the first successful socialist journal in the Vojvodina) he wrote that the reorganization of Serbian society could take but two forms: either there would develop a capitalist system with its attendant division of the population into capitalists and workers, followed by a social revolution, or the small proprietors (the majority of the population) would voluntarily renounce private property and organize collectives. The latter form was, in his view, not only preferable but possible; and since it could be introduced as a result of a peaceful political reform, it would avoid social revolution. The social revolution would be unavoidable only in the Banat, where there already existed a class of capitalists-landlords, and in Bosnia-Hercegovina, where Turkish feudalism still held forth. In the rest of the Serb lands, Marković wrote, "our task is not to destroy capitalism, which in fact does not exist, but rather to transform small patriarchal property into collective property, in order *to leap over an entire historical epoch of economic development—the epoch of capitalist economy.*"[70]

The visionary socialism which Marković envisaged was outlined in a letter to the Ninković sisters: "A socialist society is one in which each member of society has the opportunity to develop to their limits all his natural capa-

[70] *C.d.*, VII, pp. 63-65.

bilities; it is a society where every individual is concerned to see that all members of the society attain this, their natural goal. It is a society in which the individual does not regard his personal labor as a means of *controlling* material goods or creating private property, but rather as a part of social labor, and the product of his labor as a part of the products of social labor, which all use in accordance with the goal which a socialist society wishes to attain."[71] The principles of a socialist society, he told the sisters, were industry and sympathy for one's fellow man. It was clear that Chernyshevsky had begun to triumph over Marx. Marković wrote at about this time: "In the whole Marxist theory of economic evolution there is only one, but an extremely important, error. The development of capitalistic society is the history of western European society; the laws which are cited as the laws of the development of this society are indeed completely accurate. But they are not laws of human society in general. It is not necessary for every society to pass through all the same steps of economic development through which industrial society (for example, England, which Karl Marx had predominantly in view) went. If the English workers had been in a different situation and at another stage of development when the machine was invented and introduced in England, they naturally would under no circumstances have permitted the development of capitalistic economy to reach perfection, but would earlier have pondered the problem of the reorganization of society. With this we wish to say that any society can reform its system of economy, founded on small-scale property, and can introduce the most perfected machine production, and absolutely does not have to go through the purgatory of capitalist production."[72]

71 *Izbrannye Sochineniia*, pp. 825-830.

72 Marković, *Načela narodne ekonomije ili nauka o narodnom blagostanju* (*po N. G. Černiševskom*) (*The Principles of Political Economy, or Science of the National Welfare* [*According to N. G. Chernyshevsky*]), Belgrade, 1874, pp. 20-21.

It was one of the earliest statements of "separate roads to socialism." Rejecting Marx's rigid determinism, Marković held that, while mankind is universally the same, society is not and each society must pursue a course dictated by its own characteristics. Backward, agricultural Serbia did not have to repeat the mistakes made in England during the Industrial Revolution; surely, Marković insisted, man's reason would permit him to profit by the mistakes of others.

Though it can scarcely be considered a criticism, it must be pointed out that Marković did not solve the problem of the "original accumulation of capital." Karl Marx held such accumulation to be possible only through the development of capitalism; latter-day Marxists in the Soviet Union have added the convenient codicil that it may be possible when a developed, industrialized, *socialist* society renders assistance to the "under-developed" nations.[73] Marković did not see, and the Marxists in the Soviet Union have ignored, the fact that the major element in accumulation is domestic—often forced—savings, i.e., accumulation at someone's expense. In Europe, whether the society be capitalist or socialist, the most likely victim is invariably the peasant.[74]

In his concept of capitalism and socialism Marković was still attempting to synthesize the teachings of Marx and the Russian socialists. In this connection Chernyshevsky's biographer has written that the Russian economist "repeatedly and persistently underlines the *historical and transient character not only of the capitalist system, but also of private property*."[75] Marx of course did likewise,

[73] Cf., for example, Karataev, *Ekonomicheskaia platforma*, pp. 54-55.

[74] Israel is perhaps the most striking example of the exception which proves the rule; in that country foreign economic aid has indeed played a significant factor in accumulation.

[75] Iu. M. Steklov, *N. G. Chernyshevskii: Ego zhizn' i deiatel'nost'* (*N. G. Chernyshevsky: His Life and Work*), I, Moscow-Leningrad, 1928, p. 561.

but Marković and Chernyshevsky both disagreed with him on the implications of the phenomenon; both Slavs insisted that their countries could avoid the capitalist stage, and both remained rather vague as to the means necessary to create socialism. Marković was not at all a social revolutionary, while Chernyshevsky (who abhorred violence) equivocated on the matter. Similarly, the thinking of both men with regard to the state was "tinged with a wariness of Leviathan,"[76] but Marković went beyond Chernyshevsky and (anticipating Kropotkin and the anarcho-syndicalists) held that not only capitalism and private property but also the state itself had an historical and transient character. Marković wanted to turn what he considered the exploiting state into a social state, whose primary function would be "the regulation of economic life and . . . the organization of work in the interest of society as a whole, i.e., for the creation of wealth to be used by the whole society."[77] Nowhere did Marković discuss the "withering away of the state," but he clearly looked forward to its ultimate reduction to the role of information bureau, serving as a clearinghouse for transactions between the autonomous local units (the communes).

Now in the summer of 1873 Marković had come back to his Russian teachers. Chernyshevsky as an economist and social reformer was of especial importance "for us Serbs," he wrote, for he "fully understands the difference between an industrial and an agricultural society, the difference in the methods they must take in order to transform private property into collective and in general to solve the social problem according to its own characteristics."[78]

76 Yarmolinsky, *Road to Revolution*, p. 96.

77 Prodanović, *Shvatanje Svetozara Markovića o državi*, pp. 39-53, 121-124.

78 Quoted in *Skerlić*, pp. 129-130.

Lavrov too was of importance to Serbian socialism, Marković added, for he had defined more clearly than Chernyshevsky the means of introducing socialism on a gradualist, legitimate basis without resorting to social revolution. Marković's activities in the last two years of his life were to prove that Chernyshevsky above all others had provided the foundation for his theory, Lavrov the method by which it might be implemented.

The largely uncritical infatuation with Marx and the International was now a thing of the past. Marković continued (though much less vehemently and dogmatically than in the *Radenik* period) to proclaim his support of Marx in his struggle with Bakunin, but he had had his doubts as early as 1871 when he wrote that Marxist theory "does not give any positive basis for the solution of the social problem in Serbia,"[79] and late in 1873 he observed that the crisis in the floundering International "lies much deeper in the very differences in industrial development among different peoples. I hold that Marx's program, which the International adopted, is in the first place *one-sided and inapplicable* to almost all nations except England. According to it the International will in all countries be in the minority and will never seize 'power.' Accordingly the tendency to create a wide socialist program is justified . . . ; the International must put forth a wide program and not just 'the struggle of the proletariat with the bourgeoisie,' or it will disintegrate and come to ruin in its own bailiwick."[80]

According to the Soviet scholar B. P. Koz'min, Marković in rejecting Marxism "made a mistake analogous to that which our *narodniki* [populists] made. Like them he was convinced of the possibility of building socialism without a proletariat."[81] The leading Soviet student of

[79] *Ibid.*, p. 145. [80] Quoted in *ibid.*, p. 139.
[81] Koz'min, *Russkaia sektsiia*, pp. 237-238.

Marković's work, V. G. Karasëv, has similarly written that "Markovich did not rise to an understanding of the conformity with law and historical conditionality with which social formations are superseded one by the other. All this compels us to draw the conclusion that Markovich approached the evaluation of the events of socio-political and socio-economic life in Serbia not as a proletarian socialist, but as a revolutionary democrat, remaining on the position of utopian socialism."[82] And, finally, the liberal Serbian historian Slobodan Jovanović has written of Marković that "he found fault with Marx's principles which, he held, are valid only for a definite class in a definite society. He did not understand the essence of the strength of Marxism. He searched for general principles which could inspire all men regardless of class, and held that in Chernyshevsky he found those principles, and he intended . . . to win the world to them. Obviously he was a victim of utopian socialism."[83]

Both Marxist and liberal views are clearly erroneous. Marković did indeed understand the "essence of the strength of Marxism" *in the industrialized West*, and he gave Marx full credit for "correctly" analyzing the development of the West and offering a "solution" to the evils of an industrialized, proletarianized society. But the "solution" did not apply to Serbia. Marković had written in the *Radenik* program that the goal of Serbian socialism was "to create *educated workers, workers with capital, to create collective capital and collective production*." Why should Serbia, which had no oppressed proletariat, create one? The Marxist view of Marković absurdly depicts him as a reactionary; since Marxism holds that capitalism represents a progressive phase of economic development, Marković therefore had only two alternatives: he could either

[82] Karasëv, *Svetozar Markovich*, p. 328.
[83] Jovanović, "Svetozar Marković," p. 85.

have supported the growth of capitalism (while screaming at the workers, "You are not miserable enough for socialism!"), or he could have retired and waited patiently for several generations to create an industrialized, proletarianized society. He of course did neither. He sought a socialism based upon communal institutions and instincts rather than upon inexorable historical "laws." His was in essence an ethical rather than a materialist socialism; if it was visionary it was also humane, and on both counts unacceptable to his Marxist critics. Marković would probably have been grateful for their abuse.

Having earlier in the year decided that all his previous work had been "in error," Marković struggled in the summer of 1873 with the problem of a parliamentary policy for the socialist party (the first socialist deputies were elected to the National Assembly the following year). At one point he went so far as to reconsider the Lassallean state socialism which he had previously rejected; he praised both Lassalle and Lorenz von Stein, though criticizing the latter's "metaphysical style" and "abstract Hegelian logic."[84] The possibility of an alliance between the socialists and the state did not, however, long detain him. He set forth his own "wide socialist program" in a letter to the Ninković sisters early in November of 1873.[85] The program is here reproduced virtually in its entirety; imperfect though it was, it represented the essence of Marković's views on social reform, and it was the program pursued by the socialist deputies during their first three years in the National Assembly:

[84] *Izbrannye sochineniia*, p. 838; in the *Communist Manifesto* Marx and Engels referred to Stein's program as "feudal socialism," and Engels later called Stein a "speculating wiseacre" who "translated foreign propositions into undigested Hegelian language." Cf. *Marx and Engels: Selected Works*, I, p. 367.

[85] The 1873 program is in *Skerlić*, pp. 169-171.

1. The complete destruction, by decision of the National Assembly, of the existing system of government;
2. A provisional committee, elected from the ranks of the National Assembly, will in the beginning be the central government; later this committee will be replaced by another consisting of delegates elected from each district. . . .
3. In the districts there will be elected similar committees which will have control of the administration of economic, educational and other affairs concerning the individual districts;
4. The Central Committee will execute the resolutions of the National Assembly, and the district committees those of the district assemblies and the pertinent resolutions of the National Assembly;
5. The police administration will be transferred wholly into the hands of the individual communes [*opštinas*];
6. The existing judicial system will be liquidated completely; in its place there will be only elected judges (jurors), who it is understood will serve without pay or at the expense of the litigants.

   Note. [Marković here outlines a system providing for district courts and courts of appeal in the event that it is impossible immediately to introduce a wholly decentralized, elective judicial system.]
7. The financial system will have a particularly independent arrangement: at the head there will be a central bank, which will administer state income and expenditures; in the districts district banks will be established to administer all district financial affairs. These banks will simultaneously serve all economic needs, for example, the development of collective, communal industry, the construction of roads and construction in general, credit, etc.
8. The liquidation of all debts on the land of the agricultural class. There are various methods of achieving this:
   a) The liquidation of the national debt in the Uprava Fondova* and the invalidation of all debts owed private creditors. The obligations of the state to

* The Uprava Fondova was the central state credit institution.

orphans, paupers, and . . . others can be assumed by the people and paid from the general national income. This is the simplest and most radical method, but it is simultaneously the most dangerous;

b) The national debt of the Uprava Fondova can be assumed by the nation at large and debts owed private creditors by the communes. But beforehand judges elected from the ranks of the peasants of the district would decide whether a debt is usurious and therefore invalid, or just and therefore deserving of payment. In recompense [for its assumption of just debts] the commune will become the proprietor of the indebted land and will give it for the benefit of each member of the commune. . . .

9. Land can be held only by those who work it. All land which does not belong to those occupied in agriculture belongs to the commune in which it lies. This will be legalized by the National Assembly.

10. In order to ensure the Serbian people against proletarianization it is necessary that all private land be turned into communal. How this can be accomplished and in what length of time remains to be seen.

Note. When the [socialist] party is organized it will, in accordance with these general principles, work out a detailed plan for the future organization of Serbian society and a plan for its own practical work to achieve that end.

Marković became dissatisfied with the program, which his biographer has called "more radical than socialist,"[86] almost as soon as he had formulated it. It was justified, in his view, only by the "chaotic and disordered" conditions in Serbia and the attendant difficulties facing all political parties.[87] The program attempted to solve the problems facing the Serbian peasant through a policy of land nationalization. Such a policy had been adopted four years earlier at the Basle Congress of the International, though its impact had been diminished by the struggle between

[86] *Skerlić*, p. 139. [87] *Ibid.*, p. 171.

Marxists and Bakuninists over the right of inheritance. *Narodnoe Delo* and the Russian Section had enthusiastically embraced the concept, and called for the surrender of the Russian land to the *obshchinas*.[88] The association of his Russian "brother revolutionaries" with the policy doubtless made it easier for Marković to accept it, despite his mild disaffection with the International.

THE PLIGHT OF THE PEASANTRY

The Serbian peasant in the late sixties and early seventies was in difficult circumstances. The world-wide "Great Depression" of 1873-79 had begun earlier in Serbia, and had compounded the existing distress of the peasant class. In his address opening the 1873 session of the National Assembly Prince Milan observed that "the commercial and financial crisis which has in this year reached the greatest proportions in the largest world markets, and which has not come to an end, has placed our trade in a most difficult situation. The preceding years of poor harvests are responsible for the fact that this crisis has had a much more severe effect upon us than would normally be the case."[89] The poor harvests and the effects of the depression were only partly responsible for the plight of the Serbian peasant. Far more significant were the unsolved problems of land tenure and agricultural credit.

The disintegration of the communalist (*zadruga*) system of land tenure began when Serbia won her autonomy early in the nineteenth century. The old system was destroyed in four ways: (1) willful seizure of the land; (2) allotment of communal land to immigrants and poor members of the *opština*; (3) sale and confiscation of communal lands for debts; (4) division of collective property among the

[88] Karataev, *Ekonomicheskaia platforma*, pp. 21-23.

[89] Quoted in V. G. Karasëv, *Svetozar Markovich*, p. 64.

members of the *zadruga.*[90] The richest and most aggressive peasants seized the best Moslem lands,[91] and a small "kulak" class came into existence; the majority of the peasants, however, owned only a few acres of land.

Left to shift for himself in the wholly unfamiliar world of a competitive economy lacking the security of the patriarchal *zadruga,* the average Serbian peasant was slowly driven toward disaster. He was now obliged to purchase on his own the tools, seed, and household items he required. He was moreover required to purchase these items, and pay the taxes necessary for the support of the bureaucracy and the army, in cash rather than in kind. High taxes, inefficient farming and poor harvests, reckless buying on credit, and the absence of regulated credit facilities forced the peasant to turn to the village usurer.

Despite legislation under Miloš and Michael Obrenović (1836, 1860-62, 1865) to protect peasant holdings, peasant indebtedness had by the seventies reached serious proportions and many peasants were being deprived of their land in settlement of debts. The state credit institution (*Uprava Fondova*) founded in 1862 had proved a miserable failure; it had no branches in the interior of the country, and the illiterate peasant who went to Belgrade was obliged to fill out a maze of documents in order to receive a loan.[92] Five district savings banks were opened in 1871 with the aim of helping the peasant by eliminating his dependence upon the usurer, but they likewise proved

[90] M. S. Shikhareva, "Sel'skaia obshchina u serbov v XIX-nachale XX v." ("The Serbian Village Commune in the 19th and Beginning of the 20th Century"), *Sovetskaia Etnografiia,* 1959, no. 6, pp. 103-104.

[91] Slobodan Jovanović, *Ustavobranitelji (The Defenders of the Constitution),* Belgrade, 1912, p. 14.

[92] P. A. Rovinsky compared the situation in Serbia, where "in all affairs, even the most minor details among simple people, all had to be on paper, with lawyers handling everything," with that in Russia, where "innumerable commercial transactions take place without any kind of written documents," "Belgrad," part II, p. 164.

ineffectual. The original maximum loan was five hundred Austrian ducats, and small loans were effectively discouraged. As a result the usurers themselves borrowed large sums from the banks at a low interest rate, then made small loans to the peasants at high rates. In 1874 the banks were reorganized and empowered to issue loans ranging from five to one hundred ducats, but bureaucratic corruption and inefficiency remained; the ubiquitous usurer was not seriously hampered nor the peasant significantly helped.[93]

The peasant remained unprotected from both his own folly and the clutches of the usurer, but though he was ignorant he was not wholly powerless. As he had occasionally resorted to banditry during the centuries of Turkish rule, so he now, in the 1870's, organized mass armed demonstrations of protest. In December of 1873 two hundred armed peasants gathered in Kragujevac to demand that the government call a temporary halt, pending new legislation, to all legal actions against the peasantry. Led by Jevrem Marković,[94] the demonstrators complained that many of their number were being forced into bankruptcy and forced to sell all their possessions (at a fraction of their value) in order to settle debts.[95] Numerous other demonstrations, most on a smaller scale, were held in the years 1873-78; occasionally there were arrests, but in at least one instance the peasants forcibly freed one of their number who had been seized by the police.[96]

Coincidentally with the December demonstration in Kragujevac (the seat of the National Assembly) the Serbian government again attempted to halt the process which was rapidly transforming Serbia into "a country of predominantly dwarf farms."[97] On Christmas Eve (Old

93 *Vlada Milana*, I, pp. 189-190; Karasëv, "Osnovnye cherty," pp. 217-241.
94 *Vlada Milana*, p. 213.
95 Milutinović, "Agrarna problematika," pp. 84-85.
96 Karasëv, "Osnovnye cherty," p. 226.
97 Stavrianos, *The Balkans Since 1453*, pp. 261-262.

Style), 1873, the National Assembly passed the unique "Six-day Land Law" which prohibited the alienation from the peasant (even at his own wish) of the amount of land he could plow in five days plus his household plot (one day's plowing). The assumption being that 5,760 square meters constituted the amount of land that one man could plow in one day, the peasant was thus to be guaranteed a minimum of 3.456 hectares (about 8.6 acres) of inalienable land. The law further stipulated that certain items of movable property could not under any circumstances be seized in lieu of payment of debts: one plow, one cart, two oxen or working horses, a hoe, an axe, a pickaxe, a scythe, ample grain for food, fodder, and seed. An exception to the law was provided for those who wished to abandon farming altogether; it was a loophole which the usurer immediately seized upon to trap the perplexed peasant into giving up his land. The alienation of peasant land proceeded, albeit at a reduced pace.[98]

The "Six-day Land Law" was passed by a National Assembly dominated by peasant deputies who felt that legal protection of a minimum of land was the only solution to the ever-worsening problem of peasant indebtedness.[99] They, and the Serbian government which sponsored the law, failed to see that their "solution," which did nothing but attempt to prevent further pauperization, would inevitably have the effect of imposing a rigid legality upon the existing system of subsistence farming. Since the "guaranteed minimum" of less than three and a half hectares of land was not even half the amount required to support a family of five, the "Six-day Land Law" was in many respects worse than useless. It confirmed rather than solved the problem, but remained in force until 1945.[100]

[98] *Vlada Milana*, I, pp. 185-186; Karasëv, "Osnovnye cherty," pp. 222-223. On the methods used by the usurers to circumvent the law, see Petrović, *Okućje ili zaštita zemljoradničkog minimuma*, pp. 278-284.

[99] *Vlada Milana*, I, p. 187.

[100] Cf. Tomasevich, *Peasants, Politics and Economic Change*, pp. 42-45.

A conservative minority of well-to-do peasants and merchants in the National Assembly argued that peasant indebtedness was not a cause but a consequence of impoverishment. In their view the process of pauperization could not be checked by denying credit facilities to the peasant (the law prohibited the use of land for collateral).[101] The conservative deputies (some of whom were moneylenders) recognized the fundamental character of the credit problem, but in their zeal to uphold the rights of property they aligned themselves with the usurious creditors against the peasantry. Their shortsighted and truculent stand could only benefit the radical-socialists, who presented themselves as the defenders of the peasant against bureaucrat and usurer.

In the Marxist view Serbia's difficulties lay in the problems of her "unfinished bourgeois revolution." Marković adopted the "bourgeois" slogan of land nationalization, it is argued, because he and his radical-socialists "appeared in the historical arena at that moment when, in the course of Serbia's social development, there was placed on the agenda the task of the completion of the bourgeois revolution. The solution of this task would clear the way for the free development of capitalism and the opening of the class struggle."[102] There are a number of serious objections to such a glib interpretation. In the first place, the Serbian Revolution began as an attempt to restore the benevolent paternalism of Hadji Mustapha, and in its later stages (1804-30) was manifestly national rather than bourgeois. What followed after the winning of autonomy was bourgeois evolution rather than revolution. Secondly, the dialectical materialist argument can only with diffi-

101 *Vlada Milana*, I, p. 186.

102 Karasëv, "Osnovnye cherty," p. 241. The same author has written that Marković, despite his adoption of the "bourgeois" slogan of land nationalization, was, nevertheless, "head and shoulders above his contemporary bourgeois sociologists." Karasëv, "Revoliutsionno-demokraticheskaia programma Svetozara Markovića" ("The Revolutionary-Democratic Program of Svetozar Marković"), *UZIS*, VI, 1952, p. 66.

culty be applied to nineteenth-century Serbia, for there was no strong feudalism to challenge the evolving capitalism. Serbian feudalism had never been of the classic variety, for the reciprocal contracts were between lord and commune (through the village elder) rather than lord and peasant, and there was no manorial economy. Certainly there were feudal survivals after the Serbs became masters in their own country, but to attribute them to an "incomplete bourgeois revolution"[103] makes it impossible to explain why they were *maintained* by the *bourgeoisie*.[104]

The major shortcoming of the Marxist interpretation is its insistence upon the emergence of a massive class struggle. In Serbia, as in every society, some exploitation of man by man did indeed exist, but it was due far more to monumental ineptitude and inefficiency on the part of the government, the illiteracy of the population, and individual greed and corruption rather than to a struggle between classes. In the largely undifferentiated Serbian society of the nineteenth century Serbian nationalism remained a vastly more important force than class conflict.[105] Ideologies appeal at least as much to temperament as to class, and the Serbs had had more than four hundred years of psychological conditioning in the complex and powerful ideology of a suppressed nationalism.

Svetozar Marković himself, as his "wide program" clearly indicated, had by now rejected a Marxist approach. His adoption of a policy of land nationalization allied him with a wide variety of Western socialist schools, but like those schools he was unable to develop a satisfactory con-

[103] So argue M. S. Shikhareva, "Sel'skaia obshchina u serbov," p. 100, and V. G. Karasëv, *Svetozar Markovich*, pp. 33-34, "Osnovnye cherty," p. 208.

[104] Tomasevich, *Peasants, Politics, and Economic Change*, pp. 102-104, 189-190.

[105] V. G. Karasëv admits that "the task of the completion of the bourgeois revolution in Serbia was interwoven in the closest manner with the national-liberation struggle of the South Slav peoples," "Osnovnye cherty," p. 241.

clusion from his basic premise; his new shibboleth proclaimed a policy but not a program. Certainly it was useless in his struggle to reconcile the nationalism of his countrymen with his theories of social justice.

In the final months of his life Marković was to make one last attempt to rally both alienated intelligentsia and peasantry to the cause of socialism. He spent those final months in the feverish development of a sweeping program of communalism.

CHAPTER VI

Svetozar Marković and Zadruga Socialism

DURING his absence from Serbia Svetozar Marković had finally come to realize that he could neither shame nor cajole the government into accepting his program for social reform, and that the only possible way to achieve his goals (given his rejection of the social revolution) was to secure a parliamentary majority for his party. Even then, as he knew, success would not be assured; the prince was not obligated to appoint his ministers from the ranks of the majority party, and indeed Milan frequently chose a minority prime minister. Furthermore, effective ministerial responsibility to the National Assembly did not, as Marković himself often pointed out, exist. Nevertheless, he chose the path of parliamentary reform; he followed Lavrov rather than Bakunin or Tkachëv.

When Marković resumed his active work in the autumn of 1873 no radical-socialist deputy had yet been elected to the Assembly. Growing peasant unrest, however, indicated that the prospects for the election of 1874 were not without promise. Marković himself had no political ambitions; he preferred to remain the ideologist rather than the politician of the radical-socialist party. It was a fateful choice. Though he could have been elected in any of several constituencies, he considered himself of more value to his cause as a journalist and publicist, and the law prohibited editors from standing for election.[1]

[1] One of Marković's friends, Uroš Knežević, was later prosecuted under the law which forbade editors to engage in political contests; cf. *Budućnost*, Belgrade, no. 91, November 9, 1874.

During Marković's absence from Serbia his colleagues had not been idle. Preparations for the revolt in Bosnia-Hercegovina had proceeded steadily, and a considerable store of small arms was collected and hidden in various parts of Serbia.[2] Socialist agitation among the students and peasants, interrupted by the brief and relatively mild repression which followed the closing of *Radenik*, resumed during the winter of 1872-73. Such agitation increased greatly during the months following the death of the regent Blaznavac; a high point was the peasant demonstration in Kragujevac in December of 1873.

The cause of the radical-socialists was aided by a new split in the ranks of their chief opponents. The liberals in southern Serbia, the Šumadija region, had become increasingly dissatisfied with the opportunism of the Belgrade branch of the party, which the southerners accused of breaking faith with the traditions of the 1858 St. Andrew National Assembly.[3] The southern liberals, who were to make common cause with the radical-socialists in the period 1873-76, thus allied themselves with the opposition liberals in Belgrade. The latter, led by Ljubomir Kaljević and Uroš Knežević,[4] founded a newspaper in 1873 as a forum for their disagreement with the government. The newspaper, *Budućnost* (*The Future*), despite the fact that it had among its writers the ideologist of the *government* liberals, Vladimir Jovanović, became the outstanding voice of the liberal opposition. Modeled to a great extent upon Svetozar Miletić's *Zastava*, *Budućnost* criticized the government-liberal and conservative press severely for their slavish adherence to the government line and their defense of the corrupt and inefficient bureaucracy.[5]

[2] *IAB*, Svetozar to Jevrem Marković, December 20 [1873], Kragujevac, letter no. 11.

[3] *Skerlić*, p. 93.

[4] I have been unable to determine whether Uroš Knežević was related to Marković's St. Petersburg roommate, Aleksa Knežević.

[5] Cf. *Budućnost*, nos. 4-9, January 11-23, 1873; nos. 71-74, 1874; no. 1, January 1, 1875.

RETURN OF THE SOCIALIST PRESS

Early in the autumn of 1873 Svetozar Marković found an ideal vehicle for his own work. The previous March a group of "progressive bureaucrats, officers and citizens, free-thinking liberals, socialists and ordinary, well-intentioned 'friends of enlightenment' "[6] had founded a society, the Kragujevac Social Printing-Works, for the establishment of a press and a newspaper in Kragujevac, the seat of the National Assembly and the heart of south Serbian radicalism. Pera Todorović, one of the leaders in the Bosnia-Hercegovina revolutionary plot, turned over his inheritance of 2,500 Austrian ducats to the society; another of its leaders was the army officer Sava Grujić, who had studied in St. Petersburg concurrently with Marković, been one of the mainstays of *Radenik*, and who now managed the Kragujevac arms factory. Grujić later abandoned the socialist movement, held many high posts in the government, and served two terms as prime minister.

Todorović wrote to Marković in Aranđelovac of the excellent opportunities for work in Kragujevac. He noted that the town contained many potential supporters of the radical-socialist movement, and he urged Marković to accept the invitation of the society to edit the newspaper it proposed to publish. Marković did so immediately. His intention was, according to Jovan Skerlić, to work with the Todorović-Grujić group temporarily, editing an innocuous journal; at the proper moment he would seize full control and give the publication a "wholly red color."[7]

The first issue of the newspaper, *Javnost* (*The Public*), appeared on November 8, 1873. Svetozar Marković was the "paid and responsible" editor (thus earning his own living for the first time in his life) and the Kragujevac Social Printing-Works the publisher. *Javnost* differed from *Ra-*

6 *Skerlić*, p. 93.
7 *Ibid.*, pp. 93-94.

denik in many respects. Where the latter journal had placed overwhelming importance upon socialist theory, and had devoted (with the exception of its discussion of the railroad issue) its columns to propagandizing the Commune, the International, and an attenuated Marxism, *Javnost* relegated theory to a secondary role and discussed the multitude of political and economic problems which confronted Serbia. The November 8 issue outlined those problems: peasant indebtedness and bankruptcy, usury, bureaucratic corruption, the strangling of the *zadruga* and *opština* by the oppressive police regime.[8] *Javnost* promised to work for the elimination of such evils by "educating public opinion, giving it a scientific direction, and creating out of public opinion a force which will have a strong influence on the solution of all problems concerning our national life."[9]

Despite its sharp criticism of the régime, the tone of *Javnost* was coldly objective rather than demagogic. It was a more mature and logical Marković who edited the journal; gone was the bombastic approach he had followed in *Radenik*. If the *Radenik* days be considered (admittedly a somewhat dubious analogy) his Jacobin period, *Javnost* now clearly marked him for the Girondin (more precisely, the Lavrovian) he was.

A new conservative government had come to power two weeks prior to the appearance of *Javnost*, and for a time it seemed that the newspaper would be allowed to publish in peace. Marković wrote of a "honeymoon" between the radical-socialists and the new government,[10] and, secure

[8] *Javnost*'s comment on the *zadrugas* and *opštinas* was confirmed by P. A. Rovinsky, who wrote in 1870 that the *zadruga* "is absolutely paralyzed by the police." Cf. "Belgrad," part II, p. 164.

[9] *Skerlić*, p. 95; I have been unable to locate a copy of the first issue of *Javnost*.

[10] *IAB*, Svetozar to Jevrem Marković, December 2, [1873], Kragujevac, letter no. 10; see also letter no. 11.

in its provincial headquarters, in such circumstances *Javnost* flourished.

Provincial life was, as the Russian commentator P. A. Rovinsky noted, far more progressive and stimulating than that in Belgrade: "In Belgrade there is too much cringing before the government and there is no free public opinion, while in the provincial towns public opinion is expressed so freely that time and again it has come into conflict with the local powers. In the provinces there is more enterprise in all affairs. . . . In the provinces I found more freedom in family relations and less seclusion of women."[11] The freer and more independent atmosphere which obtained in the provinces, especially in the Šumadija, was in part due to the fact that the farther from Belgrade, the fewer of the former Habsburg Serbs (*prečani*). Such individuals, reared in the ordered and civilized Habsburg domains, flocked to Serbia by the thousands after the principality won its autonomy. Educated (at least through the *gimnazija* level) and relatively "cultured" in the Western sense, they were a race apart from the Serbian Serbs. They quickly insinuated themselves, in many cases by default rather than ability, into all levels of the bureaucracy and educational system. Like all bureaucrats, their goal was the capital, Belgrade, and they resisted transfer to the provinces. Bureaucratic scandals, of which Svetozar Marković was the most perceptive and effective critic, were a common phenomenon and a major reason for the transfer of the National Assembly to Kragujevac in 1871.[12]

In addition to being the seat of the National Assembly, Kragujevac offered other advantages to the radical-socialists. The arms factory managed by Sava Grujić was the largest industrial establishment in the principality (and

11 "Belgrad," part 1, pp. 570-572.

12 Zh. (Živojin Žujović), "Serbskoe selo" ("The Serbian Village"), *Sovremennik*, St. Petersburg, no. 5, May, 1865, p. 126; Karasëv, "Osnovnye cherty," p. 231; Slobodan Jovanović, "Svetozar Marković," pp. 105-132.

one of the half dozen deserving the name "factory"), and its two or three hundred workers represented a sizable fraction of the tiny "industrial proletariat." A teachers' school had been founded in 1871, and its students were receptive to the radical-socialist program. The workers and students, together with the rebellious peasants and several dissident army officers, gave *Javnost* a relatively large audience.[13]

Despite the fact that Kragujevac had half the population (approximately 10,000) of Belgrade, the new journal of the radical-socialists attracted nearly nine hundred subscribers in the first month of its existence and the number grew steadily.[14] Svetozar Marković wrote most of the leading articles in the journal; Sava Grujić, Pera Todorović, Nikola Pašić, and others contributed shorter pieces, and Jevrem Marković regularly reported local news from his home in Jagodina.

Marković's plans to edit an innocuous journal notwithstanding, *Javnost* became extremely critical of the government during the first month of its existence. Marković openly challenged the intentions not only of the government but also of the prince, accusing both of pursuing a policy of flagrant opportunism. He scoffed at the feeble legislation proposed by the government to protect the peasants (the "Six-day Land Law"), and in a lengthy, serialized article he discussed the problem of poverty, which he was careful to distinguish from the "worker problem" of his polemic with Vladan Đorđević. He traced poverty to the twin evils of usury and bureaucracy. Usury, he pointed out, could be liquidated immediately by government decree; the bureaucracy was another matter but not

13 *Vlada Milana*, I, p. 201; Miloš B. Janković, *Đački socijalistički pokret u Srbiji* (*The Student Socialist Movement in Serbia*), Belgrade, 1954, p. 21.

14 *Skerlić*, p. 95, notes that by the beginning of 1874 *Javnost* had 1,100 subscribers, many of whom, as Marković complained (*IAB*, letter no. 10), were slow in making their payments.

an insoluble one. Marković admitted the necessity for a bureaucracy, but insisted that it could be held to a minimum and that proper supervision and legal restraint would eliminate abuses and scandals.[15]

He went on to amplify his "wide program," and outlined a system of local self-government based on the *zadruga* (which he proposed to rehabilitate and modernize) and the *opština*. By eliminating bureaucratic abuses and usury, Marković maintained, productive labor would triumph over unproductive, and "the producer, who now earns barely enough to keep himself alive, would receive a greater stimulus to work if he could see more benefit from his work. Besides that, each individual would have a greater sense of human dignity if he could feel that he was a *citizen* of his country, into whose hands is given the care of himself, the commune, the district, and the state in the authentic sense of the word. . . . In the district assemblies the people would discuss their economic affairs, their fields, their livestock, and in general the betterment of their situation. And this would not be merely empty sounds or words on paper, for if the people in each district have in their own hands legislative and financial power, that is, pooled capital, they would strengthen their decisions with the force of *money*."[16] "*The problem of bread,*" Marković concluded, "*is the problem of self-government.*" Communalism had become his panacea, and in the period of his work for *Javnost* he attempted to show how such a system could solve Serbia's problems.

A major campaign of *Javnost* in November of 1873 was its fight for the freedom of the press. The basic press law in Serbia was that of October 1871, which allowed the police to determine what constituted antigovernment or

[15] Marković's article, "Od kuda dolazi naša siromaština?" ("Whence our Poverty?"), appeared in *Javnost*, nos. 3, 6, 8, 9 of November 14-23, 1874.

[16] *Ibid.*, no. 9, November 23, 1874.

antidynasty journalism; a capricious local censorship was thus established, and *Javnost* frequently appeared with blank spaces, to indicate that the police had excised objectionable passages. The socialist journal devoted a series of penetrating articles (apparently not the work of Svetozar Marković) to the press law and demanded its revision; *Budućnost*, which itself frequently suffered from the censor's scissors, joined in the call for a more liberal attitude on the part of the government.[17]

In December *Javnost* increased the severity and frequency of its attacks on the government, and singled out the minister of the interior, Aćim Čumić, for special abuse. The journal particularly condemned what it called Čumić's equivocation on land reform and his abuse of his ministerial powers.[18] Čumić had earlier been a renegade conservative; he had joined with Jevrem Marković and Vasa Pelagić to draw up a political program calling for extreme decentralization,[19] and until 1873 had been extremely critical of the liberal régime in Belgrade. He was persuaded by Prince Milan to enter the conservative government of Jovan Marinović which followed that of Ristić.

Čumić replied to *Javnost*'s attack with a letter which the radical-socialist journal printed on December 12. He insisted that the proposed "Six-day Land Law" was sound and progressive, and he challenged the claim that he had opposed the concept of ministerial responsibility. He pointed out that it was impossible to accept the proposal (made by Svetozar Marković) that the National Assembly as a unit review every single item of business that came before it, since the bulk of parliamentary work was of necessity done in committee. He defended the supremacy

17 *Ibid.*, nos. 8, 10, 11, 12 of November 22-27, 1873; see also *Budućnost* for November of 1873.

18 *Javnost*, no. 17, December 6, 1873.

19 See above, p. 155.

of the ministers, claiming that theirs was a greater responsibility than that of the Assembly to the nation and the prince.[20]

Marković refused to accept Čumić's argument. He repeated his objections to the proposed "Six-day Land Law," claiming that the arguments he personally had heard in the Assembly in defense of it were "worthless." He objected to the law on three counts: it was proposed by supporters of the government rather than by the people themselves in their district councils; it did not guarantee the peasant secure title to his land; it provided loopholes for unscrupulous usurers. Marković demanded that the Assembly consider the problems of land tenure and usury separately and, further, that the proposed "guaranteed minimum" of 3.456 hectares be doubled. He renewed his attack on the government and on Čumić personally, and insisted that Serbia could not be said to have a free and independent parliamentary government until the principle of full ministerial responsibility to the National Assembly was accepted.[21]

Serbian ruling circles were not disposed to permit such outbursts in *Javnost* indefinitely. A liberal government had permitted *Radenik* to publish for nearly a year, but since that journal had been concerned with what were considered outlandish alien theories it was regarded as comparatively harmless; it was suppressed because of Marković's alleged intrigue with Montenegro rather than for its communism. *Javnost,* however, largely ignored theory and concentrated its attention upon the political and economic life of Serbia. Its attacks on the government and the prince were unrelenting. In a series of articles Marković insisted that the prince was but the servant of the people, who had the right to depose a "bad" prince. The people were the

20 *Javnost,* no. 20, December 12, 1873.
21 *Ibid.,* no. 23, December 17, 1873.

supreme authority in the land, he declared, and through their elected representatives in the National Assembly were (or should be) the masters of both prince and government.[22]

Possibly anticipating the coming conflict with the government, Svetozar Marković relinquished the editorship of *Javnost* to his colleague Dimitrije Stojković late in November. The government began to act soon after. Early in December the minister of the army ordered the dismissal of Captain Sava Grujić from the service, citing his "treacherous" association with *Javnost* and the Kragujevac Social Printing-Works. All officers on active duty were forbidden to participate in the activities of the Printing-Works, which published not only *Javnost* but also numerous brochures and pamphlets written by the radical-socialists.[23] Since the officers as a group had provided the bulk of the financial support of the enterprise, their withdrawal was a serious blow. In a letter to his brother Marković noted that "the 'honeymoon' with the new government is over; now everything is again the same old story."[24]

Sava Grujić contested the order for his dismissal, claiming that he exercised no control over *Javnost* or the Printing-Works, despite the fact that he was titular president of the latter. The government rejected his defense and he was temporarily retired from the service.[25]

Svetozar Marković was the next to feel the wrath of the government. On December 20 he was summoned to police headquarters in Kragujevac to answer for his criticism of the government. He was merely interrogated, however,

22 *Ibid.*, nos. 7, 12, 13, 23, November 20-December 17, 1873; Marković's articles in these issues were presented in evidence against him at his trial.

23 In 1874 the Printing-Works published Sava Grujić's *Vojena organizacija Srbije* (*The Military Organization of Serbia*).

24 *IAB*, Svetozar to Jevrem Marković, letter no. 10; *Vlada Milana*, I, pp. 203-204.

25 *Javnost*, no. 27, December 29, 1873; *IAB*, Svetozar to Jevrem Marković, letter no. 11.

and he wrote to his brother that he probably would not be summoned again.[26] His optimism was unfounded. The local authorities, after consulting with Belgrade,[27] issued an order for Marković's arrest on January 8, 1874; he was immediately lodged in the filthy Kragujevac jail. Dimitrije Stojković was also arrested; under the law it was not necessary to find an indictment immediately, and the two men were held without charge on a detention order signed by a local judge.[28] For the police records Marković gave his occupation as writer; the local authorities, however, jeeringly recorded that he was "nothing but a tramp."[29]

MARKOVIĆ'S TRIAL

Marković's health had already begun to suffer in the unusually cold winter, and the damp, poorly heated cell of the Kragujevac jail was sheer torture for him.[30] His friends attempted to secure his release on bail, but their requests were rejected.[31] He was denied books and writing materials, and was frequently interrogated.[32]

The trial of Svetozar Marković and Dimitrije Stojković for "press crimes" began before a large audience on February 19, 1874.[33] In his opening statement the state prosecu-

26 *IAB*, letter no. 11.

27 The permanent offices of the various ministries remained at all times in Belgrade.

28 *DANRS,* PO k/108, order dated Kragujevac, January 9, 1874, and PO k/110, order dated Kragujevac, January 8, 1874.

29 *Javnost*, no. 18, February 10, 1874.

30 *IAB*, Svetozar to Jevrem Marković, n.p. (but Kragujevac), n.d., letter no. 15.

31 *Budućnost*, no. 3, February 12, 1874.

32 Živan Milisavac, "Svetozar Marković i Matica Srpska" ("Svetozar Marković and Matica Srpska"), *Letopis Matice Srpske*, vol. 358, 1946, p. 185; *Skerlić*, p. 97.

33 The official transcript of the trial is contained in *DANRS*, PO k/102-114. The transcript gives the government case in full but leaves out several key points made by Marković and Stojković in their defense. A full account of both prosecution and defense cases appeared in *Javnost*, nos. 21-25, 1874; *Budućnost*, nos. 15-35, 1874; *Zastava*, nos. 25-33, 1874.

tor, Đoka Stefanović, identified the defendants as the chief writer and responsible editor of *Javnost*, and noted that their journal had pursued a socialist policy "wholly hostile to the laws of this country." Turning first to Marković, Stefanović observed that he "imagines himself that awaited messiah who will reform this country on the basis of socialist principles, and has with his venomous pen . . . recklessly attacked the most important national institutions: the National Assembly, its deputies and ministers; he has charged the National Assembly with breaking the laws of the land; he has justified the raising of a revolt against the ruler of the land; and finally . . . he has not even left in peace the constitutional laws of the founding fathers, but has attacked and insulted even them."[34] In *Javnost* of November 20, 1873, Stefanović charged, Marković had referred to the National Assembly as a mere debating society whose members were more interested in displaying their paragraphical knowledge[35] of the law and their oratorical skills than in working for the good of the nation. He had also criticized in intemperate language Prince Milan's address opening the 1874 session of the National Assembly; therefore, Stefanović charged, he was guilty of violating Paragraph 104 of the Criminal Law of October 24, 1870, which made it a criminal offense to insult the prince or the National Assembly.[36]

In Part II of the indictment Stefanović quoted from Marković's November 30, 1873, article in *Javnost* in which he had written that "the people have always held that they have the right to overthrow a prince who does them evil and replace him with a good one." Clearly it was a call for revolution, Stefanović insisted, and Marković was guilty

[34] *DANRS*, Trial, PO k/102.

[35] The Serbs often referred to bureaucrats as "Mr. Paragraph"; *Oslobođenje*, Kragujevac, no. 21, February 16, 1875.

[36] *DANRS*, Trial, part I of the indictment; see also *Javnost*, no. 21, February 22, 1874; *Zastava*, no. 25, 1874; *Budućnost*, no. 15, 1874.

under Paragraph 92 of the Criminal Law, which made it a felony to preach the overthrow of the prince. Part III of the indictment claimed that Marković had compounded his guilt by accusing the National Assembly of intimidating the press and by "advocating socialism."

The state prosecutor noted that, in the pretrial investigation, Marković had denied that he had called for the overthrow of the prince. He had maintained that the prince's authority was based only on the *Hatt-i Sherifs* of 1830 and 1833 (still technically in force in 1874), and that no reasonable man could believe that those documents any longer had genuine legal significance. To the charge that he had insulted the National Assembly, Marković had not, Stefanović noted, made any defense.

Finally, turning to Stojković, Stefanović claimed that he had pleaded innocent to the charges against him, insisting that he was a mere figurehead. Editorial control of *Javnost*, according to Stojković, had resided solely with Svetozar Marković.[37] It was at first glance a cowardly defense, an impression strengthened when the prosecution produced a letter (which does not appear in the transcript of the trial) from one of the members of the Kragujevac Social Printing-Works purporting to show that Stojković's role had indeed been a minor one on *Javnost*.[38] During the course of the trial, however, it became obvious that Stojković's "defense" had been conceived and foisted upon him by Marković, who wished to be alone in his martyrdom. Marković had seen in Russia how Chernyshevsky's influence had grown enormously after his own imprisonment and exile, and he was convinced that the radical-socialist movement would benefit greatly by his persecution at the hands of the Serbian government.

Marković had deliberately sought arrest. He had returned to Serbia in March of 1873 knowing that he would be seized

37 *DANRS,* Trial, parts II and III of the indictment.
38 *Ibid.,* part III of the indictment.

by the police, and he was probably disappointed when he was released the same day on Ristić's order. *Javnost* was scarcely two weeks old when his articles took on a militant character certain to provoke retaliation: his assertion that the Serbian people "have the right to overthrow a prince" could not possibly have been ignored by the authorities. Marković was not obsessed by any martyr complex, and it is unlikely that he envisioned sacrificing his life for the radical-socialist cause. But he was aware of the political advantages of being considered a victim of oppression, and, partly due to his undeniable egoism, partly to genuine concern for Stojković, he wished to be alone in the dock. His plans were upset, however, and Stojković's defense during the actual trial was as militant and uncompromising as his own.

In the afternoon of the first day of the trial Marković began his defense. Though he had no legal training he displayed a thorough knowledge of Serbian law, and despite its frequent verbosity his defense was closely reasoned and logically sound. To the charge that he had insulted the National Assembly by criticizing its endless debates and vulgar displays of legal knowledge, Marković replied that he had merely written the truth; the distress of the Serbian peasant, he observed, could not be alleviated by speeches. Citing verbatim the sections of the law which he was accused of violating, and quoting his own articles in *Javnost,* Marković refuted the first part of the indictment point by point. He further strengthened his defense by quoting from the conservative newspaper *Vidov Dan,* which had criticized the National Assembly in terms at least as strong as his own. In a moving appeal for freedom of the press, he defended the right of both *Javnost* and *Vidov Dan* to review and evaluate the actions of the Assembly, the government, and the prince.[39]

[39] *Ibid.,* part I of Marković's defense.

Concerning his alleged call for the overthrow of the prince, Marković asserted that he was speaking in the abstract of the concept of popular sovereignty, and that he had not specifically directed his comments at the reigning prince. The Serbian people, he maintained, had indeed always had the right to overthrow a prince with whom they were dissatisfied: they had done so, through their National Assembly, in 1839, 1842, and 1858. Why, he asked, was it now held that they no longer had that right? His defense of the rights of the people, he insisted, was not a crime but a duty; if the government and the prince persistently ignored the National Assembly, the only logical conclusion was that they were guilty of usurping the rights of the Serbian people.[40]

Finally, in his defense Marković declared that his socialist beliefs had nothing whatever to do with the case against him. He insisted that his call for the replacement of "bad laws" by laws embodying socialist principles involved only the question of whether or not the laws he challenged were indeed bad; socialism was not on trial. Marković equated socialism with justice, and in a passionate conclusion challenged "the ruling forces of this state" to go before the people and admit that they had, by arresting him, condemned justice.[41]

According to the accounts published in *Javnost, Zastava,* and *Budućnost,* it was only with difficulty that the three presiding judges maintained order in the courtroom when Marković collapsed into his chair after concluding his defense. Peasants from the surrounding countryside, workers from the local arms factory, students, and ordinary townsmen had crowded into the room to witness the trial, and hundreds reportedly waited outside for news of its developments. Marković had by this time become a symbol

40 *Ibid.,* part II.

41 *Javnost,* no. 23, February 26, 1874; this concluding portion of Marković's defense does not appear in the official transcript.

of the dissatisfaction with the government felt by many—especially the peasants—in Serbia. The Serbian peasant knew virtually nothing of socialism, but he knew Marković as a dedicated opponent of a capricious, costly government. The peasant held the government responsible for all his distress: the government supported the usurer, who took his land and his property when he could not pay his debts; the government sent rapacious, arrogant bureaucrats to harass him; the government collected taxes which he could not afford to pay. Svetozar Marković had criticized that government, and now, barely able to stand after an agonizing month in a wretched jail, he was forced to fight for his very freedom.

The trial represented a significant departure for Marković: he had at last made an effort to create a bond with the peasantry. None of his work prior to *Javnost* had been directed toward this, the very segment of the Serbian population he wanted to help. The attenuated Marxism of *Radenik* had sought the support of the intelligentsia and a nonexistent working class; the Tkachëvian, Pisarevian elitism of his work in *Omladina* and *Pobratimstvo* was aimed exclusively at the intelligentsia.[42] Like Rousseau, Marković had clearly been under the impression that he could force men to be free; the intelligentsia was to lead the peasantry to socialism. Now, at his trial, he had in a sense attempted to atone for his arrogant attitude toward the class which would build his new society. Time was to prove that he realized his mistake too late.

[42] Chernyshevsky himself influenced Marković's earlier elitism to a certain extent; as one writer has pointed out, Chernyshevsky counted upon "a vitality which should come from the whole people and not from a select minority. The people constitute a social expression of that reality which for Chernyshevsky is prior to idea and which is the material ground out of which the idea emerges. It is the task of the enlightened minority to bring that reality to self-consciousness." Herbert Bowman, "Revolutionary Élitism in Chernyshevsky," *The American Slavic and East European Review,* XIII, no. 2, April, 1954, p. 199.

Dimitrije Stojković next took the stand. His defense, sparkling though it was, could only be an anticlimax. Stojković's presence in the courtroom was regarded by all as merely incidental; he was virtually unknown in Serbia, was on friendly terms with the prosecutor (both men used the familiar "ti"), and the case against him was purely legal rather than personal and ideological, as was that against Marković. Ignoring his pretrial "defense," Stojković" admitted full responsibility for everything that had appeared in *Javnost,* and declared that he could see nothing criminal in anything that Marković or anyone else had written in the journal. Praising Marković as a learned, dedicated apostle of "scientific socialism," Stojković defended his colleague rather than himself.[43]

The trial concluded late in the afternoon on February 19 with the prosecution and defense summations. One of the three judges, Dimitrije Lazarević, interrupted the prosecutor to direct several questions at Marković; his openly hostile attitude foreboded the outcome of the trial. The state prosecutor summed up his case with a reference to Marković's claim that he was a true Serbian patriot: "God save the country," Stefanović prayed, "from such patriots as Mr. Marković and his kind."[44]

After a day's delay due to the inability of the judges to agree, the Kragujevac district court was convened on February 21, 1874, to hear the verdict in the Marković-Stojković trial. The defendants were pronounced guilty of all charges. Marković was sentenced to eighteen months in prison, Stojković to nine months plus a fine. The two men immediately filed an appeal with the Belgrade Court of Appeals.[45] One of the three judges, Gruja Gavrilović, had

[43] *Javnost,* no. 24, February 27, 1874; Stojković's defense does not appear in the official transcript.

[44] *Ibid.,* no. 25, March 1, 1874.

[45] *Ibid.*

voted for acquittal. For his pains he was almost immediately removed from his post and "exiled" to a minor provincial town to serve as a district clerk. Several young court functionaries who had expressed sympathy for the defendants were similarly punished.[46]

Considering the nature of the charges, and the fact that conviction had been almost certain, the sentences were not excessive. A respectable merchant had earlier been sentenced to thirteen months in prison merely for possessing one of Marković's works,[47] and few in Serbia would have been surprised had the court ruled a five-year prison term for Marković.[48] The lenient sentences were a certain reflection of the support now enjoyed by Marković personally and by the radical-socialist movement. Aćim Čumić, the minister of the interior, hinted that he personally had been responsible for the mild treatment accorded Marković and Stojković, and intimated that he might use his influence in their favor when the Court of Appeals met to consider their appeal.[49]

Despite the leniency of the Kragujevac court, eighteen months in prison was regarded by many as a death sentence for Marković. His body racked by now rapidly advancing tuberculosis, his collapse at the trial had been genuine. The prefect of Kragujevac "examined" Marković and pronounced him healthy,[50] but his conclusions were disputed by all three doctors in the town. The latter demanded that he be released pending action on his appeal; despite the opposition of the prosecutor and local police, the court

46 *IAB*, Svetozar to Jevrem Marković, letter no. 14; see also *Skerlić*, p. 98.

47 See above, p. 168.

48 Under Paragraphs 92 and 104 of the Serbian Criminal Code the maximum sentence which could have been meted to Marković was ten years in prison; to Stojković, three years.

49 *IAB*, Svetozar to Jevrem Marković, letter no. 12.

50 *Javnost*, no. 30, March 13, 1874.

freed Marković on the guarantee of two prominent citizens.[51]

A major effect of the Marković-Stojković trial was its bringing of the radical-socialists and the opposition liberals into an alliance which lasted over two years. *Budućnost* had supported Marković as much as it dared during the trial,[52] and immediately after the verdict the dissident liberals sent the journal's editor, Uroš Knežević, to confer with Marković concerning the possibility of joint action. Knežević arrived in Kragujevac early in March; Marković was still awaiting the outcome of his appeal. The two men discussed at length the possibility of forming a parliamentary alliance, but the project remained rather vague since no radical-socialists were then sitting in the National Assembly. Knežević told Marković that a society had been formed in Belgrade for the purpose of publishing a new journal on which the opposition liberals and the radical-socialists could collaborate. Several prominent deputies had agreed to support the society, and one (Milan Piroćanac, later founder of the Progressive party) had donated a large sum of money. It would be some time before the society could begin to publish a newspaper, Knežević observed, but in the meantime he promised to step up the intensity of his attacks on the government in *Budućnost*.[53]

The prospect of collaboration with the opposition liberals delighted Marković, and he rightly regarded the support of Knežević and Ljubomir Kaljević as a signal victory for his radical-socialist movement. The two men dominated the opposition liberal group, and their increasingly intransigent attitude toward the government forced Marko-

[51] *IAB*, Svetozar to Jevrem Marković, letter no. 12; *Skerlić*, p. 98.

[52] Under the law the press could not discuss a criminal trial until after its conclusion; *Budućnost* risked suspension by referring to Marković's trial several days before it began (no. 3, February 12, 1874).

[53] *IAB*, Svetozar to Jevrem Marković, n.p., n.d. (but Kragujevac, March 1874).

vić's old opponent, Vladimir Jovanović, to abandon his connection with *Budućnost*.[54]

The trial of the radical-socialist journalists attracted attention even outside the Serb lands. In its evening edition of February 18, 1874 (New Style), the Vienna *Neue Freie Presse* commented on the discovery in Kragujevac of a "very significant plot" aiming at the overthrow of Prince Milan and the annexation of the Vojvodina and the Banat. The journal noted that the conspirators, led by an artillery captain (i.e., Sava Grujić), were well financed, being friends of "those who administer all monastery property in Serbia." *Javnost* discussed the Vienna account, and asked, "Who gave this weird story to the foreign press?"[55]

Javnost continued to publish after the arrest of its chief writer and editor. Though no documents have been published, it is clear that those connected with the journal maintained close ties with Liuben Karavelov and the Bulgarian revolutionaries in Bucharest. *Svoboda* had been suppressed for the second and final time at the request of Constantinople, but in February of 1873 Karavelov had founded a new journal, *Nezavisimost* (*Independence*).[56] He was joined in the venture by the young poet and revolutionary Hristo Botev, who in 1874 assumed the leadership of the Bulgarian Revolutionary Committee.[57]

On February 1, 1874, one of the Bulgarian revolutionaries in Bucharest—the style and timing indicate Botev's authorship, although it is not certain—wrote an extremely interesting article which *Javnost* published three weeks

54 Jovanović was further compromised in his association with *Budućnost* by his appointment in May of 1873 as first secretary to the minister of internal affairs. Cf. his *Avtobiografija*, pp. 32-33.

55 *Javnost*, no. 26, March 3, 1874, and no. 30, March 13, 1874.

56 Konstantinov, *Vođi bugarskog narodnog pokreta*, pp. 142-143.

57 *Izbrannye proizvedeniia bolgarskikh revoliutsionnykh demokratov*, pp. 45-53; see also Konstantinov, *Vođi bugarskog narodnog pokreta*, pp. 187-199.

later.[58] According to the article, a Dalmatian legal journal[59] a few weeks earlier had printed an "Open Letter to Mr. Marinović" (then prime minister of Serbia) signed by a mysterious "Macedonian Society."[60] The Budapest *Pester Lloyd* and several Austrian newspapers had reprinted the letter, claiming it proved that the Bulgarians and Montenegrins would never permit Serbia to liberate the Balkan Peninsula. The Bulgarian writer quoted *Pester Lloyd* as saying that "this letter is to us a precious document, for it reveals not only the relations of the Bulgars with Serbia, but also the futile direction of Ristić's ["Great Serbia"] propaganda."

The article which *Javnost* printed scoffed at the claim of *Pester Lloyd* that a Serbo-Bulgarian union was merely a fantasy: "We are prepared to state thousands of facts to show that that union is natural, and necessary, and open and inevitable; that that union existed, exists, and will exist, and that *honest and intelligent Serbs and Bulgars will never be ready to think otherwise.*" The writer further insisted that it was untrue that the Bulgars were dissatisfied with members of the Serbian government for having tried to foment revolution in Bulgaria; on the contrary the Serbian government had not been revolutionary *enough.* The Bulgarian writer quoted *Javnost* to the effect that there was *no* Serbian propaganda in the Bulgarian lands; it was a strange situation, Marković's journal had observed, in view of the recognition by both Serbs and Bulgars that liberation depended upon their cooperation. *Zastava,* the article noted, had written in a similar vein, and had found it incredible that the "Open Letter"

58 *Javnost,* no. 22, February 24, 1874; in a brief preface to the article *Javnost* noted that it had promised its readers to print the views of *Nezavisimost* on the "Open Letter."

59 *Pravo* (*Jurisprudence*), published monthly in Zadar and Split.

60 I have been unsuccessful in the attempt to identify the "Makedonska družina" which wrote the letter published in *Pravo.*

had ever seen the light of day and fantastic that anyone believed it.

Although the article did not directly comment upon the "Macedonian Society," it did identify several Serbs and Bulgarians who apparently subscribed to ultranationalist views which brooked no cooperation between the two peoples. In Serbia Miloš Milojević had previously been identified by *Javnost* as "a writer, the product of a certain Moscow school, who would like to Serbianize the whole world."[61] One unidentified Popović[62] was added to the Milojević school by the Bulgarian writer, who noted that among his own people their counterparts were Balabanovats and Sapunovats. The latter two were possibly members of the "Macedonian Society," but positive identification of both society and membership must await further research.

Finally, the article from the Bulgarian revolutionary circle in Bucharest noted and agreed with *Javnost*'s comment that there was "only one society *which would lay the preparations for an uprising to achieve Bulgarian independence*."[63] That society was obviously the Bulgarian Revolutionary Committee, and it was further obvious that the committee was in close touch with *Javnost* and the radical-socialist movement in Serbia.[64]

The article from Bucharest was dated February 1, three weeks after Marković's arrest and about the same length of time before his trial. It stressed the "historical and

61 *Javnost*, no. 22, February 24, 1874; its earlier comment is quoted in the article from Bucharest. Milojević was a writer, bureaucrat, and historian; the *Narodna enciklopedija Srpsko-hrvatsko-slovenačka*, II, p. 919, refers to an article by R. Popović, "Miloš S. Milojević," in *Bratstvo*, Belgrade, vol. 8, 1899, pp. 379-400. The reference to "a certain Moscow school" is perplexing; in view of Milojević's allegedly violent Serbian nationalism the "school" could hardly have been Pan-Slavism.

62 Possibly the editor of *Vidov Dan*, Miloš Popović, an ardent Serb nationalist with no known enthusiasm for the Bulgars.

63 *Javnost*, no. 22, February 24, 1874.

64 See above, p. 145.

natural" ties between Serbs and Bulgars, a concept long preached by Svetozar Marković and one which had not found any genuinely effective support in Serbian ruling circles. The article had not criticized the Serbian government, pointing out, rather, that "we positively know that not one Serbian government has participated in the work of Miloš Milojević." In view of these circumstances, it is interesting to speculate briefly whether the Bulgarians had timed their article to gain a favorable verdict in Marković's trial; clearly the *quid pro quo* was cooperation against the Turks. In the absence of any substantive evidence in support of such a theory, the timing of the article can perhaps be attributed to coincidence. But the ties between the Bulgarian revolutionaries and Marković's radical-socialists are undeniable, and a great deal of research remains to be done in the Yugoslav and Bulgarian archives.

While Marković and Stojković awaited the outcome of their appeal the Kragujevac authorities made life miserable for *Javnost*. The journal continued to publish all through the spring of 1874, with Stojković still officially the editor. After careful research the prefect of Kragujevac summoned Stojković (who had also been released pending the appeal) and charged him with violating Article 39 of the Press Law, which made it illegal to print any news of a criminal trial prior to its completion. The prefect insisted that the Marković-Stojković trial could not be considered over until the appeal had been acted upon. Stojković and Pera Đorđević, the *Javnost* writer who had reported on the trial, successfully disputed such an absurd interpretation of the law, but the prefect had the last word: "We will see," he commented, "just how long it [*Javnost*] will continue."[65]

The radical-socialist journal increased its circulation

[65] *Javnost*, no. 30, March 13, 1874.

significantly as a result of the trial, and by March of 1874 it had agents in at least fourteen towns throughout Serbia.[66] The government continued to harass the newspaper, however, and resorted to "losing" copies in the mails. *Javnost* complained bitterly of such treatment, and was then forced to print an "Official Correction" in which the authorities attempted to explain the disappearance of certain issues. The journal dutifully printed the explanation, but observed that the police were better at producing such "official corrections" than at anything else.[67] When the Kragujevac prefect wrote a letter on the matter, *Javnost* printed a notice stating that it could not publish it. Its press did not have certain letters of the alphabet[68] which the prefect had used in his letter, and "according to the Press Law, Article 18, to which you refer, we dare not correct or change anything."[69]

Svetozar Marković meanwhile remained at liberty, despite the best efforts of the local prefect to have him returned to jail. The prefect claimed that Marković frequented smoky cafés at all hours of the day and night, and asked the judges who had freed him because of his health to reconsider their action. Marković could scarcely be ill with tuberculosis, the prefect noted, if he was able to spend all his time in such places; furthermore, the authorities had only the letter of the court as proof of Marković's illness.[70] The prefect published his views in a new letter to *Javnost*, and the journal answered him in the same issue.

First of all, *Javnost* noted, Marković was not in the habit of frequenting public places; he lived with a friend in a

[66] *Ibid.*, no. 31, March 15, 1874; one of the towns was Požarevac, where Marković and Stojković were to spend their sentences.

[67] *Ibid.*, no. 33, March 20, 1874.

[68] The prefect, Nikola Đorđević, had used some letters from the Old Serbian alphabet in his letter.

[69] *Javnost*, no. 32, March 17, 1874.

[70] *Ibid.*, no. 33, March 20, 1874.

small room, and only went out to take his meals at a café. Secondly, his illness was genuine; while he was waiting for the verdict to be announced in his trial, he had been unable to stand and had been forced to sit on the damp ground outside the city hall. Finally, he went out only once a day, usually around noon, and at that hour there were few people and little smoke in the cafés; the only time he had gone at a different hour, the journal noted, the three judges in his trial had happened to be in the café he entered.[71]

Marković wrote to his brother early in March that it was rumored in Belgrade and Kragujevac that the Court of Appeals was "favorably disposed" toward the petitions he and Stojković had filed. He noted that he had "no faith" in Čumić's "promise," and that he owed no thanks to Čumić for the fact that he was at liberty now.[72] Čumić indeed had no intention of intervening to secure leniency for Marković. Though he had earlier collaborated with Jevrem Marković, Čumić caught the attention of Prince Milan in 1872 and became a trusted sycophant. Far from seeking to free Marković or reduce his sentence, Čumić, apparently on the orders of the prince, attempted to prevent the Court of Appeals from altering the decisions of the Kragujevac district court.[73]

Despite Čumić's efforts, the Belgrade Court of Appeals announced on March 20, 1874, that it had reduced Mar-

71 *Ibid.*

72 *IAB*, Svetozar to Jevrem Marković, letter no. 12.

73 *Vlada Milana*, I, pp. 204-205. Čumić served briefly as prime minister (November 1874-January 1875) and was responsible for the persecution of Svetozar Marković which followed his release from prison; Pera Todorović's *Rad* blamed him for Marković's death (no. 9, March 1, 1875). Čumić fell from Prince Milan's favor early in 1875, and became a bitter opponent of his former benefactor. He rejoined forces with Jevrem Marković, and together they participated in an abortive military rebellion at Topola in 1877. Marković was executed by a military tribunal, but Čumić, after being sentenced to death, was reprieved by Prince Milan and served only a seven-year prison term.

ković's sentence to nine months (dating from February 20) and Stojković's to three months and a small fine. The two men immediately took the last legal step open to them and filed a further appeal with the Belgrade Court of Cassation, the highest appellate court in Serbia.[74]

The Kragujevac authorities, almost pathologically anxious to be rid of Marković, attempted to send him to the state prison in Požarevac immediately after receiving the decision of the Court of Appeals. The prefect, who had conceived an intense personal hatred for Marković, insisted that he was perfectly well and able to travel to the prison, and that there was no further excuse for his remaining in Kragujevac. Marković was forced to send a telegram to the minister of justice demanding that he be allowed to remain in Kragujevac until the Court of Cassation had acted on his appeal; his request was granted.[75]

Marković thus was able to put the affairs of *Javnost* in order before leaving to begin his prison sentence. He and his colleagues asked Sava Grujić to assume the editorship of the journal, but in March Grujić's wife became seriously ill and he was obliged to decline.[76] It was then decided that *Javnost* should be allowed to expire before Marković and Stojković left Kragujevac. The Printing-Works society was still intact, and the radical-socialists laid plans to launch a new journal as soon as an editor could be found and a competent staff assembled.[77]

On April 10 the Court of Cassation rejected the appeal made by Marković and Stojković.[78] There was nothing to do but prepare for the journey to the state prison.

[74] *DANRS*, PO k/104, Appellate Court decision dated Belgrade, March 20, 1874.

[75] *IAB*, Svetozar to Jevrem Marković, n.p., n.d. (but Kragujevac, March-April 1874); see also *Javnost*, no. 30, March 13, 1874.

[76] *IAB*, Svetozar to Jevrem Marković, letters nos. 13, 14, 15.

[77] *Ibid.*, letter no. 14.

[78] *DANRS*, PO k 105/1874, Court of Cassation decision dated Belgrade, April 10-11, 1874.

The last issue of *Javnost* appeared on April 14, and a few days later Marković and Stojković were transported to Požarevac, a small town about sixty kilometers southeast of Belgrade. Marković was near collapse on arrival, and was given a cell to himself. A young female radical-socialist, a teacher in a nearby town, visited him and immediately afterward wrote to the Ninković sisters that she feared for his life. The government flatly rejected a request by his friends that he be released and his sentence commuted to the payment of a fine.[79]

Not content with the imprisonment of Marković, the Serbian government attempted further to cripple the radical-socialist movement. In September of 1874 the minister of education sent a circular to the *Velika Škola* and other educational institutions, in which he severely criticized the materialism which had taken such strong root in Serbia. And not long after Marković's trial one of his colleagues on *Radenik* (Dimitrije Cenić) and several others were imprisoned on suspicion of plotting the overthrow of the government. Cenić and a suspected Karađorđevist lawyer, Jovan Milinković, had planned to start a political journal in the provincial town of Šabac. Two Bosnians, apparently police agents, testified concerning the "conspiratorial" nature of the proposed journalistic venture, and Minister of the Interior Čumić had all the alleged conspirators arrested and held without trial.[80]

But despite the repressive measures the Serbian government remained as inefficient as it was vindictive. Marković continued to write in prison, and in these the last months of his life produced some of his most significant works. Under the care of the prison doctor his health improved slightly, and he devoted most of his time to his writing. He had two outlets for his work. The Kragujevac Social

[79] *Skerlić*, pp. 99-100.
[80] *Vlada Milana*, I, pp. 205-206.

Printing-Works secured the services of Stevan Milićević, the last editor of *Radenik*, and in July of 1874 began to publish a new journal, *Glas Javnosti* (*The Voice of the Public*). Also in the summer of 1874 Pera Todorović, who had urged Marković to come to Kragujevac, founded a radical-socialist monthly, *Rad* (*Labor*) in Belgrade. In the pages of these two journals Marković developed his theory of a communalist society based on the foundation of the old *zadruga*.

THE ZADRUGA

Marković defined the *zadruga*[81] as a "branched-out family which lives on common property, works jointly, consumes jointly. Each member does the work assigned to him, and consumes as much as he needs. The price of labor is not fixed, for the products of joint labor belong to all in equal degree. Joint property belongs to the family; no individual can sell, give away, or mortgage his share. He has only the right to live and work in the zadruga. If he leaves the zadruga his [share of the joint] property falls to the members who remain, but if he returns he is again accepted into the zadruga. A zadruga produces almost everything it needs. It procures very little on the outside."[82] This was of course the *zadruga* of Turkish times, before disintegration began. Vladimir Jovanović, who like Marković held the ancient institution in a rather mystical esteem,[83] more succinctly defined the *zadruga* as "a sort of as-

81 The name, as Professor Jozo Tomasevich has pointed out, was a literary invention; many Serbs referred to the family commune merely as the "house" or "family"; *Peasants, Politics, and Economic Change*, p. 178.

82 "Suvremena radnička načela" ("Contemporary Labor Principles"), *Socijalistička štampa u Srbiji do XX veka*, I, Belgrade, 1951, p. 199.

83 Strangely enough, Jovanović, while holding the *zadruga* in high regard, remained closer to Chernyshevsky's views on the *obshchina* in recognizing the drawbacks and restrictive nature of the old commune, while Marković tended to follow the Slavophils in his often uncritical glorification of the institution.

sociation, founded on blood ties, which represents a co-operative society for the exploitation of the land and the communal funds."[84]

As Engels noted,[85] the *zadruga* was the best example still in existence in the nineteenth century of the patriarchal family community. The elected head of the *zadruga* was the elder (*starešina*); in the family communes he was ordinarily the grandfather, father, or oldest brother, but exceptions were not unusual. In theory the elder was responsive to the will of the majority of the male members of the commune, but in fact he often exercised arbitrary power; communal democracy was widely accepted as a tradition but frequently violated as a policy.[86]

The number of individuals in a *zadruga* varied widely. At the beginning of the nineteenth century it was not uncommon to find sixty to eighty members of one such institution, and a few had more than one hundred members.[87] The great majority, however, embraced ten or fewer individuals.[88] Usually the members were related by blood ties, but such ties were by no means obligatory and the larger *zadrugas* frequently included several separate families.[89]

The most valuable possession of the *zadruga* was land. A complicated legal structure dating back to Tsar Dušan's Code of 1359,[90] and further embracing both common law and tradition, regulated the ownership of the land. Each *zadruga* had, in addition to the arable land of its individual members, a share in the wooded and pasturelands

[84] Jovanović, *Les Serbes*, pp. 268-269.

[85] "The Origin of the Family, Private Property and the State," *Marx and Engels: Selected Works*, II, p. 199.

[86] Živojin Žujović, "Serbskoe selo," pp. 131-132.

[87] Vladimir Jovanović, *Les Serbes*, p. 269.

[88] Tomasevich, *op. cit.*, pp. 179-180; Karasëv, "Osnovnye cherty," p. 215.

[89] E. I. Tkalac, *Das Staatsrecht des Fürstentums Serbien*, Leipzig, 1858, p. 61.

[90] Cf. Stojan Novaković, *Zakonik Stefana Dušana* (*The Code of Stefan Dušan*), 2nd edition, Belgrade, 1898.

of the village commune (*opština*). The bulk of the arable land was in private hands. It should be remembered, however, that the primary occupation of the Serb was not farming but the raising of livestock; thus the *communal* pastureland was at least equally as important as the *private* cropland. Furthermore, the *zadruga* maintained a significant measure of control over the private land of its members: it fixed the dates for sowing and harvesting, and was the court of first instance in disputes involving private land.[91]

Other forms of private property existed in the *zadruga*. Some livestock was privately owned, and dowries frequently brought private movable property into the hands of separate families in the larger communes. On the whole, however, the distinguishing feature of the *zadruga* was the communal ownership and exploitation of property.[92]

Despite Svetozar Marković's tendency to identify the Serbian *zadruga* with the Russian *obshchina*,[93] there were several vastly important differences between the two institutions. Unlike its Russian "counterpart," the *zadruga* did not, after about the sixth century A.D.,[94] practice the periodic repartition of the arable land, most of which gradually fell into private ownership within the organization. Further, membership in the *obshchina* was never based upon blood ties, and private ownership of the land (despite many instances of hereditary household tenure) was never known. The *zadruga*'s functions were more limited than those of the *obshchina*: it had no political functions per se, such being reserved to the *opština*. Finally, the *obshchina* remained a flourishing institution throughout

91 Shikhareva, "Sel'skaia obshchina u serbov," p. 107.

92 The land tenure system is discussed in the Shikhareva article just cited, which includes a good bibliography; see also Tomasevich, *Peasants, Politics, and Economic Change*, pp. 179-180.

93 See above, p. 116.

94 Shikhareva, *loc. cit.*, pp. 99-100.

the nineteenth and into the twentieth century; Karl Marx wrote in a draft of a letter to Vera Zasulich that "the village obshchina, which still exists [1881] on a national scale, can free itself from its primitive traits and develop directly as an element of collective production on a national scale."[95] The *zadruga,* on the other hand, began to disintegrate immediately after the Serbs won their autonomy.[96]

During the centuries of Turkish domination the *zadruga* had served three purposes: it was an administrative-territorial entity in the feudal system, a means of defense, and a repository of Serbian culture, the importance of which was rivaled only by the Church.[97] With the winning of autonomy the removal of external pressures struck at the fundamental *raisons d'être* of the *zadruga* and the institution began to fall apart.[98] The pace of disintegration accelerated rapidly after the middle of the nineteenth cen-

[95] Karl Marx and Friedrich Engels, *Sochineniia* (*Works*), XXVII, Leningrad, 1935, p. 678; the three drafts of Marx's letter are reproduced in pp. 677-698. In the preface to a Russian edition of the *Communist Manifesto* Marx and Engels wrote that the *obshchina* "can be the point of departure of communist development." Cf. Karataev, *Ekonomicheskaia platforma,* p. 54; see also Koz'min, *Russkaia sektsiia,* pp. 251-253.

[96] The Yugoslav communist writer Veselin Masleša wrote with some exaggeration that the *zadruga* had ceased to exist in Svetozar Marković's time; "Svetozar Marković," p. 80. On the comparison of the Russian and Serbian communes see Viktorov-Toporov, "Svetozar Markovich," pp. 44-45; Karasëv, "Osnovnye cherty," p. 219; Karasëv, *Svetozar Markovich,* p. 57. Karasëv is surely aware that the *zadruga* and *opština* are two wholly separate entities, yet he has a tendency to discuss the functions of one using the terminology of the other; he translates both "zadruga" and "opština" as "obshchina," and the result is serious confusion.

[97] Cf. Tkalac, *Das Staatsrecht,* p. 61.

[98] Živojin Žujović wrote that most Serbs were convinced that the chief culprits in the break-up of the *zadrugas* were the women. Females were treated barbarously in the *zadruga*; they were invariably addressed in the third person singular, and were frequently beaten in the presence of the entire family. The women felt that *zadruga* life—where the males egged each other on—was responsible for their misery, and they did their utmost to withdraw their families from its restrictive environment. "Serbskoe selo," pp. 130-134. In his "Suvremena radnička načela" Svetozar Marković agreed with Žujović's observations.

tury. In the years 1861-63 a total of 4,439 *zadrugas* were officially liquidated and their property divided among their members; in the following three years the number of liquidations increased to an annual rate of more than 1,700.[99]

The *zadruga* was not a legal entity in autonomous Serbia until 1844. In that year the National Assembly passed a comprehensive law which gave the institution legal existence and attempted to define the rights and obligations of both *zadruga* and its members.[100] The government became increasingly concerned over the disappearance of the *zadrugas* in the middle of the century, and various laws, all of them ineffectual, were passed in a feeble effort to preserve the family communes.[101] The process of disintegration did not slacken, and by the 1880's the greater portion of the former collective lands had passed into private ownership.[102]

THE OPŠTINA

The Serbian *opština* was the second institution upon which Svetozar Marković proposed to build the South Slav state of the future. The legal status of the *opština* was defined in an Organic Law of 1839, which recognized three types of the communal municipalities: in ascending order of size and importance, the three were the church, administrative, and natural *opštinas*.[103] Every Serb had to belong to one (and only one) *opština*, for the institution was a fiscal as

99 Žujović, "Serbskoe selo," p. 131; Karasëv, "Osnovnye cherty," p. 214.

100 Tkalac, *Das Staatsrecht*, pp. 61-65.

101 *Vidov Dan*, no. 96, 1864; Žujović, "Serbskoe selo," p. 131.

102 Shikhareva, "Sel'skaia obshchina u serbov," p. 111.

103 The "church *opština*" embraced "all inhabitants of an area who have one church"; the "administrative *opština*" was composed of "a village or several villages having one conciliatory court"; the "natural *opština*" was formed from "a village having its own name and its own festival day"; cf. M. Milićević, "Serbskaia obshchina" ("The Serbian Opština"), *Russkaia Beseda*, Moscow, VI, 1859, pp. 53-54. See also Tkalac, *op. cit.*, pp. 66-77, and Svetozar Marković, "Suvremena radnička načela."

well as a political and administrative entity. The *opština* apportioned the communal lands among the *zadrugas* of which it was composed; it further collected taxes, provided for local defense, administered justice, and kept the peace.[104]

Prior to the Serbian Revolution the male inhabitants normally elected the officials of the *opština*. During the nineteenth century, however, the primitive democracy was gradually supplanted by a kind of district oligarchy. Military officers, heads of wealthier *zadrugas*, and bureaucrats began to gain control over many of the *opštinas*. Even those which maintained their internal democratic character were inexorably brought under the control of the central government, which sent police and district bureaucrats to supervise *opština* affairs.[105] The *opština* courts, originally designed to settle petty disputes, soon became tools of the oligarchs and bureaucrats and thus emerged as the *de facto* executive power.[106]

The *opština* was obliged to pay its bureaucrats (the *kmet*, or *knez*, here roughly corresponding to mayor, and his staff) and maintain public services. Its income was derived from fairs, public scales, the sale of liquor (on which it had a theoretical monopoly), public slaughterhouses, and fishing taxes.[107] Its expenditures were primarily for the upkeep of roads and (in the case of the "natural" *opštinas*) primary schools, and it also maintained all public buildings.[108]

104 In general on the functions of the *opština* see Vladimir Jovanović, "Obština" (a variant in the spelling), *Glasnik srpskog učenog društva*, XXXIV, 1872, pp. 86-150, and also M. Ć. Milićević, "Opštine u Srbiji" ("Opštinas in Serbia"), *Godišnjica Nikole Čupića*, Belgrade, II, pp. 183-239.

105 See above, p. 215. Svetozar Marković's father had been a district bureaucrat whose job it was to supervise *opština* affairs; see *Radenik*, no. 49, September 28, 1871.

106 Marković, "Opština," *C.d.*, I, pp. 128-129; Žujović, "Serbskoe selo," p. 158.

107 The fishing in the rivers Sava and Danube was under the control of the central government in Belgrade.

108 Milićević, "Serbskaia obshchina," pp. 60-62.

The *opština* fulfilled an important social function. The members of the organization (both male and female, though the latter had no vote) generally met in public session once or twice a week; their purpose was as much to visit neighbors and break the monotony of rural life as to conduct business. The old "town hall" democracy persisted in form and social structure long after it had been seriously compromised in substance.[109]

These, then, were the twin pillars which in their perfected forms were to be the foundations of Svetozar Marković's communalist system. He admitted their shortcomings, however, recognizing that the *zadruga* was perhaps deservedly fast disappearing and that both it and the *opština* had a patriarchal character which was inconsistent with socialism.[110] It was not the existing institutions he took for his model, but rather their idealized forms which he, like Rousseau, imagined to have existed in the distant past before society corrupted man. Marković provided the final outlines of his communalist theory in a series of studies which he wrote during his imprisonment in Požarevac. He completed the second part of his *Principles of National Economy*,[111] but by far the most important of his works in this period was his lengthy monograph "Socialism, or The Social Problem" which Pera Todorović published in *Rad*.[112]

"Socialism, or The Social Problem" was conceived as a polemic in answer to a work bearing the same title which Vladimir Jovanović had published the previous year.[113]

109 Žujović, "Serbskoe selo," p. 158. See also Vladimir Jovanović, "Obština."

110 *Radenik*, no. 59, October 23, 1871; *Srbija na istoku*, pp. 15-23, 77; "Suvremena radnička načela," *passim*.

111 *Načela narodne ekonomije*, Belgrade, 1874.

112 *Rad*, 1874, nos. 11-22. I have used the edition which appears in volume I of *Socijalistička štampa u Srbiji do XX veka*, pp. 355-425.

113 "Socijalizam ili društveno pitanje," *Glasnik srpskog učenog društva*, XXXIX, 1873, pp. 1-116.

Jovanović had described socialism as the "tyranny of society over the individual," insisting that the socialists considered the individual "the natural enemy of society." Marković accused Jovanović of basing his opinions on an inadequate knowledge of socialism; he knew only the work of the "bourgeois democrats" Lassalle and Schulze-Delitzsch, Marković scoffed, and had never studied the "scientific work" of Marx and Engels. His opponent was further ignorant, Marković maintained, even of the works of the "learned non-socialists" J. S. Mill, Lorenz von Stein, and Eugen Dühring.[114]

COLLECTIVISM

Marković had earlier rejected the arguments of those who would merely reform capitalism. The ownership of the means of production, of capital, must be either private or collective; there is no third form. Society has the freedom to choose which form it will have: if the majority remains convinced that it can best "fill its belly" (*sic*) under capitalism, that system will remain; if the majority becomes convinced in the superiority of communism, "communism will come."[115] Which of the two forms of capital ownership was superior? Again Marković had earlier provided his answer: "There is no doubt that any nation in Europe, including even Serbia, could immeasurably increase the productivity of its labor . . . if it would at once introduce collective production . . . in all branches of the economy."[116] By "collective production" Marković understood the "union of capital and labor"; that such a union is the true foundation of national wealth and the correct way

[114] Marković, "Socijalizam ili društveno pitanje," pp. 362-363; hereafter cited as "Socijalizam." Of Engels' works Marković apparently knew only (in addition to the *Communist Manifesto*) *The Condition of the Working Class in England in 1844*.

[115] *Radenik*, no. 14, February 6, 1872.

[116] "Suvremena radnička načela," p. 198.

to economic reform is admitted, he maintained, by "socialists, non-socialists, and even the bourgeoisie . . . who live only to make two pieces of money out of one."[117]

Like Chernyshevsky, Marković believed that the reformed commune could show the peasants the advantages of collective production. Under the leadership of an enlightened intelligentsia, the peasants would be brought to see that such a system would be far more beneficial to them than "exploiting each other for the last piece of bread," and they would voluntarily embrace collectivism.[118]

Vladimir Jovanović had insisted that there was no difference between the legal foundations of private and collective property rights, since the latter are but the sum of individual, private rights. Marković admitted the logic of Jovanović's argument: "*Each* individual has the right to property, and in order that this be a *de facto* right, and not merely a right in name, society must ensure to each of its members the opportunity to acquire property. Further: [society] must establish collective property."[119] The rules were the same in collectivist and capitalist society but the practice was different; the capitalists-exploiters, Marković insisted, did not give labor its right to property, and therefore the capitalist system had as its foundation not the preservation but the denial of the right to property.

Marković again went back to the labor theory of value, but he drew toward a Proudhonian position in maintaining that even labor does not give the *unconditional* right to property. That right, he wrote, is based upon "absolute justice"; he proposed not the destruction of the principle of property but the universalization of property itself.[120]

In a collectivist society private property would indeed exist, Marković maintained, but no individual would be

117 *Ibid.*, pp. 198-199. 118 *Ibid.*, p. 203. 119 "Socijalizam," p. 381.

120 *Ibid.*, p. 377. Marković adopted Proudhon's famous maxim, though he used slightly different language: "Property is usurpation."

in a position to exploit another. There would be no competition, for one thing, and no overpricing of goods and services. A collectivist society would have no "superfluous" production or business crises, since "production is based upon precise calculations rather than competition." Marković did not specify what kind of private property would be permissible, though he clearly would have excluded land (contrary to the existing practice in the *zadruga*) and industry.[121]

There would obviously be a transitional stage during the change from a private to a collective society, and for a time private property would continue to exist side by side with collective. During this transitional stage the bulk of private property (in land and industry) would be transferred to worker communes; the transfer would be completed as soon as all communes had introduced machine production. Marković, like Chernyshevsky before him, now considered the machine the key to the success of socialism. Large-scale agricultural and industrial production on a collective basis would ensure the well-being of society; in Britain, Belgium, and parts of France industrial worker communes would predominate, while in Serbia and Russia the agrarian worker communes would at first be in the overwhelming majority. Each commune should, however, strive to become self-sufficient (on the model of the old *zadruga*) by extending its activity into both industry and agriculture wherever possible. This would not, Marković insisted, lead to a series of mutually exclusive and independent communes: "on the contrary, we consider that the ties between separate groups will become more and more lively." Furthermore, since the law will apply equally to all individuals in all communes, every individual would have the right to share in the collective property of *any* commune. By ensuring the individual the right to

[121] *Ibid.*, pp. 394-395.

his fair share of the collective property, and guaranteeing him the right to join any commune, a collectivist society (so Marković held) demonstrated its superiority over bourgeois society.[122]

Concerning the remuneration of workers in a collective society, Marković agreed with Marx that "the machine equalizes the conditions of hiring" and that in time work could be measured strictly according to quantity.[123] The productivity of labor, Marković wrote, embodies three elements: the personal labor of the individual, the joint labor of the commune, and the labor of the entire society. Thus the only just and equitable method of distributing income was that proposed by Louis Blanc: one third to the state in return for the loan of its capital (a problem Marković did not discuss) and for its general needs; one third to the commune for its needs; one third to the workers.[124]

The worker communes were to be the foundation of collectivist society. Enjoying the widest possible autonomy, they would lead mankind to the millennium; they would create a society where "everyone works according to his capabilities and receives according to his needs," and would thus fulfill the visions of St. Simon and Louis Blanc. Eventually the state would become one large commune, which would be organized "as one family"; this, Marković said, would be "complete communism."[125]

The communes which Marković envisioned were patterned on the schemes of his teachers: Blanc, Fourier, St. Simon, and—certainly not least—Dühring. Like the German thinker, to whose views he was increasingly attracted

122 *Ibid.*, pp. 382-391.

123 Marković was willing to except doctors, teachers, learned individuals, and others from the "general rule" pertaining to the evaluation of labor and permit them to work as private individuals. He predicted, however, that such people would be in the vanguard of the collectivist movement and would voluntarily have their labor evaluated according to the rules which applied to the rest of society; *ibid.*, p. 394.

124 *Ibid.*, pp. 391-392.

125 *Ibid.*, p. 395.

in the last two years of his life, Marković based his case for socialism on absolute values. The materialism of his earlier years had been diluted by his belief in the fundamental perfectibility of man.

Marković did not advocate the use of force to establish a collective society in Serbia. He agreed with Marx that "violence is the midwife of the old society when it is heavy with the new,"[126] but the precept applied, he maintained, only to the social revolution.[127] Since in Marković's view Serbia had already undergone her social revolution when she overthrew the Turks, the task confronting the country in the 1870's was economic and political *reform*. The reforms he proposed in 1873 and 1874 clarified his "wide program" to some extent, but he admitted that his program remained incomplete. The essence of his reforms was the democratization of Serbian society through the worker communes, to which would be transferred nearly all political and economic power; in a later day his slogan might have been "all power to the worker communes."

One third of the national income was to go to the state "for its needs"; yet Marković did not specify what those needs would be. He feared the state to an only slightly less degree than did Bakunin, and his fear precluded even a tentative solution to an inescapable problem. He proposed to make the National Assembly the *supreme* legislative body with the additional right of *supreme* control over all state organs, yet in the same breath he proposed as the *supreme* state power a "Sovjet" (Council) of citizens elected by the communes.[128] Such were the contradictions which led Jovan Skerlić to conclude that Marković regressed from socialism to radicalism.

Marković's wide acquaintance with socialist theory ham-

[126] *Ibid.*, p. 411.

[127] Cf. Traian Stoianovich, "The Pattern of Serbian Intellectual Evolution," p. 269; Slobodan Jovanović, "Svetozar Marković," p. 83.

[128] *Javnost*, no. 9, November 23, 1873.

pered him more than it helped. He saw the contradictions in and between the theories of his teachers, yet he failed to see the impossibility of reconciling them. The eclectic socialism he tried to create required a profundity of thought of which he was clearly incapable. He proposed an extremely decentralized state based on the worker communes, and ignored the problems of national defense, foreign relations, and foreign trade (the latter a factor the self-sufficient communes would apparently ignore). The domestic functions of the state were largely to be usurped by the autonomous communes; yet the problems of relations between the communes, higher education, large public works, and capital investment remained unanswered. Despite his misgivings Marković had come to recognize the desirability and indeed the necessity for large-scale production in all branches of the economy; yet the decentralized system he proposed would only with enormous difficulty progress beyond cottage industry and small-scale farming.

Marković idealized the *zadruga* and the communal concept to an unreasonable degree. He was convinced that the *zadruga* was disintegrating as a system because of bureaucratic abuses and the machinations of the usurers; he tended to minimize as a contributory factor the desire of the members of the *zadruga* to seek a freer life than any commune, patriarchal or not, could provide. Marković insisted that the *zadruga* and the Russian *obshchina* embodied the purest form of collectivism and would, if revived and perfected (he was vague as to how this was to be accomplished), elevate society from egoism to altruism, from exploitation to justice. Justice was absolute, and Marković equated it with collectivism.

Finally, Marković could not answer Vladimir Jovanović on the point of individual freedom in a planned society. The "tyranny of society over the individual" remained to plague him. He had indeed written that communism would come only if the majority wanted it; yet we may question the sincerity of his statement. Certainly there was no such majority anywhere in sight in his day, and the rapid disintegration of the *zadrugas* ought to have indicated to him that the majority was on the other side and growing larger. Was Marković, with his enlightened intelligentsia, to follow Rousseau and force men to be free? Such had indeed been his implicit position until 1873, but in that year he reversed his stand in the attempt to win the peasants to his cause. For, whatever his shortcomings, Marković remained a humanitarian. His ultimate rejection of totalitarian ideologies is reflected in the criticism to which he has been subjected by modern communist writers.

That Marković was occasionally—even frequently—a visionary is manifestly obvious and needs no further elaboration. Like Marx he held that the moral ills of mankind—chief among them egoism—were caused by imperfections in the economic structure, but unlike Marx he did not lump those ills into a *bête noire* of class struggle. In the tradition of the Enlightenment he called not on a revolutionary proletariat but on reason to guide man to liberation.[129]

Always an idealist, Marković wanted to reach what can only be regarded as an unattainable Utopia. Whatever the merits of his goal, his insistence that the route to it did not necessarily pass through Armageddon reflects only credit upon him.

[129] The Marxist critique of Marković's economic theory has been admirably expressed by Miriana Iovanovich in her article "Ikonomicheskite v'zgledi na Svetozar Markovich" ("Svetozar Marković's Economic Views"), Vissha partiina shkola "Stanke Dimitrov" pri TsK BKP, *Izvestiia* (otdel istoriia), 4, Sofia, 1959, pp. 190-234. Mme. Iovanovich repeats most of the tiresome and shopworn Marxist arguments concerning Marković's alleged failure to "ascend" to dialectical materialism, yet for all the jargon her article has considerable value. The author has addressed herself directly to the problem of the pretermission of the capitalist stage (possible, in her view, with an "outside push") and has handled it more courageously than most of her Marxist colleagues; see especially pp. 228-230.

CHAPTER VII

CONCLUSION

LIKE the state penitentiaries in all Slavic countries, the damp and filthy Požarevac prison was known in Serbia as the "house of the dead."[1] Men who entered the prison in perfect health often emerged broken and racked with disease, and for those like Svetozar Marković who entered it already in poor health the prison was indeed, as Hermann Wendel wrote, a "dry guillotine."[2] The prison regime itself, however, was not harsh; Marković had no duties to perform, and was able to devote most of his time to writing. He did not lack for company: Dimitrije Stojković was with him for a few months, and after Stojković's release his cell was taken by Đura Ljočić, the former editor of *Radenik*, who was imprisoned on a charge the nature of which remains obscure.

Even in prison Svetozar Marković's difficulties with the law did not cease. Plagued all his life by financial difficulties, in September of 1874 he was named in a lawsuit brought by two Požarevac tobacconists who sought payment of a bill. Stojković (who had remained in the prison town to be near Marković) and Ljočić were named as codefendants; in October of 1874 the suit was dismissed in Belgrade court for lack of evidence.[3]

Toward the end of his sentence Svetozar Marković was physically exhausted. Despite the ministrations of the prison doctor, he had little hope of recovering his health. The scrofula which had been diagnosed in St. Petersburg developed into tuberculosis of the stomach and colon,[4]

1 *Skerlić*, p. 100.

2 "Svetozar Marković," *Nova Evropa*, XI, 1925, pp. 404-408.

3 *DANRS*, PO k 102/114.

4 *Oslobođenje*, no. 27, March 2, 1875.

and the disease was aggravated by overwork and the debilitating prison life. The Ninković sisters, who had come to Serbia to join the radical-socialist movement, visited Marković in September and found him in good spirits but extremely weak and emaciated.[5]

Marković was released from prison on November 16, 1874. He immediately left Požarevac and went on some unknown mission to Belgrade; remaining in the city only one day, he then traveled to Jagodina, where he spent a few weeks resting and recuperating with Jevrem Marković and his wife.[6]

THE SOCIALIST TIDE

During the months Marković spent in prison the radical-socialist movement had gained greatly in numerical strength and political influence. The peasants, profoundly moved by Marković's ordeal, flocked to the banner of the socialists. Many of them were converted to the cause of the radical-socialists by the shrewd and popular Adam Bogosavljević, a Croat who had recently become one of Marković's most trusted associates. Of peasant origin, Bogosavljević and his family had moved to Serbia several years previously. He graduated from the Technical Faculty of the *Velika Škola,* and settled near Kragujevac. A handsome and articulate man who spoke the Šumadija patois better than most Šumadinci, Bogosavljević translated Marković's communalist theories into language readily understood by the peasants. He was elected to the National Assembly in 1874 and quickly emerged as the parliamentary leader of a small group of socialist deputies.[7]

5 *IAB,* Svetozar to Jevrem Marković, August 11, (1874), n.p. (but Kragujevac); *Skerlić,* p. 100.

6 *Rad,* no. 9, March 1, 1875; *Skerlić,* p. 100.

7 Viktorov-Toporov, "Svetozar Markovich," p. 47; *Budućnost,* no. 91, November 9, 1874. There were 130 seats in the National Assembly. Slobodan Jovanović has mistakenly claimed (*Vlada Milana,* I, p. 228) that only

The handful of socialists in the 1874-75 session of the National Assembly were a vocal and potentially powerful minority. The groups in the legislative body had finally crystallized into definite party organizations, of which the most important were the conservatives and the liberals. Previously, deputies had been either for or against the government, and party lines were vague. It was in part due to the threat posed by the radical-socialists, who advocated Marković's program of communal autonomy and reform of the bureaucracy, that the two major parties organized on a more rational and practical basis.[8]

Bogosavljević and the small group around him were unable to accomplish any of their major legislative objectives in the 1874-75 session of the National Assembly, but their presence in that body encouraged Svetozar Marković to return to his publicist activities. He did so despite the continued persecution of his colleagues, two of whom were sentenced in 1874 to long prison terms (eight and ten years) for alleged political crimes.[9] Jevrem Marković and his wife had urged Svetozar to remain with them until he recovered his health,[10] but when his friends in Kragujevac—the Social Printing-Works group—requested that he return to the city to edit a new journal, he was unable to resist the temptation to resume his crusade.

---

two radical-socialists were in the Assembly in 1874-75. Jevrem Marković, Dimitrije Katić, Milija Milovanović, and Adam Bogosavljević formed the nucleus of the socialist bloc, which was supported by several other deputies with no party affiliation. Bogosavljević's influence in the Assembly was considerable; he was elected chairman of several important committees and worked closely with the former opposition liberals Ljubomir Kaljević and Uroš Knežević. Cf. *Protokoli Narodne Skupštine* (*Register of the National Assembly*), Belgrade, 1875.

8 *Vlada Milana*, I, pp. 227-228.

9 *Skerlić*, p. 103. The two were Mita Cenić and Jovan Milinković, who had earlier been charged with plotting the overthrow of the dynasty (see above, p. 238).

10 *IAB*, Svetozar to Jevrem Marković, January 20 (1875), n.p. (but Kragujevac).

MARKOVIĆ'S LAST NEWSPAPER

On the first of January 1875 Marković began publication of his last newspaper, *Oslobođenje* (*Liberation*). The title was symbolic in a greater sense than he realized. Having started his career with *The Worker* in a land which had few workers, he was to end it with *Liberation*, recognizing as did few of the socialists who followed him the fact that the nationalism of his countrymen was the most important single force in the country. He had not abandoned his earlier goals; rather, he had attempted to blend them with those of wider and more popular significance. His aim was, he wrote in 1874, "*internal social reorganization on the basis of national sovereignty and communal self-government, revolution in Turkey and federation in the Balkan Peninsula.*"[11]

In the leading article of *Oslobođenje*'s first issue Marković wrote: "We come before the public as old acquaintances under a new banner. We are continuing the same work which we began in *Javnost* and *Glas Javnosti* (and even earlier in *Radenik*). We are not coming out with any new program; we adhere to the old. But our new banner, 'Liberation,' aside from our own fundamental principles, has its own significance. . . . Serbian liberation has but one meaning: the liberation of the nation from every want, from material and intellectual slavery as well as from every tyranny, no matter what its origin. To achieve this goal we need certain social and political changes in this land in which we live, and besides internal change we must also have the destruction of Turkey and Austria-Hungary and a union with our brothers in those states. . . . [But] we want to achieve unity through freedom and not vice versa. We know that we remain absolutely unclear on many points. We could make ourselves absolutely clear, and we

[11] *Rad*, nos. 21-22, 1874.

could substantiate our opinions with irrefutable evidence, but we do not want to come into conflict with the criminal laws in our very first issue."[12] He ended with his version of the famous remark by Abbé Sieyès: "*Until now the people have been nothing—they must become everything.* That is our concept of liberation."

Oslobođenje lashed out at the Serbian government more immediately and more sharply than had any of the previous radical-socialist journals. Attempting to build his case for a democratic Balkan Federation, Marković severely criticized the foreign policy of the government. That policy, he maintained, was in actual fact *antinational* because Serbia appeared to the populations of Bosnia-Hercegovina, Croatia, Montenegro, and Bulgaria to be a conqueror. The result was that the peoples of those areas "are ever more in the enemy camp even though they are our natural allies."[13]

The Serbian government, driven to the limit of its patience by Marković's attacks, directed the Kragujevac police to call him to account for the "disgusting Karađorđevism" in the first issue of *Oslobođenje*.[14] The police confronted him with two specific charges: he was involved in the preparation of a "treacherous undertaking," and he was "spreading hatred against the Prince."[15] Marković ridiculed the charges and challenged the authorities to produce evidence that he had ever supported the Karađorđe dynasty or directly advocated the violent overthrow of Prince Milan. But he was not physically able to endure another trial. When the police ignored his reply and gave him the choice of leaving the country or being indicted on criminal charges, Marković submitted.

12 *Oslobođenje*, no. 1, January 1, 1875.

13 *Ibid.*, no. 5, January 10, 1875; no. 7, January 15, 1875.

14 *IAB*, Svetozar Marković to Pera Todorović, Kragujevac, January, 1875, letter no. 18; see also *Oslobođenje*, no. 7.

15 *IAB*, Svetozar to Jevrem Marković, letter no. 17.

The campaign against him personally and against the radical-socialist movement became too strong for him to resist in the last months of his life. Five peasants were arrested in Jagodina for their support of Jevrem Marković's political candidacy;[16] Stevan Milićević, former editor of *Radenik* and *Glas Javnosti,* was sent to prison for libeling a government official; numerous copies of *Oslobođenje* mysteriously disappeared in the mails; Marković himself was accused of having pocketed the 1,200 ducats left to him by his deceased friend Pera Đorđević, when in reality he had given the money to the Ninković sisters to assist them in establishing a school for women in Kragujevac.[17]

In a front-page announcement on January 22 Svetozar Marković informed the more than 1,000 readers[18] of *Oslobođenje* that his poor health obliged him to relinquish the editorship of the newspaper. He hoped to return soon, he noted, and he assured the friends of the journal and the radical-socialist movement that the editorial policy of *Oslobođenje* would not change "one iota."[19]

Having obtained a passport, Marković prepared to leave Serbia immediately. He had planned to visit his brother in Jagodina, but under pressure from the police he abandoned the idea. He wrote instead to Jevrem Marković that he was going directly to Vienna to seek medical advice: "I regret very much that we will not see each other until I return. I hope it will not be long."[20]

Fearing to travel through Belgrade, Marković went instead to the Danube port of Smederevo and took a steamer

16 Sixty-two residents of Jagodina sent an open letter to the National Assembly protesting irregularities in the 1874 elections; among other things, they noted that the district prefect had threatened to drive into Turkey anyone who voted for Jevrem Marković; *Oslobođenje,* no. 16, February 5, 1875. The Jagodina police were unsuccessful in their efforts to have Marković's election set aside; cf. *Protokoli Narodne Skupštine,* p. 5.

17 *Oslobođenje,* no. 1, January 1, 1875.

18 *Skerlić,* p. 104.

19 *Oslobođenje,* no. 10, January 22, 1875.

20 *IAB,* Svetozar to Jevrem Marković, letter no. 17.

to the Hungarian town of Baja, where he boarded a train for Vienna. In the Austrian capital he consulted several doctors, all of whom agreed that his case was virtually hopeless.

LAST DAYS

Marković refused to accept the fact that he had little time to live. He summoned the members of the Serbian student society, *Zora,* in Vienna and discussed with them the possibility of founding yet another newspaper. To his colleagues in Serbia he wrote urging them to keep up their courage and continue publishing *Oslobođenje* until his return.

His condition approached the breaking point, and the Viennese doctors insisted that Marković travel south, to Dalmatia, to seek a warmer climate. Reluctantly he obeyed their advice, and undertook the arduous journey by train to Trieste, intending to continue on to Boka Kotorska by ship.

Marković took a room at the Hôtel de la Ville in Trieste, and planned to spend a few days in the city before making the voyage down the Adriatic. The day after his arrival he collapsed in the hotel and was forced to take to his bed; for the first time he realized that his work was over. Recalling that there was a Serbian Orthodox church in Trieste, Marković, a lifelong agnostic, wrote a humble letter to the priest asking him to visit a "brother Serb" who lay ill in a strange city. Father Bogoljub Toponarski responded to Marković's entreaty, and found the young socialist near death. He immediately had him moved to the Hospitale Civico, where the doctors agreed that the end was near.

Despite Svetozar's protests Father Toponarski sent a telegram to Jevrem Marković asking him to send money for his brother's care and to come to Trieste immediately. Early in the evening on February 25, 1875, the priest visited Svetozar and asked if there was anything he could do for him. Marković replied that he would "arrange everything" when his brother arrived; he further promised to admonish his brother to be a good Christian.

Father Toponarski bade the rapidly sinking Marković farewell and left the hospital. A few hours later, at four o'clock in the morning on the twenty-sixth of February, Svetozar Marković died. He was twenty-eight years old.

THE JOURNEY HOME

Since Jevrem Marković had not arrived, Father Toponarski made arrangements for the funeral. He appealed to the Serbs in Trieste to attend the burial of their famous countryman, but none responded. The priest and the caretaker of the Church of St. Spiridon were the only mourners.

Jevrem Marković arrived in Trieste a day or two after his brother's burial. He ordered the body disinterred for transfer to Vienna, and thence to Jagodina. Arriving with the coffin in the Austrian capital, he found that the Belgrade police had wired the authorities requesting them to seize his brother's notebooks; he was forced to relinquish them. Traveling on by rail and steamer with his burden, he finally reached Jagodina on March 16. There, on the following day, Svetozar Marković was buried in the presence of hundreds of his fellow Serbs, some of whom shouted at the police assigned to maintain order to remove their hats in the presence of a saint.[21]

[21] The numerous obituaries which appeared in the Serbian press are the major source for Marković's last days: *Oslobođenje*, nos. 26-35, February 28-March 21, 1875; *Rad*, nos. 9-12, March 1-15, 1875; *Istok*, no. 23, March 3, 1875; *Budućnost*, no. 28, March 16, 1875 (a lengthier obituary appeared in nos. 24, 25, and 26, all of which were confiscated); *Zastava*, nos. 26 and 31, March 2 and 14, 1875. Most of the newspapers also printed letters from friends and admirers of Marković. Jovan Skerlić has made a synthesis of the obituaries and letters in his biography of Marković, pp. 104-107. Foreign obituaries were quoted in *Rad*, no. 12, 1875, which I have

MARKOVIĆ IN RETROSPECT

The Balkan Peninsula, perhaps the most famous disputed ground in the world, has in the past century and a half been the scene of a momentous ideological and political conflict. Since the era of the French Revolution, Russia and the West have competed for the allegiance of the Balkan peoples. In this protean struggle the battle lines have often become blurred as a result of shifting emphasis and priorities, but the basic issue has remained unchanged: East and West, each convinced of the moral superiority of its cause, have been determined to win the Balkans.

None of the Balkan nations, excepting the Greeks, had a flourishing and unique culture deeply rooted in a civilized and brilliant past. Thrust suddenly into the modern world upon the collapse of the Ottoman Empire, they were confronted with the necessity of orienting themselves toward one of the cultures and political psychologies which demanded their allegiance—toward East or West. The outcome would depend upon many factors, not the least of them the political decisions of the great powers; but in the final analysis it would depend largely upon the Balkan peoples themselves.

Each of those peoples had its own special problems. The Greeks, whose ancient civilization had to a great extent determined the pattern of civilization throughout the West, had little reason to look to the East, despite the religious heritage they shared with the Orthodox Slavs.

---

not seen. The incident at the graveside in Jagodina is recorded in Veselin Vukićević, "Svetozar Marković, ideolog seljačke klase" ("Svetozar Marković, the Ideologist of the Peasant Class"), *Nova Evropa*, XI, no. 13, May 1925, pp. 393-398. Finally, there are some interesting observations in Oskar Davičo, "Pesme u spomen na tamnovanje i smrt Svetozara Markovića" ("Poems in Memory of the Imprisonment and Death of Svetozar Marković"), *Književnost*, I, 1946, pp. 45-52.

At the other end of the scale the Albanians, perhaps the most primitive people in Europe, had virtually no ties with either East or West and were faced with the still unsolved problem of finding their identity; the search has led them in strange and occasionally preposterous directions. The Rumanians attempted, on the basis of a questionable interpretation of history, a rather artificial identification with the West; but it is significant that the Rumanians, until the occupation of their country by the Red Army, stoutly maintained their incompatibility with the East.

The Balkan Slavs were in a peculiarly complex situation. The Bulgarians, closely linked to Russia by language and politics if not, as is so often forgotten, by ethnic origin, clearly demonstrated their desire to follow their own path independent of Russian tutelage. The Croats, Slav but almost wholly Western in culture and religion, have attempted to remain a part of the West; in their case the ethnic tie has been no match for the psychological and the religious. The Serbs, whose proud nationalism has often seemed to border upon an overbearing arrogance, were confronted with an exceedingly difficult dilemma. Despite their undoubted ethnic, religious, and psychological ties with Russia, the Serbs were strongly influenced by the West (although certainly to a much lesser extent than their Croatian brothers). Unwilling to submit to domination from either East or West, the Serbs vacillated; they feared that a decision either way might commit their national and spiritual independence.

For himself and for Serbia, Svetozar Marković chose the East. But in so doing he allied himself with the philosophy of those in the East who were most strongly influenced by the social teachings of the West. Marković, like his Russian teachers, attempted to apply in a backward and undeveloped society theories originally designed for the advanced and industrialized West. It was a difficult path made still more formidable by the fact that Marković was not a profound thinker in any field. But, to give him credit, he did not pretend to be something he clearly was not; his greatest ambition was to be a "Balkan Chernyshevsky," to propagate Chernyshevsky's teachings in the Balkan lands and prepare the ground for the introduction of socialism.

Despite his untimely death Marković's career encompassed an amazing amount of work in the service of socialism. Publicist, literary critic, polemicist, national revolutionary, parliamentary reformer, political strategist, and founder of the cooperative and socialist movements in the Balkans, Marković was a dynamic and gifted individual who did much—perhaps more than any other single individual—to wrench the Serbian educated class from its complacent provincialism and direct its attention to the new intellectual currents in Europe. His predecessors Dositej Obradović and Vuk Karadžić had sought to introduce their countrymen to the ideas and ideals of the Enlightenment and the romantic movement; Marković's work reflected the teachings of the new age of materialism, realism and socialism.

That Marković became an adherent and propagandist of *avant-garde* social and economic theories was due chiefly to his position as an alienated intellectual in a society which, by and large, rewarded conformity and mediocrity. Even before his departure for Russia Marković had sensed that the majority of the Serbian intellectuals became sinecurists rather than servants of the people. Determined to renounce their example, Marković was inexorably drawn to the teachings of the Russian alienated intelligentsia—to socialism. The Russian version of Western socialist theories remained the dominant influence upon him throughout his life. Seeing many points of similarity between backward, agrarian Russia and his own Serbia, Marković adopted the peasant socialism of N. G. Chernyshevsky, a brand of socialism which owed much to the Western visionaries, especially Fourier. Marković agreed with Chernyshevsky that the very backwardness of a country could be a blessing; in Serbia as in Russia there was but an inchoate, weak capitalism which could be arrested and eradicated. Under the leadership of an enlightened intelligentsia the capitalist stage of economic development could be avoided, Marković held, as the backward Slav states moved directly to socialism.

Marković's views were colored by the Marxism with which he came into contact first briefly and superficially in Russia, then in depth in Switzerland. During the first two years after his return to Serbia Marxism seemed to overshadow the "Russian socialism" Marković had learned from Chernyshevsky's disciples in the Smorgon Academy. He accepted *in toto* Marx's analysis of the capitalist system, supported Marx in his struggle with Bakunin, and in his newspaper analyzed the Paris Commune from a largely Marxist point of view. But Marković was unable to strike a compromise with Marx's rigid determinism; as early as 1871 Marković expressed doubts as to whether it was indeed necessary for *all* societies to follow the path of the industrialized West. Having temporarily shunted into the background the teachings of Chernyshevsky, Marković found himself, after 1871, obliged by what he considered the objective realities of the Serbian situation to return to the agrarian socialism of his Russian master.

An audacious, bold, and relentless social reformer, Marković sought to create a society in which the collectivism of the peasant and the altruism of the enlightened intellectual would supplant the egoism and selfishness of the merchant and bureaucrat. But Marković was not consistent in his work. The discrepancy between his social diagnosis and his prescription for social ills was genuinely disturbing. On the one hand, he presented a frightening analysis of the evils of modern society; on the other, he frequently proposed mere palliatives to correct those evils. And though in some cases his palliatives might conceivably have had a beneficial effect, he did not pursue his treatment to the necessary and logical conclusions. Marković was one of those countless unhappy intellectuals too high-principled to descend to demagoguery and not realist enough to be successful in politics. His radical-socialist movement might have been able to weather its theoretical weaknesses, but it could not survive without a politician; Serbia was to be guided not by humanitarian intellectuals like Marković but by realist politicians like Nikola Pašić.

Marković himself wrote that "parties [power elites] rule the world"; yet he persisted in dabbling in theoretical problems to the neglect of practical politics. When at the last moment he recognized his error, it was too late. The disintegration of his party was assured, for he had failed to find either a firm ideology or a successor capable of holding it together. Marković realized that he and his followers among the alienated intellectuals had to align themselves with an established "have-not" class in society, and in Serbia the description fitted only the peasantry. Yet Marković, basically an elitist in spite of his humanitarianism, never really knew or understood the peasants. His attempts to win them to his cause had to be translated by his lieutenants into language they could understand; even then his program, with its restrictive collectivism, could not long hold an appeal to a conservative and individualistic Serbian peasantry.

Marković remained a stranger to the peasants despite their admiration and respect for him. For Marković socialism meant the liquidation of privilege, and with this the peasants could readily agree; but the problem remained of determining both the means of liquidation and the kind of privilege to be liquidated. Marković wanted to build a democratic, decentralized governmental system and entice the peasants back into the *zadrugas*. But while the peasants were perhaps in favor of democracy and certainly wanted a decentralized government, they, like all peasants, were unlikely ever to be a willing party to their own collectivization.

Despite the best of intentions Marković failed to understand the peasants he wanted desperately to help. His was a passionate but unfulfilled life. He remains a tragic rather than an heroic figure in Balkan history.

Epilogue

THE death of Svetozar Marković brought forth a number of laudatory obituaries in the foreign as well as the Serbian press. The Zagreb *Radnički prijatelj* (*The Worker's Friend*), founded in 1874 by a group of Marković's Croatian adherents, called him "our most competent champion of freedom, brotherhood and equality . . . our first warrior, the greatest force in our movement . . . our Svetozar." The Leipzig *Volksstaat* praised Marković as the founder of the socialist movement in the Balkans, and the Budapest *Arbeiter Wochenblatt* wrote in much the same vein. And Marković's Russian friends had not forgotten him: Peter Lavrov published a handsome tribute to the Serbian socialist in *Vperëd!*, now published in London.[1] Even in the United States Marković's name became known to a tiny audience: in 1883 the German-American newspaper *Freiheit* ("Organ der revolutionären Sozialisten"), commenting on the suicide of Jevrem Marković's wife,[2]

1 *Vperëd!* (*Forward!*), no. 5, March 15, and no. 7, April 15, 1875. The other foreign obituaries were quoted in *Rad*, no. 12, 1875, which was confiscated by the Belgrade police (a copy was, however, available to Jovan Skerlić: *Skerlić*, p. 108). Liuben Karavelov had by this time retired from the Bulgarian revolutionary movement, but his successor, Hristo Botev, was publishing *Zname* (*The Banner*) in Bucharest; I have not seen the latter journal and, therefore, am unable to quote from the obituary which it surely must have carried.

2 On October 11, 1882, an apparently deranged Jelena Marković attempted to assassinate Prince Milan; she was immediately captured and after a trial was sentenced to eighteen years' imprisonment. She committed suicide shortly after beginning her sentence at the Požarevac state prison; cf. P. K., "Serbiia v poslednie gody" ("Serbia in Recent Years"), *Russkii vestnik*, vol. 164, 1883, no. 4, p. 745. Jevrem Marković himself was executed in 1877 for his role in a military rebellion. Having reentered the army and risen to the rank of lieutenant colonel, Marković was one of the ringleaders in an abortive plot to overthrow the government. Many Serbs felt that he received the death penalty (most of the conspirators got off with prison sentences) only because he was the brother of Svetozar Marković; cf. Božidar Kovačević, "Život Svetozara Markovića," p. 109.

devoted part of its account to a brief eulogy of Svetozar Marković.[3]

The Serbian government moved swiftly to counteract the enormous surge of sympathy and support for the radical-socialist movement which followed Marković's death. Pera Todorović's *Rad* was forced to cease publication,[4] and a similar fate befell the opposition liberal journal *Budućnost,* several issues of which were confiscated before its final suspension.[5] *Oslobođenje* soon followed; police were stationed in the offices of the journal, its pages were heavily censored, and its staff was subjected to a multitude of harassments. *Oslobođenje* ceased regular operations on March 22, 1875; two issues were published in the summer, but after August 13 Serbia was without an opposition newspaper.[6]

In the elections of 1875 the radical-socialists increased their parliamentary strength significantly, though they remained a minority party.[7] Under the leadership of Adam Bogosavljević, the radical-socialists "adopted the program of the First International, and, by their agitation in favor of free socialist communities, addressed a strong appeal to the peasant deputies, who were better acquainted with communal needs than with the exigencies of the State."[8] Bogosavljević's parliamentary victories were few in number but great in popularity with the peasants. He and his colleagues induced the National Assembly to order the closing of the Administrative Institute, "long the bulwark

[3] *Freiheit,* New York, June 16, 1883.

[4] *Oslobođenje,* no. 32, March 14, 1875; *Budućnost,* no. 28, March 16, 1875.

[5] *Ibid.*; see also *Budućnost,* nos. 28-30, March 16-23, 1875. No. 30 was *Budućnost*'s final issue.

[6] *Oslobođenje,* nos. 36-38, March 22, August 10 and 13, 1875.

[7] Viktorov-Toporov, "Svetozar Markovich," p. 47; the number of radical-socialist deputies was apparently around twenty-five (out of a total of 130).

[8] Slobodan Jovanović, "Serbia in the Early 'Seventies," *The Slavonic Review,* IV, no. 11, December 1925, p. 389.

of bureaucratism and police arbitrariness," and during the crisis of 1875-78 the government bowed to the demands of the radical-socialists and reduced the salaries of the bureaucrats.[9]

In July of 1875 the long-awaited revolt in Bosnia-Hercegovina erupted with a peasant uprising against the Turkish tax collectors in the Hercegovina town of Nevesinje. The revolt quickly spread throughout the twin provinces; despite his misgivings Prince Milan was obliged by the strong tide of Serbian public opinion to declare war on Turkey in 1876. Russia entered the conflict the following year.[10]

Svetozar Marković's followers played active and important roles in the Balkan Crisis of 1875-78. Vasa Pelagić was an effective agitator among the peasants in Bosnia-Hercegovina; Đorđe Vlajković led the Serbian volunteers in the two provinces; Jevrem Marković and Sava Grujić were battalion commanders on the southern front. In the National Assembly, Adam Bogosavljević and the radical-socialists gave their wholehearted support to the revolutionary movement and the war, though their motives were not strictly patriotic: "They thought of attempting, on the plea of war danger, to establish a dictatorship of the National Assembly and of using the powers thus acquired to carry out a radical reform of all existing political institutions. This

[9] *Ibid.*; see also Viktorov-Toporov, "Svetozar Markovich." On the pay of the bureaucrats see Kosta Jovanović, "Činovničke plate" ("Bureaucratic Salaries"), *Otadžbina*, Belgrade, XII, 1883, pp. 96-127. Writing in Vladan Đorđević's journal, the author vigorously defends the bureaucrats against radical-socialist criticism.

[10] Concerning the military cooperation between Serbia and Russia see Voin Maksimovich, "Voennye sviazi i otnosheniia Serbii i Rossii (1806-1917)" ("The Military Ties and Relations between Serbia and Russia, 1806-1917"), *Iugoslaviia*, I, Belgrade, 1930, pp. 259-316. On the events of 1875-78 see, in addition to Vasa Čubrilović's *Bosanski ustanak*, David Harris, *A Diplomatic History of the Balkan Crisis of 1875-1878. The First Year*, Stanford and London, 1936, and Mihailo D. Stojanović, *The Great Powers and the Balkans 1875-1878*, Cambridge (England), 1939.

plan of theirs to exploit war as a means of effecting internal reforms on a large scale calls to mind the plan of the Girondins on the eve of the War of 1792."[11] The socialists kept the principality in an uproar during the first year of the Crisis. Socialist demonstrations were held throughout Serbia, and on many occasions the red flag was prominently displayed in some of the interior towns.[12] The wretched economic situation of the peasantry, coupled with revolution and war against Turkey, provided fertile ground for socialist agitation; it was said in Europe in the 1870's and 1880's that Serbia was, after Russia, the country in which socialism found its largest following.[13]

The Serbian government was, however, scarcely unaware of the socialist threat, and it took steps to divert the energies and attention of the dissident peasants. The liberals, who were in power throughout the Crisis, argued convincingly that the socialists could only be thwarted by a patriotic war against Turkey. Prince Milan, fearing socialism more than war, heeded their advice.[14] The liberal governments cleverly contrived to give wide currency to the dubious claim that opposition to the dynasty and government was synonymous with opposition to the national-liberation movement. The policy of the liberals was seemingly rewarded at the Congress of Berlin in 1878, when Serbia won complete independence from Turkey. The fact that the price was submission to Austria-Hungary was not widely publicized by Prince Milan and his ministers.

The Serbian radical-socialists, having allowed themselves to be outmaneuvered on the war question, nevertheless continued to play a significant role in Serbian politics. In

11 Slobodan Jovanović, "Serbia in the Early 'Seventies," p. 393.

12 *Glasnik Srpske Akademije Nauka*, III, no. 2, 1951, pp. 321-322; Hermann Wendel, "Svetozar Marković," *Nova Evropa*, XI, 1925, p. 405.

13 Slobodan Jovanović, "Serbia in the Early 'Seventies," pp. 393-394.

14 *Ibid.*, p. 394; for the best account in any language of Serbia's role in the crisis of 1875-78 see *Vlada Milana*, I, pp. 238-434.

1881 one group of Marković's followers formed the Serbian Radical party. Under the leadership of Nikola Pašić, the Radicals at first attempted to adhere to the socialist program formulated by Marković, and continued the fight begun in the National Assembly by Adam Bogosavljević for communal autonomy and reforms to aid the peasants. In the elections of 1883 the Radicals won a third of the 130 seats in the National Assembly. Prince Milan, seeing in the Radicals the chief threat to his rule, promptly appointed the reactionary Nikola Hristić prime minister. Hristić had personally supervised the reign of terror which followed the assassination of Prince Michael in 1868, and was cordially hated throughout the principality; even the liberals found him particularly objectionable. The Radicals in the 1883 Assembly refused to cooperate with Hristić, and the session was suspended. Hristić thereupon undertook a campaign to disarm the peasants; the Radicals incited a rebellion of the peasants in the Timok region against the government's project. The uprising was put down in bloody fashion, and the leaders of the Radical party (including Pašić and Pera Todorović) were sentenced to be shot. Twenty-one of the leaders of the rebellion were indeed executed, but Pašić escaped to Hungary and Todorović's sentence was commuted by Prince Milan to ten years in prison.[15]

The suppression of the Timok Rebellion marked the end of the Radical party's radicalism. After the rebellion and the general amnesty extended to all the surviving participants, Nikola Pašić and the Radicals adopted a policy

[15] On the Timok Rebellion see Slobodan Jovanović, "Timočka buna" ("The Timok Rebellion"), in *Sabrana dela*, IX, Belgrade, 1934, pp. 111-145, and "Pera Todorović," in *Političke i pravne rasprave*, II, pp. 299-403, especially pp. 347-363. See also V. I. Korotkova, "Timokskoe vosstanie i radikal'naia partiia" ("The Timok Rebellion and the Radical Party"), AN SSSR, Institut Slavianovedeniia, *Kratkie soobshcheniia*, II, 1953, pp. 42-48.

of bourgeois *Realpolitik* and nationalism; their major appeal to the electorate, however, lay in their unwavering opposition to the Obrenović dynasty. The Radicals profited handsomely from the fall of that dynasty in the gory upheaval of 1903: the party was in power from 1903 until 1918. Nikola Pašić was a chief architect of the Yugoslavia which came into existence under Serbian domination in 1918; he remained the strongest politician in the new state until his death in 1926.[16] The extent to which Pašić and the Radicals had abandoned the teachings of Svetozar Marković was indicated by the fact that in 1925 their official newspaper neglected even to mention his name on the fiftieth anniversary of his death.[17]

Soon after the formation of the Radical party another group of Marković's followers, who opposed what they regarded the "bourgeois tendencies" of the Pašić faction, created a socialist movement which purported to be the true heir of Svetozar Marković. Led by Dragiša Stanojević and Dimitrije Cenić, the socialists (who did not form a party) published a series of newspapers in which they attempted to propagate Marković's teachings. Despite considerable success among the students the socialists lacked a leader of Pašić's caliber and their movement ended in failure in the 1890's.[18]

As an anonymous Russian writer noted in 1883, Svetozar Marković continued, eight years after his death, to enjoy "huge authority" among the young Serbs.[19] That authority

16 On Pašić see Charles Jelavich, "Nikola P. Pašić: Greater Serbia or Jugoslavia?", *Journal of Central European Affairs*, II, 1951, pp. 133-152.

17 *Novosti*, Belgrade, March 22, 1925, noted the strange omission in the Radical journal *Samouprava* (*Autonomy*). Hermann Wendel noted that an earlier Radical newspaper had ignored the twentieth anniversary of Marković's death; "Svetozar Marković," p. 406. The Radical party did, however, publish an incomplete edition of Marković's works in the 1890's.

18 Andrija Radenić, "Dragiša Stanojević."

19 P. K., "Serbiia v poslednie gody," part II, p. 745.

was challenged in 1892, when the Serbian Social-Democratic party came into existence. Adopting the teachings of Marx, Engels, and Kautsky, the Social-Democrats regarded Marković as a figure of purely historical significance.[20] But Marković survived the assault, and his agrarian socialism retained considerable influence upon the intelligentsia. One of the early leaders of the Social-Democrats, Jovan Skerlić (who, after his expulsion from the party in 1904, joined the Independent Radicals), wrote a laudatory "best-selling" biography of Marković in 1910, and in 1920 the Social-Democrat Krsta Cicvarić admitted that " 'all of us in Serbia who are democrats or socialists learned the political ABC's from Marković.' "[21]

After the socialists came the communists, who founded a party following the First World War.[22] Since their seizure of power in 1945, the attitude of the Yugoslav communists toward Svetozar Marković has been arrogant and condescending: while praising him as the outstanding critic of the Serbian institutions of his day, the communists have maintained that Marković's rejection of Marx's determinism and theory of the class struggle was based upon imperfect understanding. Communist Yugoslavia has relegated Marković to a place of honor in an obscure shrine:

20 *Skerlić*, pp. 220-234.

21 Quoted in Hermann Wendel, "Svetozar Marković," p. 406. See also Milka Čaldarović, "Dimitrije Tucović," *Brazda*, Sarajevo, II, 1949, no. 11-12, pp. 821-829. Christian Rakovsky, the Rumanian-born Bulgarian who was active in Soviet politics (an unusual career, even for a Balkan communist) after the Revolution of 1917, claimed that his generation of Bulgarian revolutionaries was educated in the teachings of Svetozar Marković (*Skerlić*, p. 225).

22 Cf. Khristo Kabakchiev, B. Boshkovich, and Kh. D. Vatis, *Kommunisticheskie partii balkanskikh stran* (*Balkan Communist Parties*), Moscow, 1930. Boshkovich's treatment of the Yugoslav Communist party (pp. 135-167) is not terribly enlightening. A helpful if incomplete bibliography published by Ivan Avakumović ("Literature on the Marxist Movement in Yugoslavia," *Journal of Central European Affairs*, XV, April 1955, pp. 66-70) reinforces the opinion that the Yugoslav communists await their historian.

he was, it is argued, merely another well-intentioned but misguided utopian socialist.[23]

He deserves better treatment.

[23] The best Yugoslav communist discussion remains that produced by Veselin Masleša on the eve of World War II ("Svetozar Marković," *Dela,* III). Masleša's views were subjected to severe criticism in 1946 by the Bulgarian Stalinist, Todor Pavlov: "Svetozar Marković," *Književnost,* I, no. 2, pp. 161-177. Despite the advent of "Titoism" in 1948 the Yugoslav view of Marković remains substantially that set forth by Pavlov. Further, the Yugoslav communists, fifteen years after promising a new edition of Marković's works, have to date (January 1964) produced only one of a projected ten volumes; this suggests that the problem of evaluating Marković's critique of Marxism remains unsolved: *Adhuc sub judice lis est.*

Bibliography

MARKOVIĆ'S WORKS

Celokupna dela Svetozara Markovića (*The Collected Works of Svetozar Marković*). Of the several separate and overlapping editions bearing this title (none of which is complete), I have used the following:

Vol. I, Belgrade, 1911
Vol. II, Belgrade, 1912
Vol. III, Belgrade, n.d.
Vol. IV, Belgrade, 1891
Vol. V, Belgrade, 1892
Vol. VI, Belgrade, 1892
Vol. VII, Belgrade, 1893
Vol. VIII, Belgrade, 1893

Izabrani spisi (*Selected Writings*), Belgrade, 1937.

Izbrannye sochineniia (*Selected Works*), Moscow, 1956.

"Korrespondentsiia iz Belgrada" ("Correspondence from Belgrade"), *Nedelia*, St. Petersburg, 1868, no. 52, pp. 1832-1835.

Načela narodne ekonomije ili nauka o narodnom blagostanju (*po N. G. Černiševskom*) (*The Principles of Political Economy, or The Science of the National Welfare* [*According to N. G. Chernyshevsky*]), Belgrade. 1874. More translation than critique of Chernyshevsky's analysis of the theories of J. S. Mill.

Odabrani spisi (*Selected Writings*), Zagreb, 1950.

Odabrani spisi (*Selected Writings*), Novi Sad and Belgrade, 1961.

Sabrani spisi (*Collected Writings*), I, Belgrade, 1960. Promises to be the first complete collection of Marković's works; at least ten more volumes are planned.

DOCUMENTARY SOURCES

Dokumental'nye materialy o prebyvanii serbskikh urozhentsev Markovicha i Knezhevicha v Institute Inzhenerov Putei Soobshcheniia, S. Peterburg, 1866-69 (*Documentary Materials*

Concerning the Stay of the Serbs [Svetozar] *Marković and* [Aleksa] *Knežević at the Institute of the Engineers of the Means of Communications, St. Petersburg, 1866-1869*). Unpublished materials from the *Tsentral'nye gosudarstvennye istoricheskie arkhivy v Leningrade* (*Central State Historical Archives in Leningrad*); the collection includes about 100 documents from the Aziatskii Department M.I.D., Ministerstvo Putei Soobshcheniia, Institut Inzhenerov Putei Soobshcheniia, and Marković's diploma from the *Velika Škola*.

Državni arhiv Narodne Republike Srbije (*The State Archives of the People's Republic of Serbia*), Belgrade. The collection on Svetozar Marković includes numerous letters and official documents.

Istoriski arhiv Beograda (*The Belgrade Historical Archives*), Belgrade. The Svetozar Marković collection includes several of his letters and two of his notebooks from the Belgrade *gimnazija*.

Jovanović, Vladimir, *Avtobiografija* (*Autobiography*), n.p., n.d. The unpublished MS, located in the Belgrade Historical Archives, is of invaluable worth to a study of Serbian politics in the second half of the nineteenth century.

Serbian National Assembly, *Protokoli Narodne Skupštine 1874-75* (*The Register of the National Assembly*), Belgrade, 1875.

GENERAL WORKS

Academy of Sciences of the U.S.S.R., *Obshchestvenno-politicheskie i kul'turnye sviazi narodov SSSR i Iugoslavii. Sbornik statei (The Socio-Political and Cultural Relations of the Peoples of the USSR and Yugoslavia. A Collection of Articles*), Moscow, 1957. Includes the first Russian publication of Marković's article on Nechaev.

Bocharova, L. S., *Russkaia sektsiia I Internatsionala i ee sotsial'no-ekonomicheskaia platforma* (*The Russian Section of the First International and its Socio-Economic Platform*), unpublished Ph.D. dissertation, Moscow State University, 1955. Credits the Section with having made a positive approach to Marxism.

Boshkovich, B., *Krest'ianskoe dvizhenie i natsional'nyi vopros v Iugoslavii* (*The Peasant Movement and the National Problem in Yugoslavia*), Moscow, 1929. Tendentious and rather immature Marxist account.

Chernyshevsky, N. G., *Polnoe sobranie sochineniia* (*Complete Collected Works*), V, VII, X, XIV, XVI, Moscow, 1949-51.

Cicvarić, Krsta, *Svetozar Marković i birokratski sistem pred sudom Slobodana Jovanovića* (*Svetozar Marković and the Bureaucratic System in the Opinion of Slobodan Jovanović*), Belgrade, 1910. Interesting analysis of Marković's views on the bureaucracy.

Cole, G. D. H., *Marxism and Anarchism, 1850-1890*, London, 1957.

Ćorović, Vladimir, *Borba za nezavisnost Balkana* (*The Struggle for Balkan Independence*), Belgrade, 1937.

———, *Istorija Jugoslavije* (*The History of Yugoslavia*), Belgrade, 1933.

Čubrilović, Vasa, *Bosanski ustanak 1875-78* (*The Bosnian Uprising, 1875-78*), Belgrade, 1930. The best single volume covering the three-year uprising.

———, *Istorija političke misli u Srbiji XIX veka* (*The History of Political Thought in Serbia in the 19th Century*), Belgrade, 1958. Interesting and thoughtful analysis by the dean of living Yugoslav historians.

———, and Vladimir Ćorović, *Srbija od 1858 do 1903* (*Serbia from 1858 to 1903*), Belgrade, n.d.

Dimitrijević, Sergije, *Bibliografija socijalističkog i radničkog pokreta u Srbiji, sa osvrtom na ostale krajeve naše zemlje* (*A Bibliography of the Socialist and Labor Movement in Serbia, With a Survey of Other Parts of our Country*), Belgrade, 1954.

Đorđević, Miroslav, *Politički pogledi Svetozara Markovića* (*The Political Views of Svetozar Marković*), Sarajevo, 1952.

Đorđević, Tih. R., *Građa za srpske narodne običaje iz vremena prve vlade Kneza Miloša* (*Materials on Serbian National Customs in the First Reign of Prince Miloš*), Belgrade, 1913. Valuable background materials.

Dragnich, Alex N., *The Development of Parliamentary Government in Serbia, 1869-1889*. Unpublished Ph.D. dissertation, University of California, Berkeley, 1945. Excellent study.

Erikhonov, L., *Russkie revoliutsionnye demokraty i obshchestvennaia mysl' iuzhnykh slavian v 60-70-kh godakh XIX veka* (*The Russian Revolutionary Democrats and the Social Thought of the South Slavs in the Sixties and Seventies of the 19th Century*), Moscow, 1950. A tendentious product of the period of the Stalin-Tito feud; little value from a scholarly standpoint.

Fischel, A., *Der Panslawismus bis zum Weltkrieg*, Stuttgart and Berlin, 1919.

Gavrilović, Andra, *Znameniti Srbi XIX veka* (*Prominent Serbs of the 19th Century*), 3 vols., Zagreb, 1901-04. Brief portraits of many individuals.

Gavrilović, B. N., and others, *Beograd*, Belgrade, 1940.

Gavrilović, Mihajlo, *Miloš Obrenović*; I (1813-20), Belgrade, 1908; II (1821-26), Belgrade, 1909; III (1827-35), Belgrade, 1912.

Gligorić, Velibor, *O životu i delu Svetozara Markovića* (*On the Life and Work of Svetozar Marković*), Belgrade, 1946. A good example of the run-of-the-mill pre-1948 Yugoslav communist criticism of Marković's theories.

Gorokhov, V. A., *I-i Internatsional i russkii sotsializm. "Narodnoe Delo"—Russkaia sektsiia Internatsionala* (*The First International and Russian Socialism. "The People's Cause" and the Russian Section of the International*), Moscow, 1925. Uncritical praise of the Section's "Marxist position."

Granskii, S. V., *Marks i Engel's o Rossii i russkikh revoliutsionerakh (Marx and Engels on Russia and Russian Revolutionaries), Nauchnye Zapiski Voronezhskogo Instituta Narodnokhoziaistvennogo Ucheta TsUNKhU Gosplana SSSR*, I, Voronezh, 1940.

Haumant, Emile, *La Formation de la Yougoslavie*, Paris, 1930. Good general account, among the best in Western languages.

Ilić, Dragoslav, *Prve žene socijalisti u Srbiji* (*The First Female Socialists in Serbia*), Belgrade, 1956. Contains interesting information on the Ninković sisters.

Jakšić, Grgur, *Borba za slobodu Srbije 1788-1813* (*The Struggle for Serbian Freedom, 1788-1813*), Belgrade, n.d.

———, and Dragoslav Stranjaković, *Srbija od 1813 do 1858 godine* (*Serbia from 1813 to 1858*), Belgrade, n.d.

Janković, Dragoslav, *Istorija države i prava Srbije u XIX veku* (*The History of the State and Law in Serbia in the 19th Century*), 2nd edition, Belgrade, 1955.

———, *O političkim strankama u Srbiji XIX veka* (*On Political Parties in Serbia in the 19th Century*), Belgrade, 1951.

Janković, Miloš B., *Đački socijalistički pokret u Srbiji* (*The

Student Socialist Movement in Serbia), Belgrade, 1954. Not of great value.

———, *Pedagoški pogledi prvih srpskih socijalista Živojina Žujovića, Svetozara Markovića, Vase Pelagića* (*The Pedagogical Views of the First Serbian Socialists: Živojin Žujović, Svetozar Marković, Vasa Pelagić*), Belgrade, 1952.

———, *Prve socijalističke pedagoške ideje u Vojvodini* (*The First Socialist Pedagogical Ideas in the Vojvodina*), Belgrade, 1952.

Jovanović, Aleksa S., *Istoriski razvitak srpske zadruge sa dodatkom prinosci za istoriju starog srpskog prava* (*The Historical Development of the Serbian Zadruga with a Supplement on the Contributions of Ancient Serbian Law*), Belgrade, 1896. Valuable on the *zadruga*'s legal status.

Jovanović, Slobodan, *Druga vlada Miloša i Mihaila* (*The Second Reign of Miloš and Michael*), Belgrade, 1923.

———, "Svetozar Marković," *Političke i pravne rasprave*, II of *Sabrana dela*, Belgrade, 1932. An unfriendly account by the son of Vladimir Jovanović.

———, *Sabrana dela* (*Collected Works*), III, Belgrade, 1932, and V, Belgrade, 1933.

———, *Ustavobranitelji i njihova vlada (1838-1858) (The Defenders of the Constitution and their Rule, 1838-1858)*, Belgrade, 1912.

———, *Vlada Milana Obrenovića* (*The Reign of Milan Obrenović*), I (1868-78), Belgrade, 1926. One of the finest of Jovanović's many excellent works.

Jovanović, Vladimir, *Les Serbes et la Mission de la Serbie dans l'Europe d'Orient*, Paris-Brussels, 1870.

———, "Statističan pregled našeg privrednog i društvenog stanja, sa obzirom na privredno i društveno stanje drugih država" ("A Statistical Survey of our Economic and Social Situation in Relation to that of Other States"), *Glasnik srpskog učenog društva*, vol. 50, 1881, pp. 165-588. Contains valuable data.

———, *Za slobodu i narod* (*For Freedom and the Nation*), Novi Sad, 1868. A collection of articles from the Geneva *Sloboda-La Liberté*.

Kabakchiev, Khristo, with B. Boshkovich and H. D. Vatis, *Kommunisticheskie partii balkanskikh stran* (*Communist Parties of the Balkan Countries*), Moscow, 1930. With an introduction by Vasil Kolarov. Interesting but not of great value.

Karasëv, V. G., *Istoricheskie sviazi narodov Sovetskogo Soiuza i Iugoslavii* (*The Historical Ties between the Peoples of the Soviet Union and Yugoslavia*), Moscow, 1956. A product of the post-Stalin *rapprochement.*

———, *Svetozar Markovich* (*Sotsial'no-politicheskie vzgliady*) (*Svetozar Marković: Socio-Political Views*), unpublished Ph.D. dissertation, Moscow State University, 1950. A lengthy and consistently tendentious account.

Karataev, N. K., *Ekonomicheskaia platforma russkoi sektsii I Internatsionala. Sbornik materialov* (*The Economic Platform of the Russian Section of the First International. A Collection of Materials*), Moscow, 1959. Documents and commentary designed to dispute B. P. Koz'min's views of the Section.

Kecmanović, Ilija, *Vuk-Njegoš-Svetozar Marković,* Sarajevo, 1949.

Konstantinov, Georgi, *Vođi bugarskog narodnog pokreta: Rakovski-Karavelov-Levski-Botev* (*The Leaders of the Bulgarian National Movement: Rakovski, Karavelov, Levski, Botev*), Belgrade, 1939. Interesting data; contains some factual errors.

Koz'min, B. P., *Iz istorii revoliutsionnoi mysli v Rossii* (*From the History of Revolutionary Thought in Russia*), Moscow, 1961. A collection of articles written by the outstanding Soviet student of the nineteenth century Russian revolutionary movement.

———, *Nechaev i Nechaevshchina. Sbornik materialov* (*Nechaev and the Nechaev Era. A Collection of Materials*), Moscow-Leningrad, 1931.

———, *Revoliutsionnoe podpol'e v epokhu "Belogo Terrora"* (*The Revolutionary Underground in the Epoch of the "White Terror"*), Moscow, 1929. Contains much valuable information on I. I. Bochkarëv.

———, *Russkaia sektsiia pervogo Internatsionala* (*The Russian Section of the First International*), Moscow, 1957. Uncompromising Marxist-Leninist account stressing the failure of the Section to "ascend to an understanding of Marxism."

———, (ed.), *Sbornik materialov k izucheniiu istorii russkoi zhurnalistiki* (*A Collection of Materials for the Study of*

Russian Journalism), III (1870's to mid-1890's), Moscow, 1956. Brief note on *Narodnoe Delo.*

Kunibert, Dr. B. (B.-S. Cunibert), *Srpski ustanak i prva vladavina Miloša Obrenovića* (*The Serbian Uprising and the First Reign of Miloš Obrenović*), Belgrade, 1901. An account by Miloš's physician; originally published in French, Leipzig, 1850.

Lapčević, Dragiša, *Istorija socijalizma u Srbiji* (*The History of Socialism in Serbia*), Belgrade, 1922. Despite the promise of the title the work is not of great value.

Larionov, A. M., *Istoriia Instituta Inzhenerov Putei Soobshcheniia za pervoe stoletie ego sushchestvovaniia, 1810-1910* (*The History of the Institute of Engineers of the Ways of Communications During its First Century, 1810-1910*), St. Petersburg, 1910.

Marković, Milan, *Die serbische Hauskommunion (Zadruga) und ihre Bedeutung in der Vergangenheit und Gegenwart*, Leipzig, 1903. Useful for background material.

Marx and Engels, *Perepiska K. Marksa i F. Engel'sa s russkimi politicheskimi deiateliami* (*The Correspondence of K. Marx and F. Engels with Russian Political Figures*), 2nd edition, Leningrad, 1951.

———, *Sochineniia* (*Works*), XXVII, Leningrad, 1935. Contains the drafts of Marx's letter to Vera Zasulich concerning the Russian *obshchina.*

Masaryk, T. G., *The Spirit of Russia*, 2 vols., New York, 1955.

Masleša, Veselin, "Svetozar Marković," in *Dela* (*Works*), III, Sarajevo, 1956, pp. 12-100. Interesting observations by one of the better minds among the prewar Yugoslav communists.

Meijer, J. M., *Knowledge and Revolution: The Russian Colony in Zuerich (1870-1873)*, Assen, 1955.

Milenković, Vladislav, *Ekonomska istorija Beograda* (*The Economic History of Belgrade*), Belgrade, 1932. Good background material.

Milićević, M., *Dodatak Pomenika od 1888* (*A Supplement to Recollections from 1888*), Belgrade, 1901. Milićević was a contemporary of Marković; some useful material.

Mirković, Mijo, *Ekonomska historija Jugoslavije* (*The Economic History of Yugoslavia*), Zagreb, 1958.

Nedeljković, Dušan, *Naša filozofija u borbi za socijalizam* (*Our Philosophy in the Struggle for Socialism*), Belgrade, 1952. Not a profound work.

Nikitin, S. A. (ed.), *Istoriia iuzhnykh i zapadnykh slavian (The History of the Southern and Western Slavs)*, Moscow, 1957. Soviet university-level textbook.

———, *Slavianskie komitety v Rossii v 1858-1876 godakh (The Slavic Committees in Russia, 1858-1876)*, Moscow, 1960. A much-needed work the value of which is marred by its ideological bias.

Novaković, Stojan, *Die Wiedergeburt des serbischen Staates (1804-1813)*, Sarajevo, 1913. A valuable work by a leading Yugoslav historian.

———, *Tursko carstvo pred prvi ustanak (The Turkish Empire Prior to the First Uprising)*, Belgrade, 1907. Not consulted.

———, *Ustanak na dahije, 1804 (The Uprising Against the Dahis, 1804)*, Belgrade, 1904.

Pantelić, Dušan, *Beogradski pašaluk posle Svištovskog mira 1791-1794 (The Belgrade Pashalik After the Treaty of Sistova, 1791-1794)*, Belgrade, 1927. Excellent work.

———, *Beogradski pašaluk pred prvi srpski ustanak, 1794-1804 (The Belgrade Pashalik Prior to the First Serbian Uprising, 1794-1804)*, Belgrade, 1949.

Popov, Nil, *Rossiia i Serbiia (Russia and Serbia)*, Moscow, 1869. A classic account.

Popović, Jovan, *Svetozar Markovik*, Skopje, 1950. In Macedonian dialect; not consulted.

Posin, Jack A., *Chernyshevsky, Dobrolyubov and Pisarev, The Ideological Forerunners of Bolshevism*, Unpublished Ph.D. dissertation, University of California, Berkeley, 1939.

Prodanović, Dimitrije, *Shvatanje Svetozara Markovića o državi (Svetozar Marković's Concept of the State)*, Belgrade, 1961. Interesting and useful account.

Prodanović, Jaša, *Istorija političkih stranaka i struja u Srbiji (The History of Political Parties and Currents in Serbia)*, I, Belgrade, 1947.

Pypin, A. N., *Panslavizm v proshlom i nastoiashchem (Panslavism, Past and Present)*, St. Petersburg, 1878. Valuable account by a brilliant "Westerner."

Šišić, Ferdo, *Jugoslovenska Misao (The Yugoslav Concept)*, Belgrade, 1937. A thoughtful work by an outstanding Croatian historian.

Skerlić, Jovan, *Istorija nove srpske književnosti (The History of*

Modern Serbian Literature), 3rd edition, Belgrade, 1953. Valuable.

———, *Istoriski pregled srpske štampe 1791-1911* (*An Historical Survey of the Serbian Press, 1791-1911*), Belgrade, 1911. An indispensable work.

———, *Omladina i njena književnost (1848-1871)* (*"Youth" and its Literature, 1848-1871*), Belgrade, 1925.

———, *Svetozar Marković: Njegov život, rad i ideje* (*Svetozar Marković: His Life, Work and Ideas*), 2nd edition, Belgrade, 1922. An outstanding biography of one of his predecessors by a leading Serbian socialist who left the Social-Democratic party in 1904 to join the Independent Radicals. Uses archival material since lost or destroyed.

Stanischitsch, Alexa, *Ueber den Ursprung der Zadruga*, Bern, 1907. Valuable materials.

Stanojević, Stanoje. *Istorija srpskog naroda* (*History of the Serbian Nation*), Belgrade, 1910.

——— (ed.), *Narodna Enciklopedija Srpsko-hrvatsko-slovenačka* (*Serbo-Croat-Slovenian National Encyclopedia*), 4 vols., Zagreb, 19 (?)-29.

Stavrianos, L. S., *The Balkans Since 1453*, New York, 1958.

Steklov, Iu. M., *N. G. Chernyshevskii: Ego zhizn' i deiatel'nost'* (*N. G. Chernyshevsky, His Life and Work*), 2 vols., Moscow-Leningrad, 1928. The best biography available.

Stetskevich, S. M. (ed.), *Ocherki istorii iuzhnykh i zapadnykh slavian* (*Essays on the History of the Southern and Western Slavs*), Leningrad, 1957.

Tadić, Jorjo, *Ten Years of Yugoslav Historiography, 1945-1955*, Belgrade, 1955.

Tkalac, E. I., *Das Staatsrecht des Fürstentums Serbien*, Leipzig, 1858. Excellent materials; a valuable source for legal relationships in the first half of the nineteenth century.

Tomasevich, Jozo, *Peasants, Politics, and Economic Change in Yugoslavia*, Stanford and London, 1955. The best single volume on Yugoslav economic history.

Utješenović-Ostrožinski, O., *Die Hauskommunionen der Südslawen*, Vienna, 1859. Of some value for a study of the *zadruga.*

Venturi, Franco, *Roots of Revolution*, London, 1960. An outstanding work on the history of the nineteenth century revolutionary movement in Russia.

Wendel, Hermann, *Aus dem südslawischen Risorgimento,* Gotha, 1921. Interesting and valuable work by a slightly leftist friend of the South Slavs.

———, *Der Kampf der Südslawen um Freiheit und Einheit,* Frankfurt-am-M., 1925.

———, *Südslawische Silhouetten,* Frankfurt-am-M., 1924.

Yarmolinsky, Avrahm, *Road to Revolution,* London, 1957. Excellent study of the nineteenth-century revolutionary movement in Russia.

Yugoslavia, *Zadružni Leksikon FNRJ. The Yugoslav Co-operative Encyclopedia,* II, Zagreb, 1957.

Zhitkov, S. M., *Institut Inzhenerov Putei Soobshcheniia Imperatora Aleksandra I* (*The Emperor Alexander I Institute of Engineers of the Ways of Communications*), St. Petersburg, 1899.

Živanović, Živan, *Politička istorija Srbije u drugoj polovini devetnaestog veka* (*The Political History of Serbia in the Second Half of the 19th Century*), I (1858-78), Belgrade, 1923. A standard and valuable account.

Žujović, Jovan M., *Uticaj Svetozara Markovića na školsku omladinu* (*Svetozar Marković's Influence on the School Youth*), Belgrade, 1925. Recollections of one of Marković's contemporaries.

ARTICLES

Anonymous, "Partii v Serbii ("Parties in Serbia"), *Otechestvennye zapiski,* vol. 175, book I, November 1867, pp. 307-327. Excellent materials on political developments 1858-67.

Arsenijević, Olga, "Svetozar Marković i pitanje oslobođenja ženskinja" ("Svetozar Marković and the Problem of the Emancipation of Women"), *Letopis Matice Srpske,* Novi Sad, vol. 358, 1946, pp. 207-212. Useful discussion.

Avakumović, Ivan, "Literature on the First Serbian Insurrection (1804-1813)," *Journal of Central European Affairs,* vol. 13, no. 3, October 1953, pp. 257-260.

Bajić, Stanislav, "Svetozar Marković i pitanje velikih gazdinstava" ("Svetozar Marković and the Problem of Large-scale Production"), *Letopis Matice Srpske,* vol. 358, 1946, pp. 187-197. Important and useful.

Besarović, Risto, "O publicističkom radu Vase Pelagića" ("On the Publicist Work of Vasa Pelagić"), *Brazda*, Sarajevo, vol. 3, 1950, no. 7-8, pp. 550-568. Useful summary.

Bogdanović, Milan, "Milica Ninković," *Književnost*, I, 1946, no. 9, pp. 149-152. An excellent summary of Svetozar Marković's relationship with Milica Ninković.

Boškov, Živojin, "Uticaj Svetozara Markovića na srpsku književnost" ("The Influence of Svetozar Marković on Serbian Literature"), *Letopis Matice Srpske*, vol. 358, 1946, pp. 126-134.

Branković, Kosta, "Razvitak Velike Škole" ("The Development of the *Velika Škola*"), *Glasnik srbskog učenog društva*, Belgrade, vol. 18, pp. 1-24. Useful background material by a former rector.

Čaldarović, Milka, "Dimitrije Tucović," *Brazda*, vol. 2, 1949, no. 11-12, pp. 821-829.

Chuich, G., "Russkaia literatura na serbskom iazyke. Opyt bibliografii perevodnoi russkoi literatury za period s 1860-go po 1910-i god." ("Russian Literature in the Serbian Language. A Tentative Bibliography of Translated Russian Literature for the Period 1860-1910"), *Acta Universitatis Voronegiensis. Trudy Voronezhskogo Gosudarstvennogo Universiteta*, Voronezh, vol. 3, 1926, pp. 116-140. Useful but contains many gaps.

Clissold, Stephen, "Pioneer of Socialism in the Balkans," *The Central European Observer*, London, vol. 23, no. 24, November 22, 1946, p. 382. A brief appreciation.

Davičo, Oskar, "Pesme u spomen na tamnovanje i smrt Svetozara Markovića" ("Poems in Memory of the Imprisonment and Death of Svetozar Marković"), *Književnost*, I, 1946, no. 9, pp. 45-52. Interesting.

Dimitrov, Mikhail, "K voprosu ob ideologii Liubena Karavelova" ("On the Problem of Liuben Karavelov's Ideology"), *Uchenye Zapiski Instituta Slavianovedeniia* (Moscow), vol. 16, 1958, pp. 78-108. Marxist account of no great value.

Đorđević, Miroslav, "Glišićev realizam i društvena stvarnost Srbije njegovog doba" ("Glišić's Realism and the Social Reality of Serbia in His Time"), *Književnost*, IV, no. 2, 1949, pp. 68-90. Interesting account of one of the writers guided into realism by Svetozar Marković.

———, "O Svetozarevom članku 'Srpske obmane'" ("On

Svetozar Marković's Article 'Serbia Defrauded' "), *Književnost,* I, 1946, no. 9, pp. 145-149. Cites material from the unpublished diary of Kosta Mihailović.

———, "Svetozar Marković i Ujedinjena omladina srpska" ("Svetozar Marković and 'Youth' "), *Književnost,* I, 1946, no. 6, pp. 66-89. A rehash.

Đurić, Vojislav, "Svetozar Marković i srpska prosveta" ("Svetozar Marković and Serbian Enlightenment"), *Književnost,* I, 1946, no. 9, pp. 92-105.

Durman, Jovan, "Udruženja (zadruge) za uzajamno pomaganje u Srbiji" ("Associations (Zadrugas) for Mutual Aid in Serbia"), *Zadružni arhiv,* Novi Sad, I, 1953, pp. 173-180. Deals with the establishment of workers' cooperatives after 1873 under the influence of Svetozar Marković.

Džonić, Uroš, "Darwin u srpskoj nauci i književnosti" ("Darwin in Serbian Science and Literature"), *Srpski književni glasnik,* Belgrade, vol. 22, 1909, pp. 293-297. Lists works on Darwin and Darwinism in Serbo-Croatian.

Franičević, Marin, "Svetozar Marković," *Republika,* Zagreb, vol. 2, no. 9-10, 1946, pp. 697-711.

Hristu, Vasile, "Hristo Botev i Svetozar Markovich za federatsiiata" ("Hristo Botev and Svetozar Marković on Federation"), *Narodna Prosveta,* Sofia, vol. 5, no. 5, January 1949, pp. 24-34. No scholarly value.

Iakovkina, N. I., "Iz istorii rasprostraneniia proizvedenii russkikh revoliutsionnykh demokratov v Serbii" ("From the History of the Dissemination in Serbia of the Works of the Russian Revolutionary Democrats"), *Vestnik Leningradskogo Universiteta,* no. 14, 1959, Seriia Istorii, iazyka i literatury, vol. 3, pp. 113-118. Brief but useful on the acquaintance of the Serbs with radical Russian literature in the period 1860-65.

Iaroslavskii, E., "Marks i Engel's o Rossii" ("Marx and Engels on Russia"), *Istorik Marksist,* 1940, no. 10, pp. 54-80. Useful summary.

Ilić, Dragutin J., "Dah materijalizma u srpskoj književnosti" ("A Breath of Materialism in Serbian Literature"), *Brankovo kolo,* Belgrade, vol. 2, 1896, pp. 1071-1080. Useful.

Iovanovich, Miriana, "Ikonomicheskite v'zgledi na Svetozar Markovich" ("Svetozar Marković's Economic Views"), Vissha partiina shkola "Stanke Dimitrov" pri TsK na BKP,

Izvestiia (otdel istoriia), vol. 4, Sofia, 1959, pp. 190-234. The best statement of the Marxist view of Marković's economic theories.

Iovchuk, M. T., "Svetozar Markovich—vydaiushchiisia serbskii revoliutsioner-demokrat i filosof-materialist" ("Svetozar Marković—The Outstanding Serbian Revolutionary Democrat and Philosophic Materialist"), A. N. SSSR, Institut Slavianovedeniia, *Kratkie Soobshcheniia,* vol. 24, 1958, pp. 32-46. Limited value.

Jelavich, Charles, "Nikola P. Pašić: Greater Serbia or Jugoslavia?", *Journal of Central European Affairs,* vol. 11, July 1951, pp. 133-152.

———, "Some Aspects of Serbian Religious Development in the 18th Century," *Church History,* XXIII, June 1954, pp. 3-11.

Jovanović, Dragoljub, "Svetozar Marković kao društveni reformator" ("Svetozar Marković as Social Reformer"), *Nova Evropa,* Zagreb, vol. 11, no. 13, May 1925, pp. 390-393.

Jovanović, Kosta, "Činovničke plate" ("Bureaucratic Salaries"), *Otadžbina,* Belgrade, vol. 12, 1883, pp. 96-127. Defends the bureaucrats and their salaries.

Jovanović, Slobodan, "Serbia in the Early 'Seventies," *The Slavonic Review,* London, vol. 4, 1925-26, no. 12, pp. 384-395. Valuable.

Jovanović, Vladimir, "Obština" ("The Commune"), *Glasnik srpskog učenog društva,* vol. 34, 1872, pp. 86-150. Contains much useful information.

———, "Socijalizam ili društveno pitanje" ("Socialism, or The Social Problem"), *Glasnik srpskog učenog društva,* vol. 39, 1873, pp. 1-116. Excellent statement of the attitude of the Serbian government liberals towards socialism and the Serbian socialists.

K., "Semeinaia obshchina iuzhnykh slavian" ("The Family Commune of the South Slavs"), *Russkaia Beseda,* 1859, vol. 4, book 16, pp. 1-32. Lengthy review of O. M. Utješenović, *Die Hauskommunionen der Südslawen,* Vienna, 1859.

K., P., "Serbiia v. poslednie gody" ("Serbia in Recent Years"), *Russkii vestnik,* vol. 164, 1883, no. 3, pp. 289-320, no. 4, pp. 738-765. Excellent and informative analysis of political developments in the period 1875-83.

Karasëv, V. G., "D. I. Pisarev i Svetozar Markovich" ("D. I. Pisarev and Svetozar Marković"), *Kratkie Soobshcheniia Instituta Slavianovedeniia,* vol. 9, 1952, pp. 24-33. Summary of Pisarev's influence on Marković; not of great value.

———, "Dva novykh avtografa Svetozara Markovicha" ("Two New Works by Svetozar Marković"), *Slaviane,* no. 9, September 1956, p. 38. Discusses the works of Marković found on Ivan Bochkarëv at his arrest in October of 1868.

———, "Osnovnye cherty sotsial'no-ekonomicheskogo razvitiia Serbii v kontse 60-kh-nachale 70-kh godov XIX v." ("The Fundamental Characteristics of the Socio-Economic Development of Serbia at the End of the Sixties and Beginning of the Seventies of the 19th Century"), *Uchenye zapiski Instituta Slavianovedeniia,* vol. 5, 1952, pp. 206-242. Of considerable value as a clear statement of the Marxist position.

———, "Revoliutsionno-demokraticheskaia programma Svetozara Markovicha" ("The Revolutionary-Democratic Program of Svetozar Marković"), *Uchenye zapiski Instituta Slavianovedeniia,* vol. 6, 1952, pp. 60-88.

———, "Serbskii revoliutsionnyi demokrat Svetozar Markovich" ("The Serbian Revolutionary Democrat Svetozar Marković"), *Uchenye zapiski Instituta Slavianovedeniia,* vol. 7, 1953, pp. 348-377. Essentially a restatement of previous articles by the same author.

———, "Sotsial'no-politicheskie vzgliady Svetozara Markovicha" ("The Socio-Political Views of Svetozar Marković"), *Kratkie Soobshcheniia Instituta Slavianovedeniia,* vol. 6, 1951. One of the best statements of the Soviet-Marxist view in the late Stalin period.

———, "Svetozar Markovich (sotsial'no-politicheskie vzgliady)" ("Svetozar Marković [Socio-Political Views]"); a summary of his Ph.D. dissertation, published in brochure form in Moscow, 1950.

———, "Sviazi russkikh i serbskikh revoliutsionnykh demokratov" ("The Ties Between the Russian and Serbian Revolutionary Democrats"), *Slaviane,* no. 8, August, 1953, pp. 33-35.

Karataev, N. K., "K voprosu ob ekonomicheskoi platforme russkoi sektsii I Internatsionala" ("On the Problem of the Economic Platform of the Russian Section of the First International"), *Uchenye zapiski Moskovskogo Universiteta,* vol. 130, 1949, pp. 86-114.

Kautsky, Karl, "Jugoslaviens Aufstieg und Svetozar Marković," *Der Kampf,* vol. 16, no. 6; translated into Serbo-Croatian in *Nova Evropa,* vol. 11, 1925, pp. 400-404.

Kolosov, E., "P. L. Lavrov i N. K. Mikhailovskii o balkanskikh sobytiakh 1875-1876 gg." ("P. L. Lavrov and N. K. Mikhailovskii on the Balkan Events of 1875-1876"), *Golos minuvshago,* 1916, no. 5-6, pp. 301-339. Not consulted.

Komadinić, Slobodan, "Pisma Svetozara i Jefrema Markovića o organizovanju ustanka u Bosni 1872 godine" ("Letters of Svetozar and Jevrem Marković on the Organization of an Uprising in Bosnia in 1872"), *Savremenik,* Belgrade, no. 5, May 1957, pp. 615-618. Commentary and letters.

———, "Prvi socijalistički program" ("The First Socialist Program"), *Savremenik,* 1955, pp. 588-592.

Kondrat'eva, V. N., "Novye arkhivnye materialy po istorii Ob'edinennoi serbskoi omladiny" ("New Archival Materials on the History of the Serbian 'Youth' "), *Uchenye zapiski Instituta Slavianovedeniia,* vol. 20, 1960, pp. 306-330. Valuable materials from the Russian archives.

Koperzhinskii, K. A., "Serbskie deiateli 60-70-kh godov i peredovaia russkaia literatura" ("Serbs of the Sixties and Seventies and Progressive Russian Literature"), *Nauchnyi biulleten' Leningradskogo Universiteta,* no. 11-12, 1946, pp. 65-69.

Korotkova, V. I., "Timokskoe vosstanie i radikal'naia partiia" ("The Timok Rebellion and the Radical Party"), *Kratkie Soobshcheniia Instituta Slavianovedeniia,* vol. 2, 1953, pp. 42-48.

Kovačević, Božidar, "Ideje i život Dragiše Stanojevića" ("The Ideas and Life of Dragiša Stanojević"), *Književnost,* XIII, 1958, no. 11-12, pp. 472-486.

———, "Ljuben Karavelov i Svetozar Marković" ("Liuben Karavelov and Svetozar Marković"), *Letopis Matice Srpske,* vol. 358, 1946, pp. 198-206.

———, "O poslednjim danima 'Ujedinjene omladine srpske' " ("On the Last Days of 'Youth' "), *Književnost,* VII, 1952, no. 12, pp. 504-512. Contains some material on Marković's activities in the revolutionary movement in Bosnia-Hercegovina.

———, "Povodom stogodišnjice od rođenja Svetozara Markovića" ("On the Occasion of the 100th Anniversary of Svetozar Marković's Birth"), *Književnost*, I, 1946, no. 3, pp. 456-458.

———, "Studenti u Cirihu oko godine 1870—prvi srpski socijalisti" ("The Students in Zürich around 1870—The First Serbian Socialists"), *Književnost*, XI, no. 1, January 1956, pp. 80-84. A favorable review of J. M. Meijer, *Knowledge and Revolution.*

———, "Život Svetozara Markovića" ("The Life of Svetozar Marković"), *Književnost*, I, 1946, no. 9, pp. 106-135. An excellent short biographcal sketch.

Koz'min, B. P., "Po stranitsam knig i zhurnalov. Liuben Karavelov i Svetozar Markovich v ikh sviazi s russkimi revoliutsionerami" ("Through the Pages of Books and Journals. The Relations of Liuben Karavelov and Svetozar Marković with Russian Revolutionaries"), *Katorga i ssylka,* 1933, no. 4-5, pp. 145-155. An incisive critique of the article by K. A. Pushkarevich, "Svetozar Markovich v Peterburge."

Krstonošić, Triva, "Svetozar Marković i njegove veze sa zadružnim organizacijama u Vojvodini" ("Svetozar Marković's Relations with Zadruga Organizations in the Vojvodina"), *Zadružni arhiv,* vol. 1, 1953, pp. 91-114. Valuable and interesting.

Kusheva, E. N., "Iz russko-serbskikh revoliutsionnykh sviazei 1870-kh godov" ("From Russo-Serbian Revolutionary Relations in the 1870's"), *Uchenye zapiski Instituta Slavianovedeniia,* vol. 1, 1949, pp. 343-358. Of considerable value; based on archival sources.

Lapčević, Dragiša, "Svetozar Marković, 1846-1875," *Književni sever,* Subotica, September 1926, pp. 306-307.

Malon, Benoit, "Svetozar Markowitch et la socialisme serbe," *La Revue Socialiste,* vol. 8, no. 2, 1888, pp. 582-595. Valuable; contains documentary material not available elsewhere.

Marić, Sreten, "Svetozar Marković," *Politika,* Belgrade, March 10, 1945, p. 2.

Marić, Svetislav, "Svetozar Marković i prirodne nauke" ("Svetozar Marković and the Natural Sciences"), *Letopis Matice Srpske,* vol. 358, 1946, pp. 226-231. Not of value.

Marković, Todor, "Ljuben Karavelov u srpskoj književnosti" ("Liuben Karavelov in Serbian Literature"), *Srpski knji-*

ževni glasnik, series 1, vol. 24, 1910, pp. 347-359, 439-450, 534-540, 604-610, 678-687. An excellent survey.

Miletić, Momčilo, "Svetozar Marković i Đura Jakšić" ("Svetozar Marković and Đura Jakšić"), *Književnost,* III, 1946, pp. 303-305.

Milićević, M. Đ., "Opštine u Srbiji" ("Communes in Serbia"), *Godišnjica Nikole Čupića,* Belgrade, vol. 2, 1858, pp. 183-239. Valuable.

———, "Serbskaia obshchina" ("The Serbian Commune"), *Russkaia Beseda,* Moscow, vol. 6, 1859, pp. 49-64.

Milisavac, Živan, "Svetozar Marković i Matica Srpska" ("Svetozar Marković and Matica Srpska"), *Letopis Matice Srpske,* vol. 358, 1946, pp. 172-186.

Milutinović, Kosta, "Agrarna problematika prvih srpskih socijalista" ("The Agrarian Theories of the First Serbian Socialists"), *Zadružni arhiv,* vol. 1, 1953, pp. 75-90. Analyzes the views of Svetozar Marković, Živojin Žujović, and Vasa Pelagić; valuable.

———, "Odjek Pariske komune u Srbiji i Vojvodini" ("The Repercussions of the Paris Commune in Serbia and the Vojvodina"), *Letopis Matice Srpske,* vol. 367, 1951, pp. 420-437. Valuable.

———, "Proterivanje Svetozara Markovića iz Vojvodine" ("The Expulsion of Svetozar Marković from the Vojvodina"), *Istoriski časopis,* Belgrade, vol. 5, 1955, pp. 349-364. A valuable source; based upon archival materials.

———, "Prvi socijalisti u Beogradu" ("The First Socialists in Belgrade"), *Godišnjak Muzeja grada Beograda,* Belgrade, vol. 1, 1954, pp. 237-254. Analyzes the work of Živojin Žujović and Dragiša Stanojević.

Minović, D. R., "Svetozar Marković i predratna Srbija" ("Svetozar Marković and Pre-War Serbia"), *Nova Evropa,* vol. 31, 1938, no. 3, pp. 77-84. An excellent though sometimes hypercritical summary.

Mordovtsev, D. L., "Razvitie slavianskoi idei v russkom obshchestve XVIII-XIX vv." ("The Development of the Slavic Idea in Russian Society in the 18th and 19th Centuries"), *Russkaia Starina,* XXI, 1878, pp. 65-78. Not consulted.

Nikitin, S. A., "Iuzhnoslavianskie sviazi russkoi periodicheskoi pechati 60-kh godov XIX veka" ("The South Slav Ties of the Russian Periodical Press in the Sixties of the 19th Century"), *Uchenye zapiski Instituta Slavianovedeniia,* vol. 6, 1952, pp. 89-122. Valuable.

———, "Slavianskie s'ezdy 60-kh godov XIX veka" ("The Slavic Congresses of the 1860's"), *Slavianskii sbornik. Slavianskii vopros i russkoe obshchestvo v 1867-1878 godakh,* edited by N. M. Druzhinin, Moscow, 1948, pp. 16-92. A valuable work.

Nikolajević, Svetomir, "Kraljevsko-srpska Velika Škola za pedeset njenih godina" ("The Royal Serbian Velika Škola over Fifty Years"), *Godišnjica Nikole Čupića,* vol. 12, 1891, pp. 202-232. Recollections of one of the rectors.

Obradović, Vidosava, "Svetozar Marković i sestre Ninković" ("Svetozar Marković and the Ninković Sisters"), *Žena danas,* Belgrade, 1939, no. 20, pp. 7-8. No clues to the riddle.

Panić-Surep, M., "Manifest Komunističke partije iz 1871 godine" (Deals with the publication in 1871 of the first Serbo-Croatian translation of the *Communist Manifesto*), *Bibliotekar,* 1948-49, no. 1, pp. 19-21.

Pavlov, Todor D., "Svetozar Marković," *Književnost,* I, 1946, no. 2, pp. 161-177.

Pelagić, Vasa, "Avtobiografija Vase Pelagića" ("The Autobiography of Vasa Pelagić"), *Brazda,* vol. 4, 1951, no. 4-5, pp. 318-331. Not consulted.

Perović, Radoslav, "Povodom jednog izdanja prvog srpskog socijalističkog programa" ("On the Occasion of an Edition of the First Serbian Socialist Program"), published in brochure form in Belgrade, 1955. Bitter attack on Slobodan Komadinić.

Plamenac, Žarko (pseud. for Arpad Lebl), " 'Realizam' i—realnost. Nova nauka" (" 'Realism' and—Reality. The New Science"), *Pregled,* Sarajevo, vol. 13, 1937, no. 158, pp. 88-95.

Pogodin, A., "Imperator Aleksandr II i ego vremia v otsenke serbskago obshchestvennogo mneniia, shestidesiatye gody" "Emperor Alexander II and his Times in the Evaluation of Serbian Public Opinion in the 1860's"), *Zapiski russkogo nauchnago instituta v Belgrade,* Belgrade, 1936, pp. 1-38. Not consulted.

———, "Sovremennaia serbskaia literatura" ("Contemporary Serbian Literature"), *Novoe slovo,* St. Petersburg, vol. 5, no. 10, 1913, pp. 22-27.

Popović, Jovan, "Socijalizam i istinski patriotizam Svetozara

Markovića" ("Socialism and the True Patriotism of Svetozar Marković"), *Letopis Matice Srpske,* vol. 358, 1946, pp. 232-247.

———, "Svetozar Marković," in the *Ogledi iz književnosti* series, published in brochure form in Belgrade, 1949.

———, "Svetozareva buktinja nad našom književnošću" ("Svetozar Marković's Guiding Light for our Literature"), *Književnost,* I, 1946, no. 9, pp. 9-25. An excellent article on Marković's literary views.

Popović, Laza, "Šta je nama Svetozar Marković" ("What Svetozar Marković Means to Us"), *Nova Evropa,* vol. 11, no. 13, May 1925, pp. 387-390. The author is the son of one of Marković's Sremski Karlovci friends.

Pulinets, A. S., "N. G. Chernyshevskii i Svetozar Markovich" ("N. G. Chernyshevsky and Svetozar Marković"), *Uchenye zapiski Chernovitskogo Universiteta,* Chernovtsy, vol. 30, Seriia filologicheskikh nauk, no. 6, 1958, pp. 33-68. An extremely disappointing article; presents no new materials or ideas; does not utilize Serbian materials.

Pushkarevich, K. A., "Balkanskie slaviane i russkie 'osvoboditeli' (Slavianskie komitety i sobytiia na Balkanakh pered russko-turetskoi voinoi 1877-1878gg)" ("The Balkan Slavs and the Russian 'Liberators' [The Slavic Committees and Balkan Developments Before the Russo-Turkish War of 1877-1878]"), *Trudy Instituta Slavianovedeniia A. N. SSSR,* vol. 2, 1934, pp. 189-229. An extremely valuable and candid article.

———, "Svetozar Markovich v Peterburge" ("Svetozar Marković in St. Petersburg"), *Trudy Instituta Slavianovedeniia A. N. SSSR,* vol. 1, 1932, pp. 345-349. Valuable.

Radenić, Andrija, "Dragiša Stanojević—život, rad, i ideje" ("Dragiša Stanojević—Life, Work, and Ideas"), *Istoriski časopis,* vol. 7, 1957, pp. 145-212. Of considerable value.

———, "Vojvođanska štampa prema Namesništvu, 1868-1872" ("The Vojvodina Press and the Regency, 1868-1872"), *Istoriski časopis,* vol. 6, 1956, pp. 65-108. Valuable.

Rogers, J. A., "Darwinism, Scientism and Nihilism," *The Russian Review,* vol. 19, no. 1, pp. 10-23.

Rovinsky, P. A., "Belgrad, ego ustroistvo i obshchestvennaia zhizn'" ("Belgrade, Its Structure and Social Life"), part I, *Vestnik Evropy,* St. Petersburg, April 1870, pp. 530-579;

part II, *Vestnik Evropy,* May 1870, pp. 132-188. A perceptive analysis; of great value.

———, "Vospominaniia iz puteshestviia po Serbii, 1867 godu" ("Recollections from a Trip through Serbia in 1867"), part I, *Vestnik Evropy,* November 1875, pp. 5-34; part II, *Vestnik Evropy,* December 1875, pp. 699-725.

Savić, Milan, "Svetozar Marković u emigraciji" ("Svetozar Marković in Emigration"), *Branik,* Novi Sad, May 15, 1911. Valuable recollections of one of Marković's contemporaries.

Sekulić, Isidora, "Svetozar Marković—ptica bure" ("Svetozar Marković—A Stormy Petrel"), *Književnost,* I, 1946, no. 9, pp. 37-40.

Shikhareva, M. S., "Sel'skaia obshchina u serbov v XIX—nachale XX v." ("The Serbian Village Commune in the 19th and the Beginning of the 20th Century"), *Sovetskaia etnografiia,* 1959, no. 6, pp. 97-112. Valuable.

Simić, Stanoje, "Prilozi za građu o počecima socijalističkog pokreta u Srbiji" ("Contributions to the Materials on the Origins of the Socialist Movement in Serbia"), *Delo,* Belgrade, vol. 1, 1955, no. 5, pp. 576-588, no. 6-7, pp. 102-116. Valuable.

Stajić, Vasa, "Svetozar Marković i socijalisti u Novom Sadu, 1872-1880" ("Svetozar Marković and the Novi Sad Socialists, 1872-1880"), *Letopis Matice Srpske,* vol. 358, 1946, pp. 105-125. Valuable.

Stanojčić, Ilija, "O jednom dosad nepoznatom članku Svetozara Markovića o parlamentarizmu i nacionalnom pitanju" ("On a Previously Unknown Article of Svetozar Marković on Parliamentarianism and the National Problem"), printed in brochure form in Belgrade, 1957. On one of Marković's articles in *Radenik.*

———, "Prvi srpski ustanak u teoriskom delu Svetozara Markovića" ("The First Serbian Uprising in the Theoretical Work of Svetozar Marković"), printed in brochure form in Belgrade, 1957.

Stoianovich, Traian, "The Pattern of Serbian Intellectual Evolution, 1830-1880," *Comparative Studies in Society and History,* vol. 1, no. 3, March 1959, pp. 242-272.

Svatikov, S. G., "Studencheskoe dvizhenie 1869 goda (Bakunin i Nechaev)" ("The 1869 Student Movement [Bakunin and Nechaev]"), *"Nasha Strana" Istoricheskii sbornik,* St. Petersburg, no. 1, 1907, pp. 165-249. Valuable.

Tagirov, R. Sh., "Iz istorii russkoi sektsii Mezhdunarodnogo Tovarishchestva Rabochikh (Russkaia sektsiia i evropeiskoe revoliutsionnoe dvizhenie)" ("From the History of the Russian Section of the International Association of Workers [The Russian Section and the European Revolutionary Movement]"), *Uchenye zapiski Kazanskogo Pedagogicheskogo Instituta,* Kazan, vol. 2, part II_2, 1956, pp. 83-126. From the author's Ph.D. dissertation.

———, "Russkaia sektsiia Mezhdunarodnogo Tovarishchestva Rabochikh i Rossiia" ("The Russian Section of the International Association of Workers and Russia"), *Uchenye zapiski Kazanskogo Pedagogicheskogo Instituta,* Istoricheskii i literaturnyi fakul'tety, vol. 7, 1949, pp. 113-132. Likewise a chapter from the author's dissertation.

Third Section, "Revoliutsionnoe i studencheskoe dvizhenie v otsenke III otdeleniia" ("The Revolutionary and Student Movement in the Appraisal of the Third Section"), *Katorga i ssylka,* 1924, no. 3, pp. 106-121. Valuable archival materials.

Topalovich, Zh., and D. Lapchevich, "Istoricheskoe razvitie sotsial'-demokraticheskogo dvizheniia v Serbii" ("The Historical Development of the Social-Democratic Movement in Serbia"), *Nasha zaria,* vol. 4, no. 2, 1913, pp. 57-66. Of limited value.

Veljković, Momir, "Marginalije Pavla Mihajlovića na *Svetozaru Markoviću* od Dr. J. Skerlića" ("Marginalia of Pavle Mihajlović on Dr. J. Skerlić's *Svetozar Marković*"), *Književni sever,* vol. 8, 1932, pp. 178-179.

Viktorov-Toporov, Vladimir, "Svetozar Markovich," *Golos Minuvshago,* vol. 1, no. 3, March 1913, pp. 30-51. An excellent summary.

Vukićević, Veselin M., "Svetozar Marković, ideolog seljačke klase" ("Svetozar Marković, the Ideologist of the Peasant Class"), *Nova Evropa,* vol. 11, no. 13, May 1925, pp. 393-398. Contains some useful material.

Wendel, Hermann, "Svetozar Marković," *Nova Evropa,* vol. 11, no. 13, May 1925, pp. 404-408. From the author's *Aus dem südslawischen Risorgimento.*

Zaitsev, V. K., "Svetozar Markovich," *Vestnik Leningradskogo*

Universiteta, 1957, no. 14, Seriia Istorii, iazyka i literatury, no. 3, pp. 123-131. Contains a few bibliographical aids.

Zh. Sklav (pseud. for Živojin Žujović), "Slavianskii iug" ("The Slavic South"), *Sovremennik*, St. Petersburg, no. 6, June 1863, pp. 259-274. Valuable for background material.

Zh. (Živojin Žujović), "Serbskoe selo" ("The Serbian Village"), *Sovremennik*, no. 5, May 1865, pp. 125-162. Contains much valuable information.

NEWSPAPERS

Budućnost, Belgrade, 1873-75.
Glas Javnosti, Kragujevac, 1874.
Istok, Belgrade, 1874-75.
Javnost, Kragujevac, 1873-74.
Jedinstvo, Belgrade, 1871-72.
Oslobođenje, Kragujevac, 1875.
Pančevac, Pančevo, 1869-71.
Rad, Belgrade, 1874-75.
Radenik, Belgrade, 1871-72.
Vidov Dan, Belgrade, 1871-72.
Zastava, Novi Sad, 1869-75.

Index